Modern Languages Across the Curriculum

This book sets out the agenda for the future of modern language teaching in schools. It aims to look beyond the dominant methods of second language teaching to a new approach emphasising the integration of language learning within the wider curriculum. Through research and case studies from the UK, France, Spain, Italy, Germany, Belgium and Finland, the book shows how teachers and policy makers are increasingly moving towards a system where second languages are taught through other curriculum subjects, rather than just alongside them. Key areas covered are:

- Recent trends and issues in the teaching and learning of modern foreign languages
- The rationale for integrating languages across the curriculum
- How cross-curricular language teaching is developing across Europe
- Practical materials and useful ideas for teachers and policy makers.

This timely book will interest all foreign language teachers, particularly those on in-service or higher-level degree courses. Researchers and Applied Linguists will find useful the practical application of theoretical discussion and reports of this approach to second language learning. It will also be useful reading for student teachers and teacher educators, and policy makers, internationally.

Michael Grenfell is Senior Lecturer at the Centre for Language in Education, and Research Co-ordinator in the Research and Graduate School of Education at the University of Southampton.

Modern Languages Across the Curriculum

Edited by Michael Grenfell

London and New York

First published 2002
by RoutledgeFalmer
11 New Fetter Lane, London EC4P 4EE

Simultaneously published in the USA and Canada
by RoutledgeFalmer
29 West 35th Street, New York, NY 10001

RoutledgeFalmer is an imprint of the Taylor & Francis Group

Typeset in Bembo by
Keystroke, Jacaranda Lodge, Wolverhampton
Printed and bound in Great Britain by
St Edmundsbury Press, Bury St Edmunds, Suffolk

British Library Cataloguing in Publication Data
A catalogue record for this book is available from the British Library

Library of Congress Cataloging in Publication Data
Modern languages across the curriculum/edited by Michael Grenfell.
 p. cm.
 Includes bibliographical references and index.
 ISBN 0–415–25482–5—ISBN 0–415–25483–3 (pbk.)
 1. Languages, Modern—Study and teaching. I. Grenfell, Michael, 1953–

 PB35 .M5925 2002
 418'.0071—dc21   2002021323

ISBN 0–415–25483–3 (pbk)
ISBN 0–415–25482–5 (hbk)

Contents

Figures

Tables

Contributors

Kim Brown, Lucy Cavendish College, University of Cambridge, UK.

Carmel Mary Coonan, Dipartimento di Studi Linguistici e Letterari Europei e Post Coloniali, Universita Ca' Foscari, Venice, Italy.

Shirley Dobson, The Stapleford Centre, Nottingham, UK.

Michael Grenfell, Centre for Language in Education, University of Southampton, UK.

Cheryl Hardy, Education Advisory Service: South Gloucestershire County Council, UK.

Glenn Ole Hellekjaer, Department of Teacher Education and School Development, Faculty of Education, University of Oslo, Norway.

David Marsh, Workplace Communication Continuing Education Centre, University of Jyväskylä, Finland.

Carmen Pérez-Vidal, Facultat de Traducció i Interpretario, Universitat de Pompeu Fabra, Spain.

Rosanna Raimato, The Sir Bernard Lovell School, Bristol, UK.

Aud Marit Simensen, Department of Teacher Education and School Development, Faculty of Education, University of Oslo, Norway.

Claude Springer, Université Marc Bloch, Strasbourg, France.

Melanie Valet, Staunton Park Community School, Havant, UK.

Piet Van de Craen, Department of Germanic Languages, Vrije Universiteit, Brussels, Belgium.

Arthur van Essen, Department of Language and Communication, University of Groningen, Netherlands.

Dieter Wolff, Bergische Universität GHS Wuppertal, Germany.

Acknowledgements

The impetus for this book emerged from work within the European Language Council, which I would like to acknowledge with thanks; in particular, the members of the Thematic Network Project – Bilingualism and Teacher Education. I would also like to thank the following for permission to reproduce extracts: CILT for the diamond-ranking diagram on p. 139, which comes from *Pathfinder 27: New Contexts for Modern Language Learning* by Kim Brown and Margot Brown (1996); The Stapleford Centre for the materials used by Shirley Dobson in chapter 10, which first appeared in *Charis Deutsch, Einheit 1* (ACT, 1996) and *Charis Français* (Stapleford Centre); and the Development Education Project at Manchester Metropolitan University for the timeline activity on p. 144. I am also grateful to Margot Brown for the Vidas Mexicanas activity in chapter 10 and to Melanie Valet, former Head of Modern Languages, Staunton Park Community School, Havant, Hants for the learning strategy schemes in chapter 12. I would especially like to acknowledge the careful and patient work of my fellow Bristolian, Pauline Marsh, in improving both the accuracy and the style of the text. Louise Mellor at Routledge has also been supportive and understanding throughout the production of the book. Finally, I would like to thank my family and friends for their understanding and support whilst I worked on this book.

1 Introduction

Michael Grenfell

This book is about broadening horizons. It is written and published at the beginning of a new millennium. With the start of a new century and the third millennium there is a sense that nothing changes and that everything does. Nothing changes in that we do not become a different world and different people. Yet, everything is looked at anew and with a fresh perspective. We reflect on the past and lessons learnt from experience. We look to the future and its threats and opportunities.

Our focus in the book is language; in particular, second languages and the way their learning and teaching might be organised. Our book title – *Modern Languages Across the Curriculum* – refers to our concern with showing how modern foreign languages can be integrated with other subject disciplines: Mathematics, Biology, Geography, Art, Business Studies, History, Religious Education, etc. Questions of learning theory and pedagogic principle are therefore central to our discussion. Issues of learning process and teaching practice do not take place in a cultural vacuum. To learn a language is to step into another world of values, senses and points of view. To teach a language is to engage in a personal interaction with the learner which involves whole identities in the fullest sense. A major objective of the book is therefore to raise awareness of the personal and cultural dimensions of language learning and teaching and to see these not simply as a transparent medium to attain pedagogic goals but as central to their realisation.

The twentieth century was the century of language and communication. At its start, telecommunications were in their infancy. Telephones were restricted to a business minority of the world's population; the most urgent conveyor of messages was the telegram; television and radio were unheard of. The printed word was all. As the century closed, quantum leap upon quantum leap in systems had created a communications network which was fast, immediate and available to nearly all. Telephones had at first put everyone in touch with everyone else in the world; then provided the lines to access the world wide web – a virtual world of information, text, aural and pictorial; then, the mobile telephone was created, allowing personal access to talk and the Internet anytime, anywhere. Between the beginning and end of the last century, television and radio became ubiquitous and our transport, economic and socio-cultural activities were all rendered dependent on language and its systems of communication.

Language is, of course, also the medium of education and training. Each development in communication systems has impacted on teaching and learning; firstly, with the growth of audio-visual techniques in film, photography and recordings; and then, video, computing and finally the Internet. The part that language plays in learning and teaching has itself attracted attention, as well as the language used to discuss language. We can say that we have become 'language aware' at every level. At the start of the twentieth century, the human race had only just conceived the idea of what it was to study language – the science of linguistics had been born. At this stage, linguistic study proceeded in much the same way as one might chart a newly discovered country or categorise a new plant species: through systematic description and explanation. In the course of the twentieth century, these early structural studies developed into all manner of applied versions, as language connected with such disciplines as Psychology, Sociology and Philosophy to produce a multitude of hybrid variants: Socio-linguistics, Psycholinguistics, Social Psycholinguistics, etc. The philosophy of man became the philosophy of language; firstly, in political rhetoric, and then in investigations which saw the constitution of people as essentially parallel to language discourse.

This picture of the last century, and the place language held in it, is painted with the broadest of brushes. However, these trends are essential elements in understanding the motivation lying behind this book. If the last century was the century *of* language and communications, the new millennium and century kicked off in 2001 with the European Year *for* Languages: a celebration of cultural and linguistic diversity as well as language learning and teaching. A second major objective of this book is therefore to consider where we are coming from in language matters, what are our linguistic needs and exigencies, and where we are going in terms of pedagogy and language policy.

As our understanding of language developed throughout the last century, so did our approaches to teaching and learning it. At the start of the century, the learning of languages other than one's first language was essentially an academic exercise. To learn a language was a mark of finesse and culture. It showed mental agility and control. Only those few rich enough to travel experienced languages other than their own. As far as a methodology for learning language existed, it expressed classical preoccupations with analysis, memorisation and application. The content of language study also focused on literature and philosophy. Such approaches and content firstly gave way to concerns to make language learning a more social undertaking, with an intention to speak and listen to language as much as to read and study it. Next, developments in behaviourist psychology recast language as a skill-based activity as liable to training as any other habit-forming function. Then came the discovery of deep generating structures of the human mind as the source of language competence and performance. And all the while the communicative imperative increased.

These developments in the approach to language teaching and learning can be regarded as 'horizons of understanding'.

The first horizon concerns language and how we conceptualise it. A second horizon follows the track of psychology: how the brain processes and generates language. A third horizon is methodological: which approaches, methods and techniques are brought to teaching contexts and what are their guiding principles? In theory at least, what we do in teaching should reflect what we understand about learning. A fourth horizon is socio-cultural, which, by implication, is also economic; in other words, the social, cultural and political forces surrounding language learning and acting on them.

These horizons have been best exemplified in a major approach to language learning during the last quarter of the twentieth century: Communicative Language Teaching (CLT). CLT is a good example of an approach to language learning which responds to what I called above the 'communicative imperative'. A main driving force for CLT was the need people had to access information in other languages and to make themselves understood in them. These social and cultural needs also have economic consequences. The principles of CLT were the characteristics of communication as a transactional and interactive act. Moreover, it conformed to what was known about the psychological and social functions and processes of language. CLT has been a major influence on language teaching and learning in recent decades. It is therefore our starting point for the present book.

Our context in this book is European. The formation, establishment and expansion of the European Union (EU) have created the condition of language needs across its member states. Communication is needed if we are to enter into dialogue and economic relations with each other. To this extent, the EU has been a prime mover behind CLT since it suits its communicative ambitions. The linguistic profile of Europe is indeed complex. Communicative language, of course, does not necessarily mean communicative *English*. Whilst it is necessary to recognise the prominence of English in the world and its usefulness as a *lingua franca*, we must resist the temptation to see it as a linguistic *passe-partout* which undermines the need to learn any other language. Similarly, within European systems, French and German join English as the 'official' languages of office, thus giving minority status to others. To learn these as 'official' languages is implicitly to condone a linguistic hierarchy and to stray away from a vision of a multilingual future. In the twenty-first century, Europe will either be multilingual or will not be at all. Yet, to accept this statement demands recognition, not only of other major languages within Europe, but of regional and trans-national languages as well. Britain too is a multilingual society containing its own indigenous languages, for example, Welsh, as well as both European and non-European languages. It is important to realise that in most European countries, some second language learning already takes place in a context where the regional language is not the same as that of the nation state. Language learning and teaching in these situations already occurs where the social and cultural issues are heavy with implications concerning identity and identification. Elsewhere, language learning may appear to be more instrumental and culturally value free. In terms of pedagogy, identity and policy we need to think in terms of language – *which* language? – and its content.

Why Modern Languages Across the Curriculum?

This introduction opened with the promise to 'broaden horizons'. One of these horizons was methodological, and *Modern Languages Across the Curriculum* (MLAC) can be seen both as a pedagogic principle and as a practice. It addresses many of the concerns mounting from experience with Communicative Language Teaching and gives a fresh perspective to enhancing the content of language teaching and learning. Another name for MLAC is therefore CLIL: Content and Language Integrated Learning. Some of the contributors to this book have retained the CLIL abbreviation as it is the one which is applied most commonly in their particular contexts. Both MLAC and CLIL, however, designate a concern to integrate language learning and curriculum content much more fully. Immersion programmes have, of course, a long history (see, for example, Johnson and Swain 1987). However, many of these have taken place in Canada or in similar cultural contexts where there was a need to integrate more than one national language. Here, bilingualism is a must. Some of the contributors to this book write from such a bilingual perspective; others from one where there are regional languages, which are taught or learnt alongside a national dominant language. In still other cases, the question is the need to learn English, as the national language is not widely recognised and, thus, is not learnt much beyond national boundaries. In all cases, however, there are further methodological implications for considering this approach to second language learning and teaching, namely, that it offers the possibility of enhancing progress in linguistic competence. We will see how MLAC offers possibilities and approaches not normally included in traditional immersion programmes. To an extent, CLIL or MLAC can be regarded as an off-spring of CLT – it is a new version of CLT – one which is more relevant to the current twenty-first century cultural context and one which offers a better means of teaching and learning languages.

MLAC can be seen as an approach which is sensitive to the multicultural issues of an expanding European Union. It can also be regarded as developing and reapplying both pedagogic principles and learning theories towards a new style of language learning. In a sense, the modern information age is a content-handling age; probably much more than one of extended competence. But MLAC or CLIL offers the possibility of making competence itself a direct result of the quality of content in a way which has been hitherto unknown in many European countries. For example, in England, we have embarked on a steadily expanding programme of creating specialist language colleges. Such colleges are expected to offer more languages, including those of countries outside the EU. They are also expected to be sensitive to and to promote and support the languages of their own internal communities. Moreover, enhanced progression is a principal goal for such colleges. It is unlikely that these colleges will succeed with these aspirations without adopting some form of MLAC or CLIL; that is, without endeavouring to deliver at least part of the curriculum through the second language and moving away from the stand-alone language programme. Furthermore, in recent years, the English curriculum has been marked by a new emphasis on language and literacy. The National Literacy Strategy (DfEE 1998) was launched in 1998 with the explicit aim of raising the standards of literacy in English primary schools, which it has done (OISE 2001). Pupils who have followed the strategy are now moving through the secondary school system. Here, a new initiative has been launched to transform teaching and learning skills in literacy in a 'language across the curriculum' policy (DfEE 2001). This book is a timely contribution to this focus on language in the curriculum and the ways it can be used to enhance learning and teaching.

The book is divided into distinct parts and chapters in order to deal with Modern Languages Across the Curriculum from a range of perspectives. Part 1 includes two chapters on theory and rationale. Chapter 2 sets the context by describing a century – the twentieth century – of change in the teaching of modern foreign languages. Arthur van Essen sets out to show how methodologies changed over the course of the century. The advantages and disadvantages of various approaches are discussed, as well as the main issues of the day. He explains each different movement in turn, ending with a discussion of Communicative Language Teaching. We see these movements as natural developments towards common goals – the same ones which MLAC and CLIL now address: cultural empathy and linguistic competence. In chapter 3, Michael Grenfell looks at some of the learning theories behind these methodological approaches. He traces early preoccupations with language as an object of analysis and more recent psychological treatments of its processes. He also considers Communicative Language Teaching and looks at the learning principles which underlie CLT. He deals with language as a social and psychological process, and includes motivation and task design in his exploration of the way MLAC/CLIL enhances language learning.

The aim of part 2 of this book is to offer a series of short national case studies. These illustrate what second language learning looks like in practice from the vantage points of different EU member states. We see policy and practice which contrast with our own, whichever country we are working in. We see how the relative weightings of social-cultural factors and pedagogic procedures can vary from country to country. The underlying issues, however, remain the same. These case examples also report in detail on MLAC classes and assess the outcomes of adopting such an approach. Part 2 is offered as a way of developing a consensus of approach whilst at the same time respecting diversity in context and practice. The picture which emerges from the case examples offers issues and an agenda for guiding the implementation of MLAC in practice within its range of applications.

Part 3 is the 'How to do it' section of the book. This part aims to offer some guiding principles for adopting a MLAC/CLIL approach in practice. Clearly, there is a continuum between, one the one hand, simply broadening the content in language learning and, on the other, a fully developed delivery of a curriculum subject through the second language. As this book is addressed very much to those who are developing an MLAC approach, part 3 demonstrates how the content of language learning can be expanded to include a broader horizon of curriculum content. Practical examples are offered as well as commentary and pointers to keep in mind when planning for such classes.

Part 4 is concerned with teacher education. Clearly, in order to be successful with MLAC/CLIL classrooms, it is necessary to have a skilled and trained teaching force. The approach requires curriculum teachers to teach in a language other than their native one and/or second language teachers to be able to deliver curriculum content. In either case, training and support are needed. As such teachers are likely to be experienced language users, bilingual and mobile, chapter 12 discusses the sorts of institutional, national and Europe-wide training and support needed to help teachers to understand both why MLAC is productive and how to begin it. The second chapter in part 4 includes materials and activities which can be used by and with teachers in order to prepare them to teach in this way.

In the conclusion to the book, the salient features of policy and practice are summarised. We locate Modern Languages Across the Curriculum as part of an overall language policy within a European context. To guide the reader, various summaries and briefings are also included throughout the book. The book includes a range of themes and topics centring on Modern Languages Across the Curriculum. The *point de départ* for different readers might be different. After this introductory chapter, classroom teachers might start with the practical examples in part 3 and then read back to see how it operates in various European countries before considering its historical and theoretical backgrounds and the training they might need from parts 1 and 4. Teacher trainers might begin in the teacher education chapters and, again, read back to the practical materials, case examples, and rationale chapters. Researchers and policy makers will want to track through the contexts, both historical and theoretical, for MLAC, what it looks like in practice, and what needs to be done to develop teachers' awareness and abilities to work with it. There are, then, different ways to read the book, as we have constructed a discursive montage to explain and demonstrate Modern Languages Across the Curriculum.

References

Department for Education and Employment (1998) *The National Literacy Strategy*, London: HMSO.
—— (2001) *Literacy Across the Curriculum*, London: HMSO.
Johnson, R. K. and Swain, M. (1987) *Immersion Education: International Perspectives*, Cambridge: CUP.
Ontario Institute for Studies in Education (2001) *Watching Learning 2*, University of Toronto: OISE.

Part 1

Modern Languages Across the Curriculum

Theory and rationale

Introduction

Michael Grenfell

This part of the book considers the background and justification for Modern Languages Across the Curriculum. Chapter 2 takes a historical perspective and offers an account of the teaching and learning of modern foreign languages in Europe during the twentieth century. Cultural, political, pedagogic and methodological issues are compared and contrasted. We see how Modern Languages Across the Curriculum as an approach is a logical extension of and development from past trends in the teaching and learning of second languages. The evolution from grammar–translation methods to Communicative Language Teaching is explained, as are the socio-cultural contexts that acted as a background to the directions taken in language teaching. Chapter 2 provides both historical and methodological rationales for Modern Languages Across the Curriculum. Chapter 3 then considers MLAC in terms of what is known about learning languages. Knowing how things are learnt should help us prepare for how to teach. Chapter 3 looks at what we know about language learning and what this implies in terms of methodological approach. Language and content, as an integrated whole, are seen to offer a defining principle for practical implementation. How such integration addresses prime discoveries about the conditions for successful second language learning and teaching is also discussed.

2   A historical perspective

Arthur van Essen

Introduction

This chapter sets out to offer a historical background to modern languages teaching from a European perspective. I want to cover the period from what is known as the reform to the present. Such an undertaking can only ever be partial. I shall also have to restrict my primary sources to only a selection of the most important works, viz. those publications which were used by teacher trainers and classroom practitioners. Nevertheless, it is possible to identify distinct periods of pedagogic trend and development. Such periods are, of course, a product of their time. However, we shall see the unfolding search for an effective methodology for teaching second languages. I shall supplement this account with my own observations as a learner, a teacher, and a participant in some of the European developments described over the past fifty years or so.

From the reform to the First World War

In most countries of mainland Europe the teaching of foreign languages was introduced into public-sector schools in the course of the nineteenth century. In those days the living languages were predominantly taught according to the method used for the dead languages (i.e. Latin and Greek), that is by teaching grammar rules, compiling bilingual wordlists, and translating isolated sentences, which were often absurd. Growing discontent over this approach was expressed throughout the early part of the nineteenth century (see Hawkins 1987: 117), but did not come to a head until the last quarter of that century, when Viëtor's *Der Sprachunterricht muss umkehren!* (1882) was published and became a clarion call for innovation and change. The ideas it expressed had been in the air for some time, both in America and Europe, and heralded a new approach to language learning.

The Reform Movement was induced by political and economic changes in Germany and fostered by the Neogrammarians' interest in the living languages and dialects (especially their psycho-physiological side) for the purpose of explaining language change. Most, but not all, reformers were also phoneticians. From Germany the movement soon spread to the other German-speaking countries and to Scandinavia, where Francke and later Jespersen (1860–1943) became its main champions. In France and England, Passy and Sweet gave the movement an important boost. The reform did not lose its first impetus until the turn of the century (Rombouts 1937: 128), but despite the fact that in Germany so many eminent scholars lent their names to it, it did not catch on there to the extent that it did in France, where the Reform Method was introduced throughout the education system by ministerial decree in 1902 (Rombouts 1937: 163). France also had a reformer named Gouin (1831–1896), who worked independently. Today, Gouin's chief claim to fame lies in the fact that he was one of the first students of language to pose the problem of linguistics in language teaching. Since no coherent theory of language was available to him at the time, he had to work out his own. Having failed in his attempts to learn German in the classical (i.e. deductive) manner, which he carried to extremes, he tried to construct his own method by observing the language use and language development of his 3-year-old nephew. These observations led Gouin to develop a psychology of language learning and teaching that permitted the selection of topics ('themes') from reality ('Nature') that were capable of analysis into constituent events ('acts' and 'facts') and of expression in at least two basic language functions. A typical exercise would reflect the thematic unity ('series') and look like this:

> Theme: Nursemaid
> 'Walk, my pretty; That's it!
> Go towards the door; That's very good!
> Now you've got there; Bravo!
> Lift up your little arm; Capital!
> Take hold of the handle; That's the way!
> Turn the handle; How strong you are!
> Open the door; What a clever little man!
> Pull the door open; There's a little darling!'

Note the simplicity of the interlinking sentences (most of which could be the starting-point of another series), displaying a chronological order, and the centrality of the verb. The verb is like a pivot around which each constituent sentence revolves. The phrases left of the semi-colon represent 'objective language' (today mostly called the 'referential', 'propositional', 'cognitive', 'descriptive', or 'transactional' language function); those right of the semi-colon 'subjective language' (i.e. the 'emotive', 'expressive', 'attitudinal', 'interpersonal', or 'interactional' language function). Though these are strongly intertwined and developed simultaneously in natural language acquisition (Gouin 1892: 154), the teacher should begin by teaching objective language, continue by teaching subjective language, and finish by teaching 'figurative (i.e. metaphorical) language', which feeds on objective language (for example: He fell into the river – He fell into the trap). Semanticisation took place by having learners enact and verbalise the series, first in their mother tongue and subsequently in the foreign language. Pictures might also be used.

The ear being 'the master-organ of language' (Gouin 1892: 127), much emphasis is placed on ear-training, with the teacher as the learners' model. Unlike other champions of the Reform Movement, Gouin made no use of the science of phonetics or phonetic transcriptions. He favoured an inductive approach: 'all that the teacher does is simply to aid or direct, it will be the class themselves who carry out this work' (Gouin 1892: 262). Gouin's 'natural' method of teaching was rather more successful on the continent of Europe (especially in Germany and The Netherlands) during the last decade of the nineteenth and the first three decades of the twentieth century (and in America during the early part of the twentieth century) than it was in his own country.

By contrast, the Englishman Henry Sweet (1845–1912) felt himself to be a phonetician in the first place and a linguist in the second. It is clear from Sweet's early writings where he situated what he called his 'practical philology' (see Howatt 1984: 189). It lies somewhere between 'living philology', which was based on phonetics and psychology, and the 'practical study of languages', which meant learning how to understand, speak, write, and read a foreign language. In other words, 'practical philology' is the area where general linguistic principles are applied to the learning of other languages. Sweet's 'practical philology' came close to modern applied linguistics. Its cornerstones were phonetics (Sweet 1899: 4) and Herbartian associationism (ibid.: 40 and 103). He favoured an inductive presentation of grammar (i.e. one presenting sufficient examples for the learners to derive the rule themselves) (p. 117). Sweet was aware of the disadvantages of age (the older we are, the more our powers of imitation and motivation decline) and of already knowing a language (one's own). For this reason, he dismissed Gouin's 'natural' method (p. 76). Nor did he approve of the view that the native-speaker teacher is the intrinsically better teacher (p. 48).

The lasting impression after reading Sweet's book is one of emphasis on phonetic and linguistic principles. For the benefit of missionaries he had added a chapter which contained guidelines for the study of unrecorded non-Western languages. The techniques described in this chapter, such as the use of native speakers and linguistically trained instructors, really foreshadowed what the American linguist Leonard Bloomfield (1887–1949) was to propose for the language training of military personnel during the Second World War (Bloomfield 1942, 1945), and they were to make a considerable impact on language education in Europe after the war. Considerations of an educational nature are virtually absent from Sweet's book. His teachers and pupils are bloodless abstractions, and his style is that of learned discourse (see Howatt 1984: 188).

How different is Otto Jespersen's book! *How to Teach a Foreign Language* came out in 1904 and has remained popular among language teachers ever since. Small wonder, for this is a book that both teachers and students can identify with, showing as it does their strong and weak points. Not only was the Dane, Jespersen, a phonetician and a linguist, but he was one with a mission as an educator. This is evident from almost every page of Jespersen's book, which shows a lively interest in teachers and pupils. His 'inventional grammar' is based upon his precept 'never tell the children anything that they can find out for themselves' (1904: 127), a principle Sweet ridiculed (Sweet 1899: 116). If Sweet focused on linguistics, Jespersen did so on pedagogy. In his book, one frequently comes across the expression 'from a pedagogical point of view'. It is Jespersen's pedagogical perspective which determines the choice of his subject-matter and the importance he assigns to the various language skills. What was at issue for Jespersen was educating young people to become responsible world citizens. Jespersen was convinced that the modern humanities could play a big part in this (Jespersen 1904: 9). His book was influential in that it defined the principal aim of reading in terms of giving 'the pupils some insight into the foreign nation's peculiarity', as he called it (ibid.: 179). Since Jespersen wrote this, *Landeskunde* (i.e. 'area studies') and *Kulturkunde* (i.e. 'cultural studies', with an emphasis on 'national character') have been present in many continental coursebooks and teacher education programmes (see van Essen 1986). Its aims have varied from teaching just the *realia* to fostering a better understanding between peoples. Jespersen believed in the latter: 'language teachers all over the world', he wrote, 'may ultimately prove more efficacious in establishing good permanent relations between the nations than Peace Congresses at the Hague' (ibid.: 180). Following his exhortations, a network of correspondence schools (as precursors of face-to-face exchanges) was established after the First World War, on the assumption that it would be best to start with children to achieve reconciliation between nations, and schools were thus seen to play a central role in an area where politics and politicians had so obviously failed. This trend continued after the Second World War, when the increasing economic and political integration of Europe led to a considerable number of associations and programmes to promote various kinds of exchanges (e.g. Socrates, Erasmus, Comenius), working towards the ideal of a common European citizenship (see Müller-Hartmann 2000: 212).

Jespersen argued that in teaching a language, the language itself is not the aim – communication is (1904: 5). This was an encouraging noise, especially at a time when the grammar–translation method was rife. What is remarkable to read today is the statement with which Jespersen concluded his chapter on grammar teaching: 'practise what is right again and again!'. But this exhortation did not anticipate the behaviourist call for embedding languages as a habit-forming skill through repetition drills. Rather it sees that having communication as the aim of language teaching does not remove the necessity to practise for accuracy.

From 1910 on, the reform principles were increasingly coming under fire. The movement was criticised for its dogmatic exclusion of the mother tongue from the classroom and for its fixation on learning to *speak* the foreign language, whereas the majority of learners would never speak but read or write it (Rombouts 1937: 130–1). While the value of *some* phonetics was not questioned, the value of a prolonged period of practising phonetic transcriptions was. And so was the artificial divorce of the spoken from the written language. This might be acceptable for commercial courses, taught by native speakers, but not for general education, which had formative pretensions.

The interwar period

One of the the most influential of the 'natural' approaches of the pre-war period, the Direct Method, was abolished in France as abruptly as it had been introduced – by ministerial directive. France then entered upon a period of foreign-language instruction based upon the precepts of Henri Delacroix (1925), whose theory shows a striking resemblance to that put forward by some North American neurophysiologists in the 1960s: each time we learn a new language we establish a new, autonomous speech centre on the cortex (Penfield and Roberts 1959). Typical of the *Ecole française de l'enseignement des langues modernes* was the alternate use of the native and the foreign language during the lesson at elementary level. At intermediate level the translations were reintroduced. The way in which the words of a text were semanticised was new. The translation of words was avoided by giving explanations in the foreign language. To make absolutely sure that learners understood what they were reading, the mother tongue was used (Rombouts 1937: 164). At the more advanced level, the teaching of literature became more important, while some attention was also paid to cultural studies. These were very much an intellectual affair.

In Germany, the counter-reform was not as radical as it was in France, but then the reform had not been as radical as in France. The majority of German teachers opted for a method that combined what they thought were the best qualities of both the traditional and the reform methods (i.e. eclecticism). Characteristic of the German counter-reform was that it did not produce any leading figures. It rested on negative experiences with the Direct Method, on personal convictions, and on regional legislation.

In the interwar years (and after), nobody contributed more to the field than the Englishman Harold E. Palmer (1877–1949), who himself had gained a lot of teaching experience in Belgium before fleeing from the invading German troops in 1914. Palmer has left us a great many works, all of them of a practical, 'applied' nature. He was completely self-taught. The lessons he taught to adult learners at private language schools shaped Palmer as a language pedagogue. The courses he taught provided his daily income. He taught according to the Direct Method, and so without recourse to the native language of his students. His teaching experiences found their way into a number of books, and it is the principles laid down in these books that have remained the core of Palmer's language pedagogy.

In 1916, Palmer published his *100 Substitution Tables* (Palmer 1916), a work with a behaviourist slant, based on a kind of type–token relationship between the example sentence (e.g. I saw two books here yesterday) and the possible utterances that could be generated with it (e.g. You put three letters there last week, etc.). In the same year Palmer enthusiastically taught an in-service course for foreign-language teachers in London. This course proved extremely popular. Indeed, so popular that Palmer decided to write out his notes and to publish them under the title *The Scientific Study and Teaching of Languages* (Palmer 1917). It was the first time that the word 'scientific' in the title of a work on language pedagogy was explicitly associated with language education. Precisely because Palmer did not belong to any linguistic school, at least not at the time, this book contained so many idiosyncratic terms (e.g. 'ergonics') that it must have driven many a contemporary reader to despair.

Palmer (1922a) embodied a first attempt at what in the 1970s was later to be called the 'notional-functional approach' (Van Ek 1975 and Wilkins 1976). Palmer's 'everyday sentences', arranged under such language functions as 'Asking for Information', 'Giving Permission', and so on, meant a huge step forwards compared with the often absurd, isolated sentences that were still widely used in the grammar–translation coursebooks of the day. But, at the same time, they were a major step backwards compared with the connected texts of the reformers of the 1880s, as a context was wanting. The absence of context – which includes any co-text (i.e. any surrounding words), the participants in the discourse, the socio-psychological roles these participants are involved in, the setting – imparts to much of Palmer's work, just as it would to Van Ek's *Threshold Level* of the mid-1970s, the flavour of a Berlitz phrasebook (cf. Newby 2000: 450). In communication, the presence of context is absolutely vital. Just how much the process of interpreting a language form, in other words, just how much a speech act or 'language function' (in Van Ek's terminology) depends on contextual factors is evident from the following example.

A: What's the time?
B: 10.15.

As a follow-up to '10.15' at least three possibilities may be considered:

1   *A*: Thanks!
2   *A*: Well done!
3   *A*: You're lying.

'Thanks!' suggests a genuine request for information on the part of A; 'well done!' smacks of the classroom (e.g. a lesson about 'telling the time'); 'you're lying' sounds like an accusation or reproach. But it is only in the first instance that we can truly speak of a language function 'Asking for Information' (cf. Widdowson 1979: 249 and McCarthy 1991: 16).

Habit-formation was the strongest pillar of Palmer's language pedagogy (Palmer 1922b). But just as with Jespersen, and later Bloomfield, it would be wrong to attach too much importance to Palmer's behaviourism. At most Palmer was a proto-behaviourist (Howatt 1984: 240). When Palmer wrote about habit-formation, behaviourism proper was still in its infancy. Palmer's use of isolated sentences also conflicted with the precepts of Gestalt psychology, which was just then coming into its own. Gestalt psychology taught that the 'whole' of something is more important than its 'parts'. A whole text would be more important than its constituent sentences. At the same time, Palmer's use of isolated sentences put the non-native teacher at a disadvantage, since they did not have at their disposal the whole range of sentences that a native-speaker teacher would be able to access in the classroom (Palmer 1922a). In fairness, one should add that Palmer strongly promoted the view that the teacher should command both the learner's native language and the target language, just as Henry Sweet had done (Palmer 1917 (1968): 163 and 173–4). When it came to using the pupils' native language in the classroom Palmer made it clear that he was not against it as long as it was limited to the explanation of word meanings ('semanticisation').

Palmer had always looked at linguistics as a language pedagogue should, namely, with a selective eye. He always asked himself the question: what does linguistics have to offer for the solution of problems that the classroom teacher finds themselves up against? To find answers to his questions he carried on a regular correspondence, and occasionally had talks with, linguists around the world. In 1931 he attended the Second International Congress of Linguists in Geneva, having come over from Japan, where he was linguistic adviser on ELT to the Japanese Government. In Geneva he met Saussure's student Sechehaye. Following this meeting, Palmer took great pains to provide his language pedagogy with a theoretical foundation. This he did with the aid of Saussure's teachings. From that moment on, Palmer's theoretical foundation began to look as follows. Every language has a systematic aspect (which Saussure called *langue*) and an activity aspect (which Saussure called *parole*). *Langue* and *parole* could be compared to Humboldt's *ergon* and *energeia*. But instead of Saussure's terms Palmer used 'language' (or 'code, an organized system of symbols or signals') and 'speech' (or 'mode of social behaviour'). For the language user, the language system is to language use what a cookery book is to food for someone who is hungry. It is the second thing that matters. The language learner may approach the foreign language from either point of view or from both. It is true, Palmer said, that a language pedagogy that takes its starting-point in language use often leads to mastery of the spoken foreign language, especially in young children. Palmer did not expect adults to learn in the same way as children but in the same spirit. So, in an actual teaching–learning situation, he expected a mixed pedagogy to emerge. It would depend on one's aims, on the age of the learners, on the time available, which of the two aims one would like to emphasise. But irrespective of this emphasis, any language pedagogy will have to start from intensively speaking the language. Palmer did not agree at all with the assumption that it is possible to teach reading prior to, or independently of, the speaking skill (Palmer and Vere Redman,1932 (1969): 72). For the learner will have to go through the Saussurian *circuit de la parole* (Saussure 1915: 27–9) time and time again, and attentive listening should be the starting-point. The principal aim of this, as Palmer saw it, was to establish in the mind a direct and permanent bond between the sound (*image acoustique, signifiant*) and the meaning (*concept, signifié*) of a language sign (*signe*). It is by emphasising this direct bond that the term 'Direct Method' took on a special significance with Palmer. For if this direct association of sound and meaning does not take place before the learner ventures into reading, there is the danger that the learner will start translating, that is, that they will make associations between the words of the foreign language and any supposed equivalents in his own language. Instead of reading, the learner will start 'deciphering'. And that is not what Palmer had in mind.

Palmer's language pedagogy is perhaps best characterised as 'eclectic', aimed at learning another language as efficiently as possible. If anything, his eclecticism meant pluralism. His 'multiple line of approach' (Palmer 1922b (1964): 108) offers the possibility of using drill-work as well as free work, of mobilising spontaneous capacities for learning as well as conscious learning, of intensive reading as well as extensive reading, and so on. Whether the teacher opts for one approach rather than another, or for an alternation of the two types, depends on the circumstances and the learner. With his methodological pluralism, Palmer was way ahead of his time. He anticipated a number of distinctions that have recently received renewed attention or have become topical issues in our field, like Krashen's unconscious acquisition and conscious learning (Palmer 1922b and Krashen 1982) and the presence of an incubation period in unconscious acquisition (Palmer 1917: 97) – similar to Krashen's 'silent period'. In the same way, he distinguished what were later to be called 'learning strategies' and 'cognitive styles'.

With Palmer we entered the interwar period. And so far our discussion has been dominated by the three reformers who mainly wrote in English. This should not lead us to believe that in the two decades roughly making up the period between the two World Wars nothing of interest or importance to us had been going on on the continent of Europe. On the contrary, one only needs to name some of the better-known German and Russian psychologists, peda-gogues, and linguists of the period (Philipp Aronstein, Karl Bühler, Erich Drach, Otto Selz, Lev Vygotsky, and Leo Weisgerber) to demonstrate that mainland Europe had not been wanting in interesting and visionary educational thinkers. However, for reasons known to all of us – the exodus of European scholars to the US after 1933, the educational monopoly (*Gleichschaltung*) by the Nazis, the physical isolation of mainland Europe during the last war and of part of it during the Cold War – the impact of European scholars on the development of our field has been negligible. Compared with the relevant literature of today, the works of the continental scholars from the 1920s and 1930s just mentioned breathe a totally different atmosphere. They almost exclusively refer to European sources in languages other than English, whereas modern Anglo-Saxon publications in linguistics almost exclusively refer to sources in their own language (cf. van Essen 1989 and Block 1996). What the continental European scholars of those days had at heart was educational ideals (*Bildungsideale*). This attitude is obvious from almost every page of their writings.

At the end of the First World War, almost everything in Germany had ground to a halt, and so had language teaching. It took the Germans some time to get going again. And when they did, they retained in their coursebooks some phonetics and a very sparing use of phonetic transcription (usually of their own making, with a lot of diacritics). They also kept the connected text as the starting-point of the teaching–learning unit. In Germany, texts (a short story or a dialogue) remained the mainstay of foreign-language coursebooks through-out the interwar period and long after. Their position within the unit shifted from the beginning to the middle, where they became sandwiched between introductory and exploratory exercises (Butzkamm 1973: 78ff.). Where the

German eclectics differed crucially from the reformers is in the place they assigned to grammar. They were not content to deal occasionally with points of grammar, for example, as they occurred in the text: no, grammar was the ordering principle of the whole course! The treatment of grammar was not altogether retrograde, however. The text was used as a grammatical treasure trove, and any specimen found there was dealt with inductively. Anti-reform also meant the use of translations, as did the deliberate use of the mother tongue.

What was true of Germany was true of many other European countries. In Belgium and The Netherlands, the situation was not essentially different (see van Essen 1989). Denmark, however, produced a very interesting figure, Flagstad. A teacher from Copenhagen, he was the very opposite of Jespersen. Drawing on Wundt's psychology of language (i.e. *Völkerpsychologie*), Flagstad made a strong plea for literal translations into the native language in order to assess the learners' understanding of the meaning involved. He also condemned the dogmatic exclusion of the mother tongue in the learning of vocabulary. Flagstad was in favour of teaching the spoken language, even if reading was the only aim. He advocated the free use of serials and penny dreadfuls as reading matter, as they represented topics of interest to less sophisticated learners. Flagstad did not believe in a 'silent period', but he did believe in the explicit treatment of grammatical structures that differed from those in the native language. Where there were no differences, grammar rules could be dealt with implicitly. Flagstad translated his work (Flagstad 1913) from the Danish himself, and it is the most comprehensive psychology of language teaching to date (Carpay 1975: 19; Butzkamm 1973: 193).

During the Second World War, the method debate in the professional journals of mainland Europe at first continued unabated but then stagnated, because of paper rationing or a ban by the Nazis.

The Second World War and its aftermath

With the weaknesses of the reform method exposed, and not knowing what to do next, European language pedagogues began to look to the New World for guidance. But they gained little from looking at the United States. Rather the reverse was to be the case.

In the US, foreign-language teaching had long been aimed not at learning to speak another language (there were no opportunities to do it anyway) but at learning to read it. For this reason, the methodology of teaching the spoken language had badly lagged behind in compulsory schooling. It was not for nothing that the commercial private language schools were booming in America.

Both Bloomfield 1914 and Bloomfield 1933 devote a separate chapter to foreign-language education in the US. In both books, Bloomfield shows himself to be familiar with the works by Sweet, Jespersen, and Palmer, discussed above. Indeed, in the final chapter of his *Language*, to which he gave the title 'Applications and outlook', Bloomfield pointed to the 'vastly greater success of foreign-language instruction in Europe' when it came to useful language mastery (1933: 504).

Therefore, when war broke out in the Pacific in 1941, the Americans found out to their cost that very few military personnel spoke any foreign languages. But now the armed forces were in need of people who, in addition to the more common foreign languages, also spoke the more exotic ones, not taught at schools or universities. These people now had to be put through crash courses. In setting up such courses, the trainers could make use of the experience American linguists had gained in the study of American Indian languages. In 1945 Bloomfield described how he, like so many other linguists, had got involved in these intensive language programmes. And earlier on in the war, in 1942, Bloomfield had produced a pamphlet setting out the guidelines for anyone wanting to undertake the study of a language for which there was no formal training available. In writing this very practical pamphlet, whose title bore a strong resemblance to Sweet (1899), Bloomfield had in effect made a liberal use of Sweet's, Palmer's, and Jespersen's works. For anyone familiar with these works, Bloomfield's pamphlet contains very little that is new, not even his emphasis on habit-formation. But, as it became required reading for the instructors in the intensive language programme, along with Bloch and Trager (1942), the Audio-lingual Method soon became *the* model for any type of language learning, even after the war (Howatt 1984: 266).

It is ironic that where the reformers had failed, the Audio-lingual Method should have been more successful in conquering Europe. But by the time it *was* more successful, a number of things had happened to change the climate of opinion. The Americans had won the war. They had entered continental Europe as victors. Their technological superiority could not but impress the dazed Europeans. In the wake of other consumer goods, tape-recorders and language laboratories found their way into the European markets. In some countries a fierce resistance was put up by those who argued that the Audio-lingual Method had been developed and tested in intensive courses for selected adults and that the European school situation was a totally different one. They also pointed out that the adoption in European schools of a unilingual Audio-lingual Method was at variance with the precepts of one of its chief proponents, the American linguist Charles Fries (1887–1967), who had insisted on a careful comparison of the source and the target language. This contrastive position was exactly the one adopted by most continental language pedagogues. The Prague School, for example, was very early in making use of the so-called Confrontational Method, which was worked out by the Czech language scholar Vilém Mathesius in the late 1920s. Mathesius's approach invites an interesting comparison with the notional-functional approach of the 1970s as far as the functions are concerned. Thus, Mathesius speaks of communicative needs and wants that are to be expressed and which are roughly analogous in all language communities. But, as he points out, languages differ in the way they give linguistic expression to these needs and it is the comparison of these expressions that gives each language its own character (Fried 1972: 24).

After the Second World War, the Poles too built up an impressive tradition in contrastive studies, and one may well say that the revival in contrastive studies is in large measure due to them. And the Poles have been far from parochial; numerous scholars from outside Poland have been drawn into their projects. The Yugoslavs evolved their own tradition of contrastive studies (the 'Zagreb Project', led by Filipovic) with links all across Europe. In Germany (East and West) new grammars, both scholarly and pedagogical, appeared in the course of the 1980s (e.g. Graustein 1986; Ungerer 1986). All of them took the learner's native language into account. The same can be said of work produced in Belgium and the Netherlands (Dirven 1986; Aarts and Wekker 1987). Contrastive linguists took much encouragement from the findings of the large Swedish GUME-project, which showed that adult learners benefitted most from a contrastive presentation of the language (van Els et al. 1984: 259).

In a joint venture, the French and the Yugoslavs developed their own variety of the Direct Method from 1954 onwards and, by 1960, they were joined by the Belgians. Their approach was called the Structuro-global Method (Boyer and Rivera 1979: 23). Linguistically, it was oriented towards Prague School structuralism, while psychologically it relied heavily on Gestalt psychology. Pictures, slides, or films were used to represent the global meaning and pragmatics of a situation in which structural drill took place. Auditory perception was seen as a 'global' process, and for that reason a good deal of attention was paid to prosodic features, such as intonation and rhythm, rather than to minimal pairs (Renard 1975). Because it gave explicit attention to semantic and pragmatic factors, many European teachers intuitively felt a greater affinity to the Structuro-global Method than to the behaviouristic Audio-lingual courses. This may explain the comparative popularity of the Structuro-global courses in countries like the Netherlands.

In (West) Germany, unilingualism became both the dominant trend and the official policy for much foreign-language teaching (especially English teaching) after the war. But since the older, eclectic coursebooks that were still in use did not fit into the new unilingual conception, and since coursebooks have a tendency to determine what goes on in the classroom, a group of German-language pedagogues, united around the new journal *Praxis des neusprachlichen Unterrichts* (1953), began to bring course design into line with the principle of unilingualism. The older lesson with a connected text as the starting-point of grammar and vocabulary learning made way for a teaching–learning unit in 'phases', with passages for reading situated in the central or 'contextual' phase. Hans-Eberhard Piepho pioneered the first English-language courses along these lines. An adapted version of one of them was used in the Dutch English-in-the-primary-school project.

The movement for unilingualism in Germany was criticised for a lack of interest in its theoretical foundations and origins. It was reproached for a blatant disregard of a whole body of literature on the shortcomings of the Direct Method produced during the counter-reform of the 1920s (Aronstein 1924); in particular, as regards the use of the native language in the process of semanticisation. It was also blamed for misrepresenting the tenets of American Audio-lingualism, which did admit the use of the mother tongue to supply meaning to the learners

(Butzkamm 1973: 98). Viëtor admitted the necessity of using the native language when it came to providing the learners with the broad meaning of a text or with the specific meaning of a word (Viëtor 1905: 138). A moderate use of the native language was no longer anathema to the more enlightened unilingualists. Even the Dutch psychologist Van Parreren, who in a sense became the unilingualists' ideologist during the 1960s, and who remained quite adamant in his rejection of bilingual wordlists, in the end permitted the marginal use of the native language as a 'cognitive foothold' in the memorisation of words (Schouten and Van Parreren 1979). Yet it is easy to see the point that Van Parreren made over and over again: that any use of the native language during a foreign/second-language lesson is bound to reactivate the native-language systems within the learner's memory, thereby increasing the risk of interlingual errors (Van Parreren 1975: 113).

The 1970s and after

The 1970s and subsequent decades are characterised by concerted efforts towards a common European policy for language education. Thus, collaboration across national boundaries that had already been going on here and there now increasingly became a feature of European course design, curriculum development and in-service training (i.e. teacher development). Both the Swedes and the Germans have produced many coursebooks that have become popular in other European countries, such as Belgium, France, and the Netherlands. But few of these coursebooks were adopted without having been adapted to the receiving markets. More often than not, teams of authors from several countries worked together on a revision.

In a similar spirit, a team of scholars from the UK and other European countries, working under the auspices of the Council of Europe, from about 1970 took a lead in developing a more semantic, a more social, a more functional, in short, a more communicative syllabus for language teaching within the EEC. In designing their syllabus, these scholars were handicapped by the fact that they were running ahead of, or unaware of, any existing theories and/or predecessors. Wilkins, in his study of notional syllabuses, states that there was no available semantic (notional) framework on which to base such a syllabus. Therefore, he felt that he had to step in and provide a taxonomy of notions for this kind of syllabus (Wilkins 1976). For Wilkins, 'notional' is a blanket term for a semantic or communicative approach to language description, which is further subdivided into semantico-grammatical categories, categories of modal meaning, and categories of communicative function.

Van Ek's *Threshold Level* (1975) provided the distinction between, and definition of, the notions and functions as we know them today. Van Ek's 'functions' bear a strong resemblance to the speech acts of the ordinary-language philosophers (principally Austin and Searle) working in the 1960s. Van Ek distinguishes between 'language functions', which the learner will have to fulfil, and 'notions', which the learner will need to refer to things, to people, to events, etc., and to talk about them (Van Ek 1980: 8). A further distinction is made between 'general notions' (i.e. general abstract categories such as 'identification', 'duration', 'shape', 'colour') and 'specific notions', which are topic-related and can be of a grammatical or lexical nature (e.g. 'name' is related to the general notion 'identification', 'red' to 'colour', etc.).

Some of the objections that had been levelled against Palmer's 'phrasebook approach' (see above) might also be brought against the notional-functional syllabus. One of them is that the notional approach sought to redefine familiar grammatical and lexical categories. Not only did descriptions and lists already exist for these, but the categorisations intended to supplant them were formulated in rather abstract and sometimes unwieldy terms. This made them somewhat inaccessible to teachers and learners. Also, there is, at least in some cases, no clearcut dividing line between the notions, whereas in other cases there may be overlaps, as between 'topics' and 'specific notions'. It is perhaps not for nothing that the notional taxonomy has found little acceptance among materials writers and practitioners, whereas the 'language functions', which could be easily understood, found a ready acceptance among them, obviously filling a long-felt need. As Newby (2000: 451) points out, for an international, multilingual body like the Council of Europe, working from non-language-specific, notional categories has an obvious ideological appeal and practical application, as the many versions of the *Threshold Level* have subsequently proved. But, for writers of coursebooks and syllabuses for specific languages, it was more convenient to bypass the 'notions' and work from existing checklists of grammatical and lexical items. Indeed, within the area of vocabulary study, corpus analysis has since provided an alternative way to lexical specification and grading, which is arguably more scientific and more efficient than the 'brainstorming' approach of using notional checklists (Willis 1990 as quoted by Newby 2000: 451).

The *Threshold Level* has proved readily adaptable to languages other than English (in which it was originally conceived). This is because it is specified in terms of what learners can do in a language rather than what they *know* about a language. So, since 1975 separate versions have been developed for over a score of European languages, including such diverse ones as Basque, Irish, Maltese, Norwegian, Russian, Spanish, and Welsh. These versions are not mere translations. They take account not only of those notional categories obligatorily represented in the grammar of the language concerned, but also of differences in socio-cultural context. But they are all strictly comparable in their common use of the original model (Van Ek 2000: 631).

It is no exaggeration to say that the *Threshold Level* has left an indelible mark on foreign-language education in Europe, as a glance at the contents pages of modern coursebooks and national syllabuses will confirm. The 1980s and 1990s may be characterised as decades in which the ideas of the 'Communicative Approach' or Communicative Language Teaching, emphasising content rather than form, communicative effect rather than structural correctness, were implemented. One such implementation took place in the context of foreign-culture studies and may be viewed as an attempt to put cultural flesh on the culturally bare bones of the *Threshold Level* as it was originally conceived. For, as we noted above, the *Threshold Level* was specified in terms of functions and notions, the latter of which were implicitly assumed to be identical in all Western languages. By conducting interviews on parallel topics in parallel settings in different languages, Meijer was able to show, however, that many concepts which are handled at the *Threshold Level* are culture-bound, in the sense that they depend for their interpretation on socially and institutionally transmitted knowledge (Meijer 1983).

The Communicative Approach succeeded where all its Direct-Method predecessors had failed: it definitively shifted the pedagogical focus from language form to language user, from language as a code to language as a form of socio-cultural behaviour: *that* is its lasting credit. The latest development in the evolution towards a common European language policy for schools concerns a type of teaching variously called 'immersion teaching', 'content-based language instruction', 'content and language-integrated learning', 'teaching content in a foreign language', or 'teaching modern languages across the curriculum'. The latter term is the one adopted in and for this book

Conclusion

That content-based language instruction should enjoy a relative popularity in Europe is due to an upsurge of interest in many countries (e.g. Austria, Belgium, Finland, France, Germany, Italy, the Netherlands, Sweden, the United Kingdom) in this type of education as a means of helping learners to achieve a higher level of proficiency in a foreign language. The European Union has recognised that effective language teaching and learning are essential if every citizen is to benefit from the single market. For this reason, foreign-language education has a firm place on the agenda of the European Commission. The EU also sees languages as holding the key to a better understanding between nations and cultures, a fact that takes on even greater significance as the EU prepares to admit new member states. This will increase even further the number of languages spoken within its borders. The issue of language teaching in the EU was debated in depth in 1995, when all member states agreed on a resolution seeking improvements in the quality and diversity of language teaching throughout the EU. The ensuing White Paper, entitled *Towards a Learning Society*, carried a clear commitment to promoting and extending language learning throughout life. It also recognised the potential of teaching school subjects through the medium of a foreign language as a means of moving towards a society in which every young person can speak at least three Community languages. The European Commission, in short, is working towards societies in which every citizen is multilingual (Vlaeminck 1996). It is against this backdrop that teaching through the medium of a foreign language is gaining in importance. The advantages of this type of teaching are obvious. If the modern foreign language is used as the medium of instruction in a subject other than the language itself, there is more time available for other subjects in the curriculum. And perhaps even more importantly, learners will

CLIL

more readily realise the full potential offered by the language if they actually have to communicate in it, rather than seeing it as just another dry, academic subject.

In each of the countries mentioned above, schools are faced with similar problems and challenges. For the most part, however, they are working independently of one another. But rather than reinventing the wheel, schools across the EU could be working together to learn from each other's experiences, to tackle common problems and work towards common solutions. For over a century now, foreign languages have been taught alongside each other in schools across Europe. During all these years, language education has been an extensive testing ground for all sorts of innovations that people wanted to introduce (van Els et al. 1984: 156). In this way, a large body of collective experience accumulated. We now look to see how Modern Languages Across the Curriculum will be interpreted by policy makers and implemented by classroom practitioners across the member states of Europe.

References

Aarts, F. and Wekker, H. (1987) *A Contrastive Grammar of English and Dutch*, Leiden: Nijhoff.

Aronstein, Ph. (1924 (1926)) *Methodik des neusprachlichen Unterrichts*, 2 vols, Leipzig/Berlin: Teubner.

Bloch, B. and Trager, G. L. (1942) *Outline of Linguistic Analysis*, Baltimore: LSA.

Block, D. (1996) 'Not so fast: some thoughts on theory culling, relativism, accepted findings and the heart and soul of SLA', *Applied Linguistics* 17 (1), 63–83.

Bloomfield, L. (1914) *An Introduction to the Study of Language*, London: Bell.

—— (1933 (1935)) *Language*, London: Allen & Unwin.

—— (1942) *Outline Guide for the Practical Study of Foreign Languages*, Baltimore: LSA.

—— (1945) 'About foreign language teaching', in C. F. Hockett (ed.) *A Leonard Bloomfield Anthology*, Bloomington: Indiana University Press, 426–38.

Boyer, H. and Rivera, M. (1979) *Introduction à la didactique du français langue étrangère*, Paris: CLE International.

Butzkamm, W. (1973) *Aufgeklärte Einsprachigkeit*, Heidelberg: Quelle & Meyer.

Carpay, J. A. M. (1975) *Onderwijsleerpsychologie en leergangontwikkeling in het moderne vreemde-talenonderwijs*, Groningen: Wolters-Noordhoff.

Delacroix, H. (1925 (1930)) *Le Langage et la pensée*, Paris: Félix Alacan.

Dirven, R. (1986) 'Towards a pedagogical English grammar', in G. Leitner (ed.) *The English Reference Grammar*, Tübingen: Niemeyer, 89–102.

Ek, J. A. Van (1975) *The Threshold Level*, Strasbourg: Council of Europe; reissued as *Threshold Level English* (1980), Oxford: Pergamon.

—— (2000) 'Threshold level', in M. Byram (ed.) *Routledge Encyclopedia of Language Teaching and Learning*, London/New York: Routledge, 628–31.

Els, T. van, Bongaerts, T., Extra, G., van Os, C., and Janssen-van Dieten, A.-M. (1984) *Applied Linguistics and the Learning and Teaching of Foreign Languages*, London: Arnold.

Essen, A. J. van (1986) 'Vijfenzeventig jaar grammatica in het vreemde-talenonderwijs', *Levende Talen* 411, 282–89.

—— (1989) 'The continental European contribution to EFL, past and present', in C. Edelhoff and C. N. Candlin (eds) *Verstehen und Verständigung*, Bochum: Kamp, 113–26.

Flagstad, C. B. (1913) *Psychologie der Sprachpädagogik*, Leipzig: Teubner.

Fried, V. (1972) *The Prague School of Linguistics and Language Teaching*, Oxford: OUP.

Gouin, F. (1880 (1892)) *The Art of Teaching and Studying Languages*, London: Philip.

Graustein, G. (1986) '*English Grammar* – a scholarly handbook in teacher-training in the GDR', in G. Leitner (ed.) *The English Reference Grammar*, Tübingen: Niemeyer, 25–44.

Hawkins, E. (1981 (1987)) *Modern Languages in the Curriculum*, Cambridge: CUP.

Howatt, A. P. R. (1984) *A History of English Language Teaching*, Oxford: OUP.

Jespersen, O. (1904) *How to Teach a Foreign Language*, London: Allen & Unwin.

Krashen, S. (1982) *Principles and Practice in Second Language Acquisition*, London: Pergamon.

McCarthy, M. (1991) *Discourse Analysis for Language Teachers*, Cambridge: CUP.

Meijer, M. L. J. (1983) *Civilisation in het voortgezet onderwijs*, Groningen: Wolters-Noordhoff.

Müller-Hartmann, A. (2000) 'Exchanges', in M. Byram (ed.) *Routledge Encyclopedia of Language Teaching and Learning*, London/New York: Routledge, 211–14.

Newby, D. (2000) 'Notions and functions', in M. Byram (ed.), *Encyclopedia of Language Teaching and Learning*, London/York: Routledge, 449–51.

Palmer, H. E. (1916) *Colloquial English. Part 1. 100 Substitution Tables*, Cambridge: Heffer.

—— (1917 (1968)) *The Scientific Study and Teaching of Languages*, London: Harrap.

—— (1922a) *Everyday Sentences in Spoken English*, Cambridge: Heffer.

—— (1922b (1964)) *The Principles of Language-Study*, London: Harrap.

—— and Vere Redman, H. (1932 (1969)) *This Language-Learning Business*, London: Harrap.

Parreren, C. F. Van (1975) 'First and second-language learning compared', in A. J. van Essen and J. P. Menting (eds) *The Context of Foreign-Language Learning*, Assen: Van Gorcum, 100–16.

Penfield, W. and Roberts, L. (1959) *Speech and Brain-Mechanisms*, Princeton: PUP.

Renard, R. (1975) 'Do the differences between native language and second language constitute a handicap to second-language learning?', in A. J. van Essen and J. P. Menting (eds) *The Context of Foreign-Language Learning*, Assen: Van Gorcum, 143–51.

Rombouts, S. (1937) *Waarheen met ons vreemde-talenonderwijs?*, Tilburg: RK Jongensweeshuis.

Saussure, F. de (1915 (1965)) *Cours de linguistique générale*, Paris: Payot.

Schouten, M. C. and Van Parreren, C. F. (1979) 'De verwerving van een vreemdtalige woordenschat', *Levende Talen* 341, 259–70.

Sweet, H. (1899) *The Practical Study of Languages*, London: Dent.

Ungerer, F. (1986) 'Guidelines for a multi-purpose grammar', in G. Leitner (ed.) *The English Reference Grammar*, Tübingen: Niemeyer, 103–24.

Viëtor, W. (1882 (1905)) *Der Sprachunterricht muss umkehren!*, Leipzig: Reisland.

Vlaeminck, S. (1996) Foreword to G. Fruhauf, D. Coyle, and I. Christ (eds) *Teaching Content in a Foreign Language*, Alkmaar: Europees Platform, 5–6.

Widdowson, H. G. (1979) *Explorations in Applied Linguistics*, Oxford: OUP.

Wilkins, D. A. (1976) *Notional Syllabuses*, London: OUP.

3 Theoretical justifica

Michael Grenfell

Introduction

The last chapter dealt with the various methodologies which were adopted at different periods of the last century and the issues surrounding each of them. Reform followed counter-reform as the forces of progressivism and conservatism ebbed and flowed in the course of pedagogic developments. The background to this discussion was the distinction between teaching and learning. Teaching is concerned with pedagogy, or what rationale is applied to guide and shape classroom practice. Learning is what happens in the learner's brain. Of course, teaching and learning are intimately connected but do not necessarily influence each other in a linear manner. Nevertheless, the various approaches covered in chapter 2 involve individuals designing teaching on the basis of what they understand learning to be. Clearly, if we understand better how languages are learnt, then we can orientate our teaching practice accordingly. This chapter considers various learning theories and their implications for recent pedagogic trends in second language teaching. Ultimately, my purpose is to show why MLAC may be justified as an approach which can enhance both teaching *and* learning. To do this, we need to look at what we know about language and its processes. Modern linguistics has much to tell us about the interrelationship between the form and content of language and the role each of these plays in the learning and teaching context. Chapter 2 dealt with second language learning from the perspective of teaching and methodology. This chapter is about all language learning in the first instance, what distinguishes second language learning in the second, and then the implications this distinction has for organising learning.

Learning to communicate

Chapter 2 brought us through a century of change and concluded with a brief reference to Communicative Language Teaching (CLT). Since MLAC can be regarded as daughter (or perhaps grandson) of the communicative approach, I shall take it as my *point de départ*. What is clear from the discussion so far is that it is a long time since languages were learnt simply as an academic exercise. In a sense, all of the methods and approaches considered had, as a principal aim, the acquisition of some facility or practical mastery over a language – in short, to communicate. Language learning emerges from a concern to access and make available information to and from cultures with languages other than the originating native tongue. Chapter 2 referred to the 'semanticisation' of linguistic study and how many of the early linguistic reformers saw their task as facilitating international relations; whether diplomatic or missionary. But it was not until the later 1960s and then the 1970s that the word 'communication' featured in an internationally recognised approach to the learning and teaching of modern languages. But what is 'Communicative Language Teaching'? And why, several decades after the Direct Method, did it become the guiding approach to second language learning and teaching in the last decades of the twentieth century?

Brumfit (1988) lists the characteristics of CLT as:

1. A focus on the needs of learners, and attempts to define their needs;
2. An emphasis on the content of the activity, rather than on overt language learning;
3. A tendency to specify syllabuses in terms of meaning ('notional' or 'semantic' syllabuses) or speech acts ('functional' syllabuses);
4. Encouragement and tolerance of language variation in the classroom, even to the extent of mixing mother tongue and target language use;
5. Individualized work;
6. Errors tolerated as a natural part of the process of language acquisition;
7. A supportive environment, to encourage guilt-free participation; a reduction or suspension of the teacher's judgemental role;
8. Use of techniques which encourage student participation in natural environments – group and pair-work, simulations, information gap exercises;
9. Presentation of language items in contexts of typical use rather than in isolation;
10. Materials which are either 'authentic' (i.e., not originally intended for language teaching at all), or which simulate authenticity;
11. For much, if not all, of the time, a lack of prediction by the teacher of exactly what language is to be used by learners, because they will be engaged in simulated 'natural' language activity – whether reading, listening, conversing or writing.

These principles very much mirror a common-sense notion of communication: that it is based on making meaning and exchanging information in a personalised way; that it contains elements that are unpredictable; and that understanding and being understood generates degrees of tolerance of mistakes. However, these principles also situate language firmly in its cultural context. One concern of CLT is therefore 'legitimacy'; that language used is appropriate and relevant for a particular situation. Another concern is 'authenticity'; that language used should be based on real linguistic sources, not simply contrived for pedagogic purposes.

CLT might be seen as an analogy of communication: it describes the charac-teristics of what it is to communicate and uses these as the guiding principles of how to teach language through communication.

The focus on meaning goes back and beyond the Direct Method of the early twentieth century, which had become so criticised for its lack of systematic structure. Linguists from the 1920s and 1930s discussed in chapter 2, such as Palmer and Jespersen, sought to ground language teaching methodology in what they saw as scientific principles; in this case, linguistics. There was then the control of lexical input derived from frequency counts of vocabulary, and grammar based on graded structures and substitution tables. These preoccupations reigned in one form or another well into the 1970s. Indeed, it could be argued that their influence is still evident in much second language learning classroom practice. Predominant features of such practice are that language is analysed and a selection is made for teaching and learning purposes. Teaching occurs through the presentation and practice of lexis and structure – which are graded in syllabus design. Such work is often complemented by deductive grammar–translation methods and therefore the explicit learning and application of syntactic rules.

Since the 1950s and 1960s, across the range of European countries, it is possible to see variations and adaptations for particular learning contexts (some of these can be seen in the case studies in part 2 of this book). In behaviourist extremes, language is simply drilled in decontextualised forms. In grammar–translation extremes, rules are studied and applied in rote fashion. In both cases, material content is also often 'semanticised', making it more meaning-based, whether in terms of situational dialogues, stories, or personal narratives and uses. All these approaches, however, seem to be based on essentially a structural approach: to language analysis, to pedagogy and to application. And it is in this aspect that Communicative Language Teaching distinguishes itself.

The starting point for CLT is not structure but meaning in communication. This focus is evident in the functional-notional syllabuses (Wilkins 1976), which guided the early development of curricula and syllabuses. Here, language progress is charted less in terms of the gradual command over language structures and vocabulary than an increasing range of operational contexts. It is also evident in the Threshold Level (Van Ek 1975): the get-by minimum linguistic competence needed for effective communication. The starting point in both cases is less linguistic analysis than communicative context.

It is easy to exaggerate a polarisation here. As already mentioned, in its broad sense, all language learning *is* for communication. Howatt (1984) writes of a 'strong' and 'weak' version of CLT. The strong version is an attempt to stimulate the natural language learning processes themselves through an inductive process of exposure. The weak version is simply a concern to offer learners opportunities to use their language to communicate in real-life situations. And between these two extremes, there lies a myriad of practice. Such a broad range of interpretation might tempt us to leave the issue to pragmatism; to say that the teacher must do what suits for a particular learning context. In one sense, this is of course true and will always be the case. However, if we are to understand the *raison d'être* for Modern Language Across the Curriculum it is worth probing a little further in order to consider the issues surrounding these polar points.

Being competent

Many of the methods and approaches referred to in the last chapter represent attempts to link the science of linguistics with pedagogy. The assumption is that knowledge about language, derived through analysis, can be imparted to the learner through a determined pedagogic plan. But the science of linguistics itself is ever changing. The biggest shift during the last century was away from a structural perspective on language – its particular components – to language as a generative process. The challenge to the structuralist approach to language came from a man who has shown very little interest in second language learning and teaching: Chomsky. His main observation was that first language learners seemingly become very competent on the basis of an input which might be termed 'degenerate' language. Learners do not 'learn' ideal linguistic structures which subsequently become reapplied but seem to possess and develop generating processes, or deep structures, which are capable of giving rise to an infinite number of variations in response to linguistic needs and exigencies. The modern idea of 'competence' was born in the 1950s as a notion to describe these deep generative structures. Chomsky also argued that they were both innate, or biologically based, and universal for all humans. Actual differences between languages were simply surface variations of deeper structural foundations. Similarly, individual linguistic utterances were instances of 'performance', which was a product of but not an expression of competence.

Chomskyan linguistics is about as scientific as the study of language structure gets. It is an approach which has dominated applied linguistics since its inception. Yet, it is a way of studying language which is noticeable for the lack of attention it gives to the content and context of language. Chomsky himself wrote that linguistics should be concerned with 'an ideal speaker-listener, in a completely homogeneous speech community, who knows the language perfectly and is unaffected by such grammatically irrelevant conditions as memory limitations, distractions, shifts of attention or interest, and efforts . . . in applying his knowledge of the language to actual performance' (1965: 3). In other words, linguistics should be concerned with something which can hardly exist in the real world. However, the notion of 'competence' had been born and entered a world of language study and took on a life of its own. Curiously, it is this very restricted notion of competence which provided one of the theoretical rationales for communicative language teaching and the heightened search for meaning in methodological practice, which became the guiding force in the second half of the last century. This concern happened through the semanticisation and socialisation of the 'competence' concept. The prime initiator in this development was the social anthropologist Del Hymes.

Social anthropology has had and still has a long tradition of studying cultural practices and traditions. One variant of this academic field proceeded by viewing cultures by analogy to language. Social structures and systems of communication were understood much in the same way as linguistic structures, and could be 'read off' accordingly. Social practice conformed to trans-temporal and trans-contextual rules which set the patterns of practice (Lévi-Strauss 1963). The purpose of social anthropology was to identify these structures and interpret their meaning. It is perhaps unsurprising to read Hymes arguing that there 'are rules of use, without which the rules of grammar would be useless' (1967: 278). There are three essential issues for language in this statement: firstly, that the Chomskyan view of competence is too narrow and lacks practical usefulness; secondly, that grammar knowledge alone is not enough; thirdly, that there are patterns of language use other than syntax which are regular enough to be described as behaving in a rule-like fashion. For Hymes, language has to be not only grammatical but also appropriate, feasible and coherent. These conditions follow 'rules' of convention and use. He coined the phrase 'communicative competence' to describe this broader definition of the Chomskyan term.

The tension between structure and meaning remains, and is at the heart of Modern Languages Across the Curriculum or Content and Language Integrated Learning. In fact, it is everywhere apparent in subsequent developments of the notion of 'communicative competence' – what it looks like in action and how it might be taught. Conceptually, what we see is the breakdown of communicative competence into a lot of little 'competencies'. So, for example, Canale and Swain (1980) formalise Hymes' arguments and develop a version which subdivides into Sociolinguistic Competence (knowledge of social conventions, situations and roles), Strategic Competence (to control and repair language where necessary), Discourse Competence (to connect the various elements of language in a coherent text) and Grammar Competence (the syntactic rules of grammar). In a further refinement of the concept of 'communicative competence' Bachman (1990) was able to identify fourteen subdivisions ranging from morphological competence to various aspects of figures of speech, including heuristic and imaginative functions. On the one hand, there are strict grammar rules. On the other, there is a wide range of linguistic conventions and practices which follow 'rules' in the wider sense. And employing the term 'competence' to describe them suggests that such rules follow similar generative procedures to deep structural grammar, and are innate, identifiable, and prone to regulation in practice.

Within this tension there appears to be a pull in two directions: one inside-out and the other outside-in. The first of these – inside-out – might also be called 'psycho-centric'. Here, the starting point is the human brain and the way it processes language. It is the Chomskyan tradition and the behaviourists before that. This approach sets out to know how language develops in the brain and the factors involved in it. It does this by studying the product of language. The second – outside-in – approach might be called 'socio-centric'. This approach could be called 'anti-linguistic' in the pure sense of the term. Its starting point is the way language operates in the world, the interactions between individuals and the effects these have on individuals' language. This approach sets out to understand the sense and meaning behind language as a social construction and how it shapes individuals' language and thinking. It does this by studying the interactive processes of language. I shall look at these in a little more detail by taking two particular examples: the work of Stephan Krashen as someone with a 'psycho-centric' perspective; the Vygotskyan tradition as a field representing the 'socio-centric' perspective.

Acquisition, learning and development

Krashen (see 1981, 1982) is a Chomskyan in all but name. Essentially, he sees language as 'competence'. He uses the phrase 'Language Acquisition Device' (LAD) to denote the innate ability of the brain to develop language proficiency and describes graphically his observations in bilingual situations. Here, he sees how learners often go through a silent period but then rapidly converge with the target language. He theorises that there is a distinction to be made between acquisition and learning. True language ability can only be acquired, and this occurs through activation of the LAD. This activation happens as a result of *comprehensible input*; that is, by giving learners language that they can make sense of. It is in this making sense that language processes in the brain are stimulated and developed. Learning – the explicit learning of grammar rules through deduction and memorisation – is likely to hinder this process and cannot affect the rate of acquisition. The two are not connected. At best, learning can act as a fine-tuning of accuracy, where acquisition has not fully occurred. Indeed, anything which hinders acquisition should be discouraged. Some of these hindrances are controllable – for example, the amount of grammar used in language teaching – and so can be reduced. Others are more connected with individual learners – for example, their affective responses – and so are less easy to control; although even here there are particular approaches which seem more or less to heighten or reduce learner anxieties. It is important to recognise that his arguments are hardly based on supposition, and he produced a large quantity of empirical linguistic analysis to support this position. For example, he has sought to show that language proficiency develops through a natural order of morpheme acquisition, which can be demonstrated from the results of relevant tests given to learners. These tests themselves have been heavily criticised (McLaughlin 1978), but the notion remains that linguistic development is not random and *ad hoc* but does appear to proceed through broadly identifiable stages.

It is easy to see how this approach connects with some of the guiding principles of Communicative Language Teaching. Indeed, the *natural* approach to language teaching which Krashen advocates seems to be a version of the strong form of CLT alluded to earlier: that it is sufficient to create meaning through communication and let the brain do the rest. Krashen seems to have offered evidence for such an approach, this time from a scientific source with falsifiable evidence to support its claims. Even Krashen, however, is not advocating throwing learners in at the linguistic deep end. There is a further condition that comprehensible input must not be too far beyond the level of proficiency of the learner. He formulates the equation $i + 1$ to designate that the level of acquisition is dependent on input (i) being just one step (1) beyond the present level of the learners. In this so-called psycho-centric situation the linguistic environment is still important.

My second perspective – the socio-centric – takes this environmental context as its starting point. Here, it is worth pausing to consider what might be called the socio-genesis of these perspectives. Krashen came to prominence in the 1970s. It was at this time that modern-day linguistics was expanding at a rapid pace, and was being formed very much in the Chomskyan mould. The need for scientific rigour was expressed in terms of empirical and experimental research procedures. The accent was on analysis and proof. The socio-centric perspective in which I am interested comes from a different world. The seminal figure here is Lev Vygotsky, a Soviet psychologist working in the second and third decades of the last century and who died in 1932. Given his national background, and the Soviet preoccupation with social conditions which is central to a Marxist point of view on the world, it is perhaps unsurprising that he should work on language as a social construction. Thirty years after his death, his most influential book – *Thought and Language* – was published in English in 1962 and, in the 1990s, was taken up by those interested in language in education. In this case, the title says it all: that he was interested in the relationships between language and thinking: does one precede the other? Is one possible without the other? How does their mutual development occur? Using empirical observation and analysis as Krashen did, Vygotsky concluded that language was an essential medium for cognitive development. Moreover, it was language which mediated between the individual and the social world. Latter-day Vygotskyans have expressed this mediation in terms of 'control'; over *self*, *others* and *objects*. In other words, language is used to establish relationships, to name the world and there- fore catalogue it for subsequent use, and develop personal thinking. He noticed these processes in first language (L1) learners. His work was developed in response to that of Piaget, who formulated the idea of the conceptual stages learners go through in developing thinking about themselves and the world. The phenomenon of 'egocentric speech' was central to both Piaget and Vygotsky: language which is free-floating and not directed at any one individual as a part of a social exchange. Both saw this as a way for individuals to reason things for themselves. However, at this point Piaget and Vygotsky differed in their views. Whilst Piaget saw this type of speech as dying away with the cognitive and linguistic maturity of the learners, Vygotsky saw it as becoming internalised; then it continued its mediating role, and could be brought out when extra control of thinking was required in demanding situations. Since most of this language and thinking was initially acquired from social situations, it stood to reason that a wide range of thinking patterns had an outer, environmental source. Vygotsky concluded that nothing appeared in the *intra*-psychological without first appearing in the *inter*-psychological. He further postulated a 'Zone of Proximal Development' (ZPD) (1978: 34). The ZPD is similar to Krashen's $i + 1$, except that here the focus is not simply on language *per se* but includes the consequent thoughts and thinking connected with it. In other words, not only language but thought itself arose as a product of the interaction between the individual learner and the linguistic and cognitive world with which they engaged.

Paradoxically, both the socio-centric and the psycho-centric perspectives set out above seem to lead to the same conclusion in terms of language learning and teaching: that sense and meaning are 'where it is at'. In order to stimulate the psychologically based Language Acquisition Device, we need meaning, and meaning also is the dynamic of social interactions: and nothing is perhaps more meaning-*ful* than communication.

Teaching, learning and communication

At this point, I want to pause to reconsider the various methodologies referred to above. In them, we saw the tension between structure and meaning. The classical version of second teaching through grammar analysis and translation is itself about finding linguistic equivalents and duality of structural meaning. The Direct Method of the early twentieth century was based on a direct association between forms and meaning in the target language. Audio-lingual approaches sought to embed the structural linguistic habits which could be used as instruments to convey meaning. Audio-visual approaches combined situational meanings with analysis of structure and lexis. Behind these approaches are tensions between induction and deduction: should language be learnt by analysis and application of rules, or through direct exposure to structures from which further language can be generated? Communicative Language Teaching contains exactly the same tensions; although their manifestations and degree of intensity depend on the particular form of CLT in operation. Moreover, while it is true that the same tensions of structure and meaning apply in the various methodological approaches, they do so for different reasons according to the developments in linguistics and learning that reigned at a particular epoch. Now, we can see that Chomskyan linguistics put a different spin on the structure–meaning tension, which was responded to by social anthropologists such as Del Hymes and psycholinguists such as Stephen Krashen. Behind the structure–meaning dichotomy lay further tensions concerning the sources of thought and language manifest in the Vygotskyan tradition. It is worth bearing these tensions or dichotomies in mind when considering the starting positions of the national case studies set out in part 2. What is clear, when the situation is viewed historically, is that methodological purity is rare. The clarity of approach suggested by various methods when presented in theory is uncommon when implemented in practice. There are periods of experiment in which a certain method is operationalised. The norm, however, is one of gradual change and influence. In Britain, for example, the average modern foreign language classroom might include elements from grammar–translation, audio-visual and lingual approaches, together with an essentially oral focus. And the whole method might well go under the banner of 'Communicative Language Teaching'. At the same time, we should not underestimate the impact on classroom practice and consequent language achievement of the shift in emphasis in the 1980s away from translation and comprehension tests to the four skills and communicative tasks. National interpretations of methodology are shaped by their particular contexts. However, the learning and teaching issues set within these individual responses remain the same. It is concerning these issues that an approach which now takes Modern Languages Across the Curriculum attempts to reconcile teaching and learning processes which seem to be pulling in opposite directions, and to do so in the name of improved principle and practice.

One of the reasons for the rise of Communicative Language Teaching is its socio-cultural context. The roots of its appearance and its growth to prominence can be traced to a number of theoretical bases, for example, social-psychological, sociolinguistic and ethnographic, as well as linguistic (see Brumfit 1988). However, as I wrote in chapter 1, the background to its emergence is the way language and communication slowly came to dominate human systems in the second half of the twentieth century. Philosophy itself took a 'linguistic turn' and, from Wittgenstein to Derrida, the philosophy of man *became* a philosophy of language. Technological systems developed from the radio to the satellite and the Internet. All of which put communication systems centre-stage. And the growth of English as an international language and the coming together of Europe within a socio-economic community gave an added boost to the notion that language was intimately connected with knowledge and power. Communication might be seen as a 'spectre' haunting Europe (Grenfell 1991). It is everywhere and yet, at the same time, it is nowhere to the extent that it is fraught with tensions, hindrances and partial articulations. Wherever there is understanding there is also misunderstanding; wherever there is communication, misinterpretation is also present (see Taylor 1992).

It is perhaps unsurprising that exactly the same processes can be observed in matters of linguistics and language teaching. Here, it is sometimes a question of not being able to see the wood for the trees. On the one hand, it seems that we have never had so much knowledge about language. On the other hand, however, it sometimes seems that this knowledge takes us away from rather than towards language. We are like the child who takes apart the hairdryer to find out how it works. In the end, we are surrounded by many, many parts, but no hairdryer! Similarly, we seem to know a lot about the features of communication but little about its content. In the eleven principles of communicative language teaching given at the beginning of this chapter, the content of communication seems almost transparent. The list contains the pedagogic principles of practice but appears to say little on *what* is to be communicated. In principle, this is not altogether true. CLT has always been complemented by lists of notions, functions and communication strategies. But these concern the medium of communication – its features – rather than its subject-content. This transparency of context follows in a long tradition of 'content-free' language teaching. In grammar–translation approaches, the meaning of content is almost arbitrary, as the main focus of work is on lexical and syntactic equivalents. The structural focus of audio-lingual approaches also defines the main goal of language teaching as structural mastery in which lexical substitution operates. The audio-visual methods of the 1960s and 1970s did locate language work within recognisable situations, and these may have had direct relevance to the learner. They include contexts with which the learner may identify or find relevance. However, such context was rarely covered in any systematic way, the goal rather being to include a range of linguistic functions and grammars. Even in Communicative Language Teaching, the content can seem notionally utilitarian and arbitrary; for example, asking questions, making notes, answering the telephone. In England, the latest version of the National Curriculum in Modern Foreign Languages is 'content-free', the accent now being placed on ' key skills' (numeracy, literacy, information technology), problem solving and vocationally based skills (DfEE 2000). But this content freedom simply allows teachers to continue to have recourse to the standard themes list from the previous version of the National Curriculum with its 'areas of experience':

1)   Everyday Activities
2)   Personal and Social Life
3)   The World round us
4)   The World of Work
5)   The International World.

(DfEE 1995: 4)

Behind such topic areas lies the notion of pupils as hosts or tourists; in other words, teaching them to get by in these situations. But what happens in teaching methodology in the name of this objective? In inductive extreme versions, there is the assumption that learners develop generative structures similar to the ones with which they are being presented. In deductive extremes, there is the assumption that learners can be taught to analyse explicitly the structures in such phrases and to use that analysis in other contexts. In behavioural extremes, there is the assumption that learners can learn such phrases by rote and reproduce them in relevant contexts. Each view has its place, but also its drawbacks. *Knowing* a language has seemed to be understood – in both learning and teaching – as two separate systems: language structure and language content. The next section considers another theoretical approach to language learning which integrates these.

Knowing language

'Competence', in fact, is only one way of modelling the way language is held in the brain; in this case, as biologically innate according to deep, generative syntactic structures. We know from our discussion of 'communicative competence' that there are other aspects of language to be identified in proficient language use: social, strategic, heuristic, semantic, etc. – knowing when to use it, how to adapt to unrehearsed situations, and how to use language in different social settings or for different purposes. The shortcomings in the competence view may be supplemented by a different model which comes from a tradition of cognitive science and sees these aspects as part of a basic operating condition of the human brain.

Cognitive theory is a psychological approach, which sees the brain as essentially an *information processor*. All of the aspects of competence, and the features of communicative competence, are understood as different sources of *information*. Certainly, these sources are different *orders* of knowledge, but are seen as information for cognitive processing none the less. Conventionally, language is often expressed in terms of a series of levels, from the relatively simple sound source to the infinitely more complex structure and meaning: phonetics, phonology, morphology, syntax and semantics. Clearly, each level operates in a different way, with varying demands in terms of the physical control needed by an individual. However, from a cognitive theoretical point of view, they are all aspects of information being processed. To this extent, the theory (in theory, at least!) offers the possibility of integrating language and content as different elements of information-processing systems.

In cognitive theory, there is a further dichotomy, which needs to be understood in order to appreciate the integrative potential of this view of language learning: that between *declarative* and *procedural* knowledge.

Declarative Knowledge (see Anderson 1983, 1985) is knowledge of facts and things that can be 'declared', although not necessarily by the knower, since not all that is known can be known to be known. It is possible to use language perfectly without being able to declare the linguistic levels of use cited above. Declarative Knowledge might also include images and temporal features in strings of events or sequences. Procedural Knowledge, on the other hand, is knowledge of *how to do things*, how to solve problems through developing knowledge about relational elements. Syntactical competence is clearly one aspect of procedural knowledge as it relates to knowing how to bring these relations together to make the desired sense.

In a world according to cognitive theory, we are constantly confronted by situations which have to be understood, interpreted and responded to according to a combination of Declarative and Procedural Knowledge. In the L1 context, the world confronts the learner and is 'declared' to them in and through their linguistic environment by the individuals surrounding them. It is not declared in terms of the technical terms of language but in naming the world and the relations existing in it. This process is part of the cognitive development of the learner and their place in the world. It includes abstract as well as concrete features. Language in an L2 context operates differently. For a start, it *double declares* the world. It names that which has already been named. Moreover, it expresses relations in a way which is different from those already familiar to the learner. This second dimension of L2 learning allows for further possibilities. For example, it is not only a question of thought and language, and the relationship between the two in a developmental process, but of thinking about language and thought and the language which might be employed to navigate this thinking. Some branches of cognitive theory have used this approach to focus not so much on 'language learning' as on 'learning to learn'. Here, the emphasis is not placed on teaching language and knowledge about language but on the strategies, tactics and activities that the learner might engage with to help themselves learn (O'Malley and Chamot 1990; Grenfell and Harris 1999). Such strategies deal with the direct manipulation of language (cognitive strategies) – for example, inferencing, using resources, visualisation and deductive reasoning – and meta-cognitive strategies – for example, the planning, monitoring and evaluation of one's language use. These are the sort of strategies 'good language learners' use (see Naimon et al. 1978/1996). However, there is another aspect of strategy use which is central to successful language learning – social strategies. The social is clearly an important source of content or meaning in language, but it is trans-mitted through a medium that is highly sensitive to affective features, attitudes, and personal dispositions.

So far, my discussion has covered the mainly linguistic aspects of language learning, that is, the way the mind might construct the components of lan-guage, hold them there and generate new language. Both the Chomskyan and Krashenite approaches deal with the psycholinguistic operations of language. The Vygotskyan perspective is also essentially psycholinguistic in that it is concerned with how language is built up and generated, albeit from and in a social environment. That social environment, however, is not neutral. The research of Wong Fillmore (see, for example, 1979) focuses on the social dimen-sions of good language learner strategies. She notes that success often occurs when individuals are highly active in their interactions, and observes when they make use of communication strategies which make the most of the language they have and the language they can acquire from their interlocutor. Learners act positively with whoever they find themselves with and give the appearance of understanding more than they perhaps do. This sort of behaviour is affectively derived but has clear linguistic consequences. The mechanics of language are just part of the story of language learning. Other important dimensions include what the learner is feeling, their social behaviour and their attitude to the learning process.

Why learn a language?

It has long since been recognised that motivation is an important part of language learning. Clearly, whatever the linguistic mechanisms of the brain, they are not going to operate unless there is the desire to achieve the goal of language learning, which in turn generates the effort to learn. Gardner (1985) expresses motivation as an equation:

Motivation = Effort + Desire to Achieve a Goal + Attitudes.

Besides achievement and effort, there is also an evaluative or qualitative aspect to motivation, summed up as 'attitudes'. These attitudes are made up of reactions based on beliefs, feelings and opinions about a particular learning option.

Language learning does not take place in a vacuum, and this early work on motivation was conducted in bilingual contexts, namely, in Canada. Here, there exist both English-speaking and French-speaking communities. To learn English or French, therefore, has very real social, cultural and economic consequences for the respective communities. Language competence opens opportunities; failure to learn the language risks isolation. In some contexts, specific language proficiency is a passport, an *entrée* into certain social milieux or professions. In their own turn, these consequences build up attitudes to the languages and to the worlds they represent.

Gardner describes two basic types of motivation: integrative and instrumental. Integrative motivation can be understood as a desire to join or link with the target language and culture for affective reasons. Instrumental motivation, on the other hand, arises from a desire to acquire a language for personal gain, especially economic and professional gain. Clearly, in reality, the two types of motivation are not totally separate: any integrative motivation can have an instrumental aspect and vice versa. This approach to languages has also led social psychologists such as Giles (1977), Bourrhis (1982) and Tajfel (1982) to conceptualise the notion of 'linguistic groups', with their implications in terms of 'in-groups' and 'out-groups' and the strength of linguistic barriers in place to open or protect group members from other linguistic influences. They see how individuals may converge or diverge from other languages for social, political and economic reasons and how these affective moves have a direct effect on the motivation to learn a particular language.

Motivation is clearly important in Communicative Language Teaching, as the latter is an approach which is based on an authenticity and legitimacy in language use, and therefore it highlights the cultural and possible power for integration in language learning. However, CLT also offers the possibility of acquiring language for practical use. Clearly, these are generalised, theoretical statements. There are lots of specific variations between different languages and language learning contexts. The sort of perspective described can be used to explore any context where two or more language meet. In the present context, it does raise the questions of 'which language?' and 'where?'. Specifically, the learning of English is often regarded as a national and personal imperative since English has become widely used. Instrumental motivation with regard to English is therefore high. How other languages rate in terms of 'motivation to learn' depends on personal and national particularities.

In a country such as England, where English is spoken, there is perhaps a different attitude to learning languages. Here, a fairly strong version of CLT has been applied. The approach is based on the four skills of listening, speaking, reading and writing, the removal of translation, the down-playing of explicit grammar study, and the definition of content in interactive-transactional terms. Yet, the results of the approach have given cause for concern. In the secondary school context, Ofsted, the national inspection agency, has reported on the decline in pupils' progression and motivation after the early years of language learning (Dobson 1998). A recent national survey (Nuffield 2000) underlines this position and notes that three-quarters of English pupils give up their second language at the age of 16, that is, when it ceases to be a statutory part of the curriculum. Of course, the reasons for this situation are many and complex, and certainly not all attributable to CLT techniques. Nevertheless, CLT has often been applied as the drilling of 'stock phrases to communicate', which are no less demotivating than the most routine language laboratory drill: contexts remain disconnected from pupils' own world and their feelings about it. It is expressed in the cliché that pupils order meals they are not going to eat, buy tickets for journeys they are not going to make, and learn about people they are not going to meet. All of this could be compensated for by strong instrumental and integrative motivation. However, the dominance of English in the world undermines both for British language learners. Connected with this issue are others concerning socio-cultural identity and affiliation which may subtract from as well as add to the desire to communicate. The content of language teaching is therefore likely to impact on motivation by the way perceived effort is calculated in terms of the desirability of the goal. To be brief: 'Do I need to know this language? Do I need to know this content?' One adult learning course book teaches the students a range of vocabulary about sawmills!

If content is not perceived as immediately relevant, this puts strain on choices about the need to know the language for integrative and/or instrumental purposes.

Content and language integrated learning

We are now a position to consider what might be the components of an effective language learning and teaching approach and the way content and language integrated learning fits into this.

Firstly, it is clear that language teaching and learning need to be based on *real meaning*. We have seen this need expressed in the 'semanticisation' of teaching methodologies throughout the last century and its culmination in Communicative Language Teaching. At the same time, we know that 'meaning' is somewhat of a holy grail in second language teaching; often aimed at but rarely achieved. It is so easy to substitute the semblance of meaning for the thing itself. It is as if meaning can be staged to have all the appearance of genuine sense, without connecting with a necessary number of levels for its potential operation. Some CLT does this with its contrived situational dialogues. Meaning is co-constructed around intent and purpose, and with a real motivation potential. This construction is central to any language use, whether viewed as psycho-centric or socio-centric. Language needs to be generated from social interactions involving psychological processes at deep linguistic levels, which shape language and thought by the way social reality is represented and interpreted.

My second point, then, is that any language teaching methodology must indeed be *interactive* – transactional is not enough. Language must interact at a social level with others and the world around us. It must support personal reflection and those feedback loops which develop a sense of identity, time and place, and relationships with surroundings. Teaching language structure is simply not enough. Nevertheless, structure must be included explicitly, and it must not simply be left to the learners' 'Language Acquisition Device' to sort out generative structures by induction. Structural knowledge is one component of knowledge about language and, like all knowledge, is always in a process of proceduralisation. To learn, it is not enough to have structure explained. However, it is unlikely that second language learners will move beyond replicating chunks of language without some metalinguistic awareness of generative schemes and how they can be put into practice. The third component of a language teaching methodology is therefore *structure*. Such knowledge of how language works goes beyond the structure derived from grammar rules. It involves an individual's patterns and routines of thought in dealing with language and their reflections on this process of problem solving and analysis. The fourth component is therefore *cognitive awareness*.

In summary, our consideration of learning theory leads us to four key elements, which must encompass any methodological approach. It must:

- contain real meaning;
- be interactive;
- support a structural understanding and its operationalisation;
- promote cognitive awareness of the learning.

Content plays a critical role in the operation of these components. Content is the subject-matter around which semanticisation takes place in a personal and group context, which implies specific language structures through which cognitive and metacognitive processes are developed. Foley (1991) writes that learners' schematic knowledge (sense and meaning of the world) needs to brought together with their systemic knowledge (syntax and lexis); mostly, schematic knowledge is way ahead of systemic knowledge in the second language. However, both are the material of cognitive processes which can facilitate the linkage of the two constituents.

At the core of Modern Languages Across the Curriculum, therefore, is a concern to teach the foreign language through a content normally dealt with in the first language. Such an approach might range from minimal to maximal versions; for example, from adopting a broader curriculum content to actual delivery of curriculum topics in a second language. The primary aim of doing so is to enhance the legitimacy and authenticity of content by using language for real purposes. However, this definition of content radically alters the structure of the classroom discourse. It is possible to identify various levels of language use within the classroom:

1   The content
2   The specialist language of content
3   The language used to discuss content
4   The language for classroom management.

In Modern Languages Across the Curriculum, the subject content might stay the same as in a mother-tongue lesson: for example, using topics in Art, Religious

Education, History, Geography, Mathematics, Business Studies, etc. However, the specialist language of content, the language used to discuss this content, and classroom management language might all operate in either the native (L1) or the second language (L2). A fifth level now comes into view, namely, the language used to discuss language. In Communicative Language Teaching, because language serves both as the content and as the medium of teaching and learning, the classroom processes can easily be short-circuited: it is as if the focus has been primarily on the language of content, and that language has often been subordinated to utilitarian objectives to 'get by in' the foreign tongue (for example, purchasing a postage stamp), or to focus on particular structural points (for example, how to conjugate a verb in the past tense). However, particular content requires thinking in *certain* ways, and this thinking in *certain* ways involves language of a *certain* sort. In other words, some content involves ways of thinking which require specific cognitive processes, which in turn call upon particular concepts and ideas and the language to express them. So, content can develop language by requiring thinking skills which need specific structures. A sensitivity to content therefore raises issues concerning the shaping of schematic knowledge about the world and the way that is expressed in systemic knowledge of grammar and vocabulary. Such knowledge is open to the mental processing skills necessary to deal with them: metacognitive, cognitive and social. The precision of a mathematical problem, for example, requires a different way of thinking, and thus language to express it, from an aesthetic judgement about art or a moral consideration from a historical event.

Work on immersion programmes (Cummins 1984; Cummins and Swain 1986) has shown that learners develop common cognitive skills and that these skills are as important as exposure to the target language in making progress in a second language. Communicative Competence becomes a group phenomenon in such classrooms, since learners must work both on sharing meaning as 'comprehensible input' and on the cognitive procedures for dealing with input. There is a relationship between gaining competence in language as a process – pronunciation, vocabulary, grammar and semantic and functional meaning – and cognitive processes – knowledge, comprehension, application, analysis, synthesis and evaluation (ibid.: 138). McGuinness (2000) considers such cognitive procedures and lists *thinking skills* available to the learner as follows:

Sequencing	Ordering Information
Sorting	Classifying
Grouping	Contrasting
Comparing	Making Predictions
Hypothesising	Drawing conclusions
Distinguishing fact from fiction	Generating ideas
Brainstorming	Formulating views
Recognising	Problem solving
Decision making	Testing
Planning	Generating options.

The point is that these ways of thinking require particular sorts of language: for example, hypothesising language is different from concluding language. Ideas formed in these two are also likely to be thought about in distinct ways. Developing the thought processes therefore develops the language by stimulating the potential for meaning and expression, for example, by thinking through and solving a problem rather than simply expressing a transactional need. Clearly, procedures vary from the more to the less cognitively demanding – compare, for example, prediction and recognising. The former is fairly mechanical and based on identification of the known. However, prediction involves much wider deductive and inferencing skills, which set in place relationships of ideas, give rise to implications, and bring into operation language for their expression.

The same is true of the *language learning strategies* listed in applied linguistic research on the cognitive processing of language; for example, inferencing is a far more demanding skill than spotting cognates (O'Malley and Chamot 1990: 119–20). Easier strategies may be acquired earlier and include the 'bottom-up' strategies of translation, repetition and use of formulaic phrases. However, they are also quite limited to specific linguistic contexts rather than involving the more advanced skills of application, monitoring and inferencing. These are more advanced skills and are more frequently found with successful language learners. Cummins (1984) sets out a continuum between cognitively demanding and cognitively undemanding tasks, defining these in terms of complexity and the degree to which they have been automatised. Obviously, more cognitively demanding tasks *pull* the learner to develop these ways of thinking. Such tasks are also set in a context, however, for which he draws out another continuum between context-embedded and context-reduced communication. In the former, 'participants can actively negotiate meaning (e.g. provide feedback that the message has not been understood) and the language is supported by a wide range of meaningful paralinguistic and situational clues'. Where context is reduced, 'linguistic cues to meaning and thus successful interpretation of the message depends heavily on knowledge of the language itself' (Cummins and Swain 1986: 138). Context-rich environments therefore provide the learner with the full range of linguistic, paralinguistic and metalinguistic material to process information in making sense in the required situations. Normally, everyday L1 language use probably takes place in 'context-embedded', 'cognitively undemanding' situations, whereas, in language learning contexts, the opposite applies – context is often reduced and the tasks are cognitively demanding. What we want in language learning situations, therefore, is context-embedded and cognitively demanding tasks. These continua can be expressed as distinct areas of activity: Context-Embedded/Context-Reduced and High Cognitive Demands/Low Cognitive Demands (see chapter 12).

The main theoretical feature of Modern Languages Across the Curriculum is that by providing a more meaningful context, it becomes possible to move learners into areas where cognitive tasks are more demanding. This is because both the language and the content tasks are designed to develop the same and complementary skills, which enhance context embeddedness.

The thinking skills and learning strategies referred to above can be applied to language *and/or* the content of language. They may be embedded in a particular task or content area, or dealt with as an object of study in themselves through 'strategy instruction' (see Grenfell and Harris 1999: 73–108). Certainly, many of them are absent in much that goes on in the name of Communicative Language Teaching. The point is, however, that by introducing these procedures as an explicit part of language teaching, the content teaches the languages by moving learners to a situation where they need the language in order to solve a particular problem to understand a particular curriculum area. Language then becomes the means to an end rather than the end in itself.

A teacher has two vehicles for developing pupils' understanding of a difficult idea: to revisit the subject context in L1; or to teach the L2 vocabulary and structure. Both might occur in Modern Languages Across the Curriculum, where the same topic is dealt with in both L1 and L2 classes, giving a multi-perspective on the topic or theme.

A cognitively attuned way of going about language learning and teaching re-establishes comprehensible input as a main focus for classroom pedagogy, but does so in such a way that it is underpinned by developing the thinking skills and strategies necessary to deal with both content and language. Of course, the possibility of pedagogic tasks providing opportunity for learners to enter into shared exchanges as a source of language learning is well known in linguistic research. For example, both 'communication strategies' (Bialystok 1990) and 'discourse strategies' (Hatch 1992) help the learner to gain language in face-to-face exchanges. This potential is also one aspect of the call to 'autonomy' (Gathercole 1990), where learners, not teachers, take charge of the learning process.

What is crucial in this approach to language teaching is the structure of the task itself, in other words, what precisely learners are required to do, and hence what cognitive procedures are developed in realising them. Long (1983) sees the structure of tasks as offering opportunities for 'negotiated meaning', that is, receiving feedback to confirm or otherwise what is being thought and said. This approach is a version of Krashen's 'comprehensible input': the learners do not learn what they are taught, but follow their own path of acquisition as an individual route. However, we have seen that, at the very least, this approach needs to be complemented with cognitive knowledge about the learning process in order to make the most of and to make sense of what is surrounding the learning in the pedagogic and everyday use of language. However, if we look at the cognitive procedures behind the tasks themselves, we can see how they might impact on the outcome of learning. Skehan (1998), for example, believes that 'negotiated meaning' is an ideal view of the actuality of learning tasks. He accepts the centrality of negotiated meaning in authentic linguistic exchanges, especially in natural contexts. However, he argues that the emphasis in such contexts is often on lexis rather than syntax. The effects of this preoccupation with 'pure' meaning rather than structural relations are very uneven and far from immediate as they do not involve higher cognitive processes. In effect, communication progresses in this process as learners become good at guessing, understanding and making themselves understood, not by developing more sophisticated ways of expressing thought and meaning. In a content-rich linguistic environment learners *do* become more communicative. However, linguistic competence also demands grammar accuracy and complexity, as well as cognitive and metacognitive skills in dealing with language and planning, monitoring and evaluating performance. Here, there is often limited space for reflection as the learners focus on the ideas. Ironically, communication actually reduces space and time for focusing on form as meaning takes primacy. It is necessary, therefore, to plan pedagogic conditions in order to build in form-focused work.

Skehan does this by what he calls 'creating supportive attentional conditions'. Such planning structures pedagogy in terms of Pre-task, During Task and Post-task activities.

Pre-task activities include rehearsal and specific language input as well as consciousness-raising work. During-task activities are planned with a view to characteristic meanings and the language needed to process them. Post-task activities are designed to raise awareness about specific language forms and strategies:

Pre-task
Rehearsal
Consciousness-raising
Preparation

During task
Task difficulty
Time pressure
Information load
New elements

Post Task
Consciousness raising
Performance
Analysis promoting

This form of pedagogic design does not so much argue against the notion of 'negotiated meaning' as enhance it since tasks are structured with a view to content, cognitive process and linguistic form and sophistication. It raises the possibility of manipulating the task to influence the language used. Skehan's research has shown how pre-task planning is a good thing as it enhances both the *complexity* and the *accuracy* of language used by learners, but accuracy is particularly sensitive to post-task conditions. In other words, time and space for reflection is a good way of raising awareness *after* the task has been completed. This structure is almost identical to the structure of the English National Numeracy Strategy lesson (see DfEE 1999), including focus on language; in this case, technical vocabulary.

In order to produce language under real-time conditions, learners have to handle a complex range of language systems. Communicative Language Teaching has shown that learners are able to process at a lexical level. However, in order to go beyond this focus on meaning, they also need to be able to achieve accuracy and fluency. Progressing in these areas depends on restructuring existent language forms as a process of gaining control. Channelling attention is the basis of achieving this. Designing tasks for linguistic complexity encourages learners to takes risks; in other words, to do what they could not do before. This complexity and fluency is particularly sensitive to input at the pre-task stage; accuracy to the post-task stage.

The conditions I listed above for successful language learning included semanticisation, interaction and structure. It is possible to see how Modern Languages Across the Curriculum deals with these in an integrative way to enhance learning. However, an additional condition was cognitive involvement. We see how planning language and content to take account of generic thinking skills, instruction for specific strategy work and task-planning tactics to provide learners with space for reflection and form-focused attention are important components of Modern Languages Across the Curriculum.

This discussion addresses the structural and cognitive aspects of language learning. It is nevertheless possible to connect the individual learner with group activities which develop context and a common cognitive approach. These group dimensions involve social features which are not directly connected with linguistic components but have an enormous impact on the way and extent to which these are acquired by the learner.

Motivation has to be high – either instrumental or integrative – for true communicative competence to develop on the basis of more limited approaches to Communicative Language Teaching. With Modern Languages Across the Curriculum, the content itself is enhanced to provide meaning which more directly engages with the learner at levels beyond memorisation or rational analysis. Broadening the curriculum content of the language learner brings in physical, aesthetic, moral, spiritual, cultural, social and political aspects. This content will itself provide opportunities for the thinking skills and learning strategies mentioned above. However, it also has the potential to improve the motivation of the learner.

Dörnyei (2001) has revised the traditional approach to motivation in language teaching outlined above. He takes a more 'situational approach' than the seminal macro-level work carried out by Gardner. He reminds us that motivation is always a site-specific feature, involving the personalities of teachers and learners and course-specific components. His 'process' approach sees motivation as communally constructed and maintained. Firstly, motivation has to be generated with a specific goal in mind. Secondly, this motivation needs to be actively maintained and protected. Finally, there is need for a retrospective evaluation, where the learner can reflect on past experiences and how they *felt* about them. Clearly, learning a second language is a demanding *process*, but it is also a demanding *experience*. At any stage, something can go wrong: the learner becomes anxious, or loses interest, or loses their way, or gets distracted, or physical conditions are poor. However, success also breeds success, learners can be clear-sighted about what they need to do, and attentional conditions can be very good. What learners feel about language learning does change according to anticipation, acute experience or retrospection of the process. Motivational factors, and expressions involving them, are then environmentally sensitive. We need to examine closely the task set for learners in terms of motivational impact as well as linguistic and cognitive potential. Does this task enhance interest, confidence and willingness to communicate? Of course, such a question might be addressed to any language-learning context. Many tasks would be found wanting on such a measure, and by tasks I mean linguistic and content features. Much that goes on in the name of Communicative Language Teaching might seem for students to be inherently lacking in interest in content, undermining confidence and missing true communication. The way context is central to content and integrated learning attempts to improve on these motivational aspects in order to enhance learning still further.

Conclusion

This chapter has set out some of the theoretical issues surrounding the case for Modern Languages Across the Curriculum. The distinction between teaching and learning is an important one. Chapter 2 considered a century of pedagogic exploration and advance. Such developments in teaching were made against a background of progress in our understanding of how languages are learnt. In this chapter, some of the main perspectives on language learning have been set out – those focusing on the psychological and the social aspects – in the light of Communicative Language Teaching, which has been the latest major methodological approach. The tension between structure and meaning was stated in pedagogic terms. Cognitive theory was used to explain a possible bridge between these two key elements. This link was forged from language, the content of language and the cognitive skills and strategies involved in both. Modern Languages Across the Curriculum draws attention to the content of language learning and teaching – the subject medium through which language is taught – and the thinking skills required to deal with both. It has the potential to improve motivation by providing common skills, interests and experiences. It is necessary to adopt a process-based approach to language learning where tasks are designed in order to develop specific cognitive skills and such linguistic features as accuracy, fluency and complexity. However, it is also necessary to generate motivation. Here the linguistic and the affective must be brought together as joint partners in a social-psychological relation. Both of these aspects need pre-planning, continued monitoring and time for reflection and evaluation, which engage with the content and language of learning.

References

Anderson, J. R. (1983) *The Architecture of Cognition*, Cambridge, MA: Harvard University Press.

—— (1985) *Cognitive Psychology and its Implications*, New York: Freeman.

Bachman, L. F. (1990) *Fundamental Considerations in Language Testing*, Oxford: OUP.

Bialystok, E. (1984) *Communication Strategies: A Psychological Analysis of Second Language Use*, Oxford: Blackwell.

Bourrhis, R. Y. (1982) 'Language policies and language attitudes: le monde de la francophonie', in E. B. Ryan and H. Giles (eds) *Attitudes Towards Language Variation: Social and Applied Contexts*, London: Edward Arnold.

Brumfit, C. (1988) 'Applied linguistics and communicative language teaching', *Annual Review of Applied Linguistics* 8, 3–13.

Canale, M. and Swain, M. (1980) 'Theoretical bases of communicative approaches to second language teaching and testing', *Applied Linguistics* 1 (1) 1–47.

Chomsky, N. (1965) *Aspects of the Theory of Syntax*, Cambridge, MA: MIT Press.

Cummins, J. (1984) *Bilingualism and Special Education: Issues in Assessment and Pedagogy*, Clevedon: Multilingual Matters.

Cummins, J. and Swain, M. (1986) *Bilingualism and Education*, London: Longman.

Department for Education and Employment (1995) *Modern Foreign Languages in the National Curriculum*, London: HMSO.

—— (1999) *The National Numeracy Strategy*, London: HMSO.

—— (2000) *Modern Foreign Languages*, London: HMSO.

Dobson, A. (1998) *Modern Foreign Languages Inspected*, London: CILT.

Dörnyei, Z. (2001) *Teaching and Researching Motivation*, Harlow, UK: Longman.

Ek, J. Van (1975) *The Threshold Level*, Strasbourg: Council of Europe.

Foley, J. (1991) 'Vygotsky, Bernstein and Halliday: towards a unified theory of L1 and L2 Learning', *Language, Culture and Curriculum* 4 (1) 17–42.

Gardner, R. C. (1985) *Social Psychology and Second Language Learning: The Role of Attitudes and Motivation*, London: Edward Arnold.

Gathercole, I. (ed.) (1990) *Autonomy in Language Learning*, London: CILT.

Giles, H. (ed.) (1977) *Language, Ethnicity and Intergroup Relations*, London: Academic Press.

Grenfell, M. J. (1991) 'Communication: sense and nonsense', *Language Learning Journal* 3, 6–8.

Grenfell, M. and Harris, V. (1999) *Modern Languages and Learning Strategies*, London: Routledge.

Hatch, E. (1992) *Discourse and Language Education*, Cambridge: CUP.

Howatt, A. P. R. (1984) *A History of English Language Teaching*, Oxford, OUP.

Hymes, D. (1967 (1972)) 'On communicative comptence', in J. B. Pride and J. Holmes (eds) *Sociolinguistics*, Harmondsworth: Penguin.

Krashen, S. (1981) *Second Language Acquisition and Second Language Learning*, Oxford: Pergamon Press.

Krashen, S. (1982) *Principles and Practice in Second Language Acquisition*, Oxford: Pergamon Press.

Lévi-Strauss, C. (1963) *Structural Anthropology*, New York: Basic Books.

Long, M. (1983) 'Native speaker non-native speaker conversation and the negotiation of comprehensible input', *Applied Linguistics* 4 (2) 126–41.

McGuiness, C. (2000) 'ACTS: a methodology for enhancing thinking skills across the curriculum', a paper given at the conference ESRC Teaching and Learning Research Programme, University of Leicester, November 2000.

McLaughlin, B. (1978) 'The monitor model: some methodological considerations', *Language Learning* 28, 309–32.

Naimon, N., Fröhlich, M., Stern, H. H. and Todesco, A. (1978/1996) *The Good Language Learner*, Clevedon: Multilingual Matters.

The Nuffield Inquiry (2000) *Languages: The Next Generation*, London: The Nuffield Foundation.

O'Malley, J. M. and Chamot, A. U. (1990) *Language Learning Strategies in Second Language Acquisition*, Cambridge: CUP.

Skehan, P. (1998) *A Cognitive Approach to Language Learning*, Oxford: OUP.

Taifel, H. (1982) 'The social psychology of minorities', in C. Husband (ed.) *Race in Britain: Continuity and Change*, London: Hutchinson.

Taylor, T. J. (1992) *Mutual Misunderstandings: Scepticism and the Theorising of Language and Interpretation*, London: Routledge.

Vygotsky, L. (1962) *Thought and Language*, Cambridge, MA: MIT Press.

—— (1978) *Mind in Society*, Cambridge, MA: Harvard University Press.

Wilkins, D. A. (1976) *Notional Syllabuses*, Oxford: OUP.

Wong Fillmore, L. (1979) 'Individual differences in second language acquisition', in C. J. Fillmore, W. S. Y. Wang and D. Kempler (eds) *Individual Differences in Language Ability and Behaviour*, New York: Academic Press.

Part 2
Modern Languages Across the Curriculum

Practical case examples

Introduction

Michael Grenfell

This part of the book offers a series of case examples of the way Modern Languages Across the Curriculum operates in various countries throughout Europe. In some countries the way language and curricular content is integrated is known as CLIL – Content and Language Integrated Learning – a phrase which is used in this part of the book synonymously with the term MLAC. Each chapter is an individual *point of view*. There is brief mention of the way modern languages teaching and learning have developed in a particular country. Various trends and developments can be noted from each national experience. These experiences include issues of policy and practice emerging from responses to the historical and theoretical developments outlined in part 1. The extent to which MLAC (or CLIL) presently features in each country is set out along with some assessment of its potential for growth. Clearly, there are questions concerning age range, level, languages, and content areas. There are also issues regarding teachers' responses to approaching languages in this way, and the sort of present and future training they might need. Methodology is also illustrated in terms of what actually goes on in the classroom. These examples represent specific contexts but raise questions relevant to anyone looking to teach languages through a wider curricular content. Issues are highlighted by each contributor, who offers some discussion of future trends and developments.

Each contributor has responded from a personal as well as a national perspective. The case examples vary in treatment and length to reflect personal orientations as well as which issues are seen as being most pressing from their perspective. Why and how any teaching context has operated with Modern Languages Across the Curriculum obviously depends on local and national factors. Each of these separate national applications might be placed on continua to reflect their differing dimensions. Just as there are weak and strong versions of Communicative Language Teaching, so we might see Modern Languages Across the Curriculum, at its simplest, as an attempt to broaden the content of teaching and learning at one extreme, and as full immersion programmes at the other. Furthermore, just as there are political, methodological, theoretical, pedagogic and social reasons for language learning and teaching – all of which overlap in any one case example – we might understand Modern Languages Across the Curriculum in terms of different elements or characteristic features. Research in Europe (Marsh, Maljers and Hartiala 2001) into the various ways in which language and content might be integrated in the classroom has identified five 'dimensions' or 'focuses':

1   The Language Dimension
    Language Competence: the ability to activate language systems – reading, writing, speaking, listening – in making sense in and of language.
    Oral Communication Skills: the ability to engage in one-to-one and group exchanges, both physical and virtual.
    Target Language: the use of a second language to process information, both formally and informally.
    Native and Target Language: both first and second language can be developed in tandem as complementary to each other.
    Plurilingual Interests and Attitudes: any context where various languages are accessed to develop and express personal interests and attitudes.

2   The Content Dimension
    Different Content Perspectives: seeing a subject discipline area from a different world view as expressed in another language.
    Target Language Terminology: language terms specific to a particular subject discipline area.
    Academic and Professional Studies: language which facilitates the formation of broader horizons for study or recruitment to specific jobs.

3   The Culture Dimension
    Intercultural Knowledge: awareness of other cultures and how they impact on each other – global mobility.
    Intercultural Communication: communication skills in trans-cultural contexts.
    Knowledge of Regions, Minority Groups and Neighbouring Countries: awareness of other countries and regions and the relationship with minorities – integration at the national and intra-national levels.
    Wide Cultural Contexts: enculturation, acculturation and cultural adaptation.

4   The Environment Dimension
    Internationalism and Integration: principles of integration at a European level and the relationship of the EU to the world at large.
    International Certification: academic qualifications recognised at an international level; for example, the International Baccalaureate and the qualifications offered by the Alliance Française and the Goethe-Institut.
    School Profile Enhancement: a wider range of certification and content options in response to socio-economic needs and expectations.

5   The Learning Dimension
    Learning Strategies: individual styles, tactics and techniques in learning languages.
    Diversification in Classroom Practice: a broader range of classroom teaching techniques with a focus on integrating language, content, thinking skills and consequent classroom organisation.
    Motivation: the incentive to learn.

Clearly, these various dimensions should not be seen as discrete elements. Rather, each relates to the other. For example, content connects with motivation and cultural awareness, which, in turn, will influence classroom methodologies. Moreover, any language learning situation will include items listed above to a greater or lesser extent. Indeed, in any particular learning context, it may be that one or more of these dimensions becomes more apparent than others. There are reasons for this which may be investigated. For the present, it is enough to keep these focuses *in mind* while reading through the various case examples. Which are immediately identifiable? Which seem to be absent? Why? How might policy and practice be altered to develop certain dimensions? Modern Languages Across the Curriculum has the potential for an enhanced provision in each of these areas. The following case examples allow us to see how far this potential has already been realised and is yet to be met.

References

Marsh, D., Maljers, A. and Hartiala, A.-K. (2001) *Profiling European CLIL Classrooms*, University of Jyväskyä: Europees Platform voor het Nederlandse Onderwijs.

4 France

Claude Springer

Introduction

Language diversification in France

As in many European countries, in France pupils learn their first foreign language when they enter the lower secondary level, *collège*. Theoretically, the French educational system provides English, German, Spanish, Italian, Portuguese, Arabic, Russian, Chinese, Japanese and regional languages. In practice, 78 per cent of pupils are enrolled in English, 15 per cent in German, 5 per cent in Spanish and 2 per cent in all the remaining languages. Pupils choose a second foreign language two years later (in the third year of *collège*). Obviously, there is more room at this stage for various languages to be chosen. We can conclude that the majority of French pupils learn two foreign languages. This picture is going to change rapidly, as the Minister of Education has decided (January 2001) that the first foreign language will be compulsory at the primary school level (age 5) and the second at the *collège* level (age 10). This new language policy follows the ambitious European plan for a multilingual Europe. In the near future (2005), all French teachers will be expected to acquire appropriate language certification (a new language certification is currently being experimented with for students and should be ready by 2003).

Diversification of language classes

The French system also offers a great variety of language classes for different types of pupils:

- classes with French as a second language: the objective is to integrate foreign pupils as quickly as possible into mainstream classes; they can be considered as immersion classes and are multicultural;
- classes for immigrants: a significant part of the curriculum is devoted to the language and culture of the pupils;
- international classes: at least 50 per cent of the pupils are French and at least 25 per cent are foreign; they provide an intensive language course (including

French as a second language for foreign pupils) and also offer some non-language courses in a foreign language (CLIL);

- bilingual classes: the curriculum provides courses in two languages. In some cases it will be a 50/50 system; two regions use this model quite extensively: the Basque Region and the Alsace Region; this is a type of immersion education;
- trilingual *collège* classes: this only means that pupils can learn two languages at the same time; pupils have more language hours and are expected to reach a good general level;
- regional classes: these classes provide regional language and culture courses (Alsatian, Basque, Breton, Catalan, Corsican, Occitan);
- European classes: this is a new type of class (1992) with a CLIL denomination (*DNL, discipline non linguistique*).

The French educational system is constantly adapting to the changing needs of French society and does its best to take into account the European dimension. European classes (CLIL) are therefore an emblematic example of the move towards European citizenship and multilingualism.

Language methodology: Communicative Language Teaching

As in most European countries, the communicative approach, as discussed in chapters 2 and 3 (see also Springer 1996), is the dominant teaching method in France. The notional and functional items were integrated into the language syllabus in 1985. Most, if not all, language books for lower secondary and upper secondary schools have the necessary 'communicative touch'. Language books for *collège* (secondary-school) pupils include many communicative and language awareness activities. For the *lycée* (16–19 years), because of the *baccalauréat* exam, the approach is more literary and cultural, but many *lycée* language books now tend to present competence-based activities. The 1996 national guidelines presented a language curriculum more open to *learning to learn* activities. The new challenge is obviously the integration of ICT and self-access environments for a more individualised type of learning.

Modern Languages Across the Curriculum

The following figures give an indication of the current situation with regard to content and language integrated learning (CLIL) in French schools:

1996–97: 1070 classes, 322 in *lycées*;
1997–98: 1426 classes (63560 pupils);
1998: 1651 classes (i.e. 1123 in *collèges* and 528 in *lycées*).

English is the first language for CLIL classes (45 per cent). Three other languages are also significant: German (33 per cent), Spanish and Italian (15 per cent).

There are also examples of CLIL in other languages: Japanese, Portuguese, Russian, and Arabic.

The most popular subjects for CLIL are history and geography (70 per cent). Others are: maths, sciences, biology and vocational subjects (technology, etc.).

Another feature to note is that two regions – Alsace and Lorraine in the east of France – make up 60 per cent of CLIL classes. I want to look at this area in detail.

CLIL in the Alsace Region

CLIL in the Alsace Region is clearly more prominent than elsewhere in France. In this section, I want to look at the region in depth as a case study in order to see the strengths and weaknesses of CLIL in practice in a French context. Some historical facts should be kept in mind. The Alsace Region has been developing its own language policy for a long time (see Petit 1993). The first efforts to reintroduce the teaching of German in primary schools date back to 1952. In 1953, 85 per cent of the Alsatian population was in favour of the early teaching of German. In 1971, a new reform was undertaken to create bilingual education in primary schools. In 1989, 81 per cent of the people still approved of the development of bilingual education in primary schools.

The early 1990s witnessed, not only in Alsace but also throughout the French educational system, the implementation of the 'early learning' of foreign languages in primary schools and experimentation with CLIL. The figures in table 4.1 show the development of bilingual education in Alsace.

A circular in 1994 defined the main objectives of bilingual teaching (cf. Blanc and Hamers 1983; Lüdi 1987) as 'leading the children, through a progressive curriculum, to gain balanced bilingualism, which enables them to acquire comparable if not totally equal competence in every domain and use of both languages: oral and written comprehension, and oral and written production.'

Priority is given to 'parity structures', meaning French/German schedule parity (13 hours in French and 13 hours in German). Continuity from primary school to secondary school is planned for, with teaching activities carried out in both languages. German is the subject studied in the language class and is a tool for some other disciplines:

> What makes bilingual teaching so special is using language as a learning medium for kindergarten activities and primary school disciplines.
>
> (ibid.)

Table 4.1 Bilingual French–German classes in Alsace

Year	No. of classes	No. of pupils
1994–95	46	not known
1995–96	73	1500
1998–99	214	4791

From September 1999 onwards, bilingual classes have been implemented in *collèges* and *lycées* to guarantee the continuity of this teaching.

CLIL classes follow the same academic framework. European classes are implemented in lower and upper secondary schools (*collèges* and *lycées*), where at least one discipline is taught in a foreign language. Theoretically, all European languages are concerned (European classes) – but oriental languages are also taught (oriental classes), and all subjects are covered (see table 4.2).

In 1998–99, the following subjects were used as a focus for CLIL classes: history and geography; life and earth sciences; mathematics; physics and chemistry; economics; physical education and sports; civic education; communication and selling; catering and cooking; commerce; marketing; electronics; electro-technical studies; secretarial studies; plastics; road construction.

In Alsace, the figures for languages taught and the number of pupils involved were approximately as shown in table 4.3.

These figures show the success of the implementation of bilingual and European classes in the Alsace Region. It seems quite clear that this success is mainly due to political engagement and a language policy scheme. Another interesting point to mention is the diversity and equality of opportunity such an implementation has afforded. Bilingual and CLIL classes should not be restricted, as is often the case, to an elite.

Implementation measures for CLIL

A circular in 1992 set out the way European sections can be implemented in secondary schools. The plan was to 'train the highest number of pupils to achieve a level close to bilingualism along with a deep knowledge of the culture of the foreign country'. The idea was not to create a new subject with a new category

Table 4.2 CLIL classes in Alsace, 1997–98

German	106
English	64
Spanish	5
Italian	4
Portuguese	2
Total	181

Table 4.3 Pupils enrolled in CLIL classes in Alsace

	German	*English*	*Spanish*	*Italian*
Lower secondary schools	2500	1150	130	
Vocational/technical schools	450	220		13
Upper secondary schools	1200	1200	100	

Source: 1998–99 local study.

of teachers, but to 'Europeanise' the curriculum and the schools. The development of the project, therefore, depended mostly on strong motivation and the involvement of all local actors. Certain measures were put in place or conditions created in order to support implementation:

- CLIL classes can be implemented from the third year of the *collège* to the last form of the *lycée* (ages 14–19). When a first language is provided at the primary level, CLIL classes can be implemented from the first year of lower secondary level;
- The language timetable is strengthened during the first two years (two extra hours a week);
- Part or all of the subject syllabus is taught in the foreign language by the subject teacher;
- Subject teachers and language teachers are required to co-ordinate and collaborate;
- Diversification of languages is provided;
- Diversification of subject matter is also provided;
- Partnerships with European countries is seen as necessary and therefore encouraged;
- A CLIL class cannot be started without a qualified subject teacher;
- CLIL pupils get a special credit in the final examination (*baccalauréat*);
- To be admitted to a CLIL class, pupils must show real motivation and demonstrate a good mastery of the foreign language.

Teacher training

The initial training of teachers is an essential part of the success of the project. In the Alsace Region, for example, since 1994, a training course has been organised for bilingual French and German teaching (primary school teachers), and more recently for the European classes in English and Spanish. Basically, junior subject teachers (trained in the teacher training schools, IUFM) can volunteer for the European and bilingual classes. They have first to pass a linguistic test. In 2005, they will have to obtain the new CLES language certification (level B2 of the European framework; for more details see this website: http://u2.u-strasbg.fr/dilanet/dlacles). If they are accepted, they will follow, in addition to their general teacher training course, a special CLIL course which is composed of four elements:

- a didactic and linguistic module of 50 hours (conferences, senior teachers' testimonies, official texts, European programmes, language course);
- a teaching practice module of 2 or 3 weeks abroad (Germany, Ireland, Spain: countries having a partnership agreement with the Academy of Strasbourg);
- a teaching practice module of 'accompanied practice' with a senior teacher and education adviser (20 hours) in a French school;
- a CLIL assignment on a question specific to the teaching of a non-linguistic discipline within the framework of the European classes.

This initial training is minimal and, at present, omits important topics: the various forms of bilingualism; the necessity of plurilingualism and European citizenship; language acquisition theories (L1 and L2); the difference between interactions in a natural environment and interactions in secondary school; the use of ICT. These topics and themes would need to be included in a full programme of teacher education for CLIL.

Remaining difficulties

The 'European option' depends essentially on a strong commitment on the part of the schools. The help and incentives provided by the Ministry of Education or the Rectorat are mostly symbolic. Schools must count on their own willingness and energy in order to implement a CLIL programme. The 'European option' provides schools with a kind of framework which enables them to develop and rationalise a European and a language policy. Schools are required to promote diversification of languages and European exchanges. The costs incurred in starting European classes therefore prove prohibitive for many schools, which slows down the further growth of this type of bilingual education in Alsace. These difficulties raise the issue of the status and the impact of CLIL in the general curriculum and in the whole school policy.

Methodologies and curricula

What is CLIL methodology, exactly? How does a teacher plan and conduct a lesson? Are there any similarities and/or differences between a traditional lesson and a CLIL lesson? In this section, I want to look at a particular example of CLIL in practice in order to answer these questions (see Springer 1999). It is based on the teaching of mathematics in a foreign language – in our case, English.

What is a mathematics class in France?

There are generally three separate areas specified in a French mathematics upper secondary syllabus: geometry, algebra and statistics. To cover the syllabus, pupils get approximately four hours per week. For those who choose maths as their major, a further two hours per week are provided. The teacher has to find ways of making these three subjects interact with each other so that the pupils can see the links and transfer knowledge and skills. The teacher is free to plan and conduct the lessons as he or she wishes. The teacher judges what is necessary according to the needs and capacities of the pupils. Above all, the teacher is expected to develop clarity of expression in his or her pupils, both written and oral, and their precision in mathematical reasoning. In short, mathematical methodology should develop a scientific linguistic competence, i.e. a rigorous and precise mathematical discourse. In a maths class, very little time is given to 'free' expression, simply because maths develops a specialised discourse and special communicative situations.

In a typical upper secondary mathematics class, the teacher asks his or her pupils to work on a mathematical problem. In the following example, geometry is being taught to boys in the upper secondary school. After a while, the teacher wants to know if they managed to find a solution:

Avez-vous tous réussi à le dessiner?

Then, she asks at random:

Qu'avez-vous trouvé?

The pupils answer spontaneously and without lifting their hands. Pupils feel free to ask a question or put a mathematical argument together when they can. It can go like this:

Teacher: Quelle autre trace peut-on trouver ?
Pupil: EG.
Teacher: EG, oui. Donc une fois encore . . . la droite . . . est . . .
Pupil: Incluse.

The sequence is mainly initiated and conducted by the teacher. Teacher and pupils collaborate to build a mathematical argument. Pupils fill in the blanks left by the teacher, finish a sentence and sometimes risk a statement in their own words. The teacher confirms the pupils' propositions. This type of maths activity requires the pupils to follow the teacher's reasoning. They have to acquire the right language. Pupils do not use complete sentences to answer the teacher. Their concentration is on the mathematical content and discourse. Maths lessons train pupils to deal orally with mathematical concepts and reasoning.

If the teacher maintains this type of teacher-centred methodology, interactions will be limited and the communicative environment quite poor. In a content- and teacher-centred methodology what counts first is accuracy and precision. Pupils are aware of this demand and react when they feel sure of their answers. It happens in a language class, and it also happens in a maths class. Here is another example:

Teacher: Donc là vous voyez que les arguments sont identiques le travail est le même . . . la limite de U_n vaut -1 mais cela ne suffit pas pour dire qu'elle est minorée par moins un . . . qu'est-ce qu'il faut ajouter?
Pupil: Décroissante.
Teacher: Qu'elle est décroissante . . . c'est parce que U_0 vaut -1 qu'elle est forcément minorée par -1 . . . il faut préciser qu'elle est décroissante . . . bon bien enfin dans ce cas là je ne m'attendais pas à un argument . . . on n'a pas encore parlé de limite . . .

In this example, the teacher focuses on the mathematical argument, on the right way of reasoning. The pupils' contribution is not important. They learn by imitation and by listening to an expert. When pupils react, they do not try to use complete sentences; they focus on content and accurate terminology. Once the pupils have that discipline and those regular thought patterns in their mind, it will be easier for them to get a grip on what the teacher is saying and anticipate what comes next. They are then ready to enter into a communication situation in mathematics.

A CLIL mathematics class

In France, a CLIL teacher is always a subject teacher who is fluent in a second language. Maths in English is, in theory, not unlike maths in French. The teacher initiates and conducts the mathematical demonstration that is expected. Pupils give short answers to complete the argument in progress. But, if we pay closer attention to what really happens, we will see many differences.

One important problem concerns the use of the mother tongue/the second language and language error correction. A CLIL teacher cannot avoid this problem and finds himself or herself in the same position as a language teacher:

Teacher: Do you know what a temple is?
Jean (a pupil): Yes.
Teacher: What is it?
Jean: Temple [in French].
Teacher: No, no, no, not in French!

In this example, the demand for a word definition is not justified from a mathematical point of view. This shows that in a CLIL class, teacher and pupils are always aware that they work with two languages. The focus is on language, and the teacher asks for a language metacognitive activity, which is unusual in a maths class. The pupil's reaction is quite understandable: he interprets the question like this: 'The teacher wants to check the French word.' This type of ambiguity is always present in any CLIL class.

What seems interesting here is that the teacher is concentrating on the mathematical argument, and this leaves him no room for concentration on language correction. The fluency of the pupil's speech depends both on his language level and on his competence in maths. This is a very important point. We can draw a parallel with a language class: when pupils are engaged in authentic speech, they are completely absorbed by communicative strategies and have little room for language control (Bange 1992). This point was made in chapter 3, where the theoretical background to CLIL was discussed.

A CLIL maths class is obviously both a language class and a maths class. In the following example we might think that we are in a traditional language class. The teacher corrects all the mistakes:

Teacher: Why would you call this point C a turning point, Michel?
Michel: Because it changes *signe* [French pronunciation].

Teacher:	Sign [corrects the pronunciation].
Michel:	At point X1 from being *négative* [again French pronunciation].
Teacher:	Negative.

We can give another example of this focus on the second language in a CLIL class. Such cases prove that pupils continue the language-processing necessary to second language acquisition.

Teacher:	Do you understand what the root is?
Pupil:	. . .
Teacher:	Come on, class, please help him! Tell him what the roots are.
Pupils:	4 and 12.
Teacher:	Did you hear that? 4 and 12. Now tell me more about them.
Pupil:	The root is positive in this euh . . .
Teacher:	Interval.
Pupil:	Interval and is negative in this interval.

The pupil concentrates on the content but cannot find the solution. He is not yet sure how to deal with this topic. What is particularly interesting here is the teacher's reaction. The pupil starts a sentence but is stopped because he does not remember the right word, even though it is a 'transparent word'. The teacher knows that the pupil has to face a double difficulty: getting the mathematical reasoning right and phrasing his argument in the second language. And here, he simply helps the pupil because what counts in this case is the content and not the language. But the pupil, instead of continuing the argument, as would be the case in the mother tongue, feels it necessary to repeat the word to memorise it. This reveals his unconscious language learning strategy of assimilating lexical items by repetition. He takes the opportunity to mouth the word while it is fresh in his memory.

Code-switching in a CLIL class is not exceptional at all (this is also the case in a language class). A fair amount of code-switching is always present in CLIL classes – for example, pupils go back to French to do mental ordering and to make sure that they have understood the mathematical problem. In these cases, they are not focused so much on improving language and communication as on improving their maths. Success with the content is vital and cannot be sacrificed to the aim of language learning. Therefore, pupils need to be reassured and know what is going on and what they have experienced even more than when a mathematical lesson is in their mother tongue. The problem in a CLIL class when the content is known to be difficult is the choice of the language to make sure that the pupils have understood. Teachers therefore often recapitulate in both English and French, as we can see in the following example:

> The most interesting point in this exercise is that you have different ways to express the same point and all these ways are equivalent Right? Ça va c'est à peu près clair pour tout le monde? Bon comme dit le plus dur était de faire ça de voir comment on peut réécrire en fait dans différents langages.

Written tasks and other written work in exercise books must be done very carefully. Most of the time, in upper secondary schools, pupils are supposed to be autonomous and teachers seldom control pupils' note-taking. In a CLIL maths class, the teacher has to make sure that pupils write the definition of a theory correctly. In the following example, the teacher asks the class to rephrase a definition and then to write it down in their notebooks. It is important to remember that the maths programme in English covers and develops the official French mathematical syllabus and that pupils will have to sit the same examination as the non-CLIL pupils for the *baccalauréat*.

Teacher: I'm waiting for your sentence.
Pupil 1:   If the gradient function F' . . .
Pupil 2:   Equals zero at X_0 . . .
Teacher: And changes sign from positive to negative or the opposite, then . . .
Pupil 3:   There is a . . . a . . .
Teacher: Something using maximal point, maybe?
Pupil 4:   Then the function has a maximum point.
Teacher: Yes, at point X_0. Céline can you repeat the whole theory, please?

This is a good example to show that the CLIL maths teacher, because he or she is a maths teacher and responsible for his or her pupils' success in the final examination, is preoccupied with giving a correct formulation and ensuring the comprehension of a particular theory. Note-taking is an important strategy or thinking skill (see chapter 3) and must be guided. Pupils are aware of this too and do their best to provide a correct formulation. The need to construct mathematical discourse in a collaborative manner creates an authentic situation and the need to use appropriate link words and terminology.

A CLIL perspective can be beneficial for the subject, but the type of subject matter can restrict opportunities for language discourse. Sometimes foreign language terminology is very helpful for a better comprehension of a concept. The teacher can then take advantage of the situation to explain the concept differently:

Teacher: Turning point. Do you understand what this expression means? [. . .] Je trouve que l'expression anglaise 'turning point' illustre bien le phénomène concret qu'élabore la courbe en rapport direct avec la variation de la dérivée.

But mathematical language implies a more restrictive type of discourse. An English teacher who collaborated with the CLIL maths teacher in the above example used to help to correct the pupils' homework. The two teachers also noticed that all the CLIL pupils were extremely good in structuring their discourse when speaking or writing in English on a general subject. On the other hand, their grammar and vocabulary were rather poor. There was no variety in the way they said things. This is understandable. English must serve the mathematical discourse and reasoning. It is a tool for the pupils' thought. The right terminology and link words are necessary to express their mathematical thought accurately and therefore to judge their competence in mathematics. The problem is that they are not able to transcend the safe routine and structure patterns they have learnt in the maths environment. This would be different in a CLIL history or arts class.

Group work is often a problem in a language class because pupils do not naturally converse in the second language. This can also happen in a maths class, but for different reasons. When pupils work together on an exercise they have to discuss it in a co-operative way because they want to find the right solution. They have to solve a real problem as negotiated meaning. It seems more natural to use the mother tongue also because they are concentrating on the mathematical content. But when the teacher comes to help them they progressively switch to English:

Pupil 1:   Elle gagnera 1000F puis elle remettra rien . . . mettons elle gagne rien la première année elle gagne 80F parce que c'est 8 pou cent
Pupil 2:   Ouais donc elle remettra 1080F.
Pupil 1:   Non, elle remet 80F.
Teacher: No, she would save the same amount of money every year. Each year she invests £1000.
Pupil 1:   Alors elle gagne juste 80 fois.
Pupil 2:   Huit fois la note.
Teacher: And at the same time you have interest – the first year she would have £1000.
Pupil 2:   The second year . . .
Teacher: And she earns interest and then next year she invests £1000 again.
Pupil 1:   So she has £208.
Teacher: She earns what she has plus . . .
Pupil 1:   Plus the interest.
Pupil 2:   So she has £2080.

When the two pupils talk together they use the mother tongue because it seems more natural. But, when the teacher arrives, it seems more natural to speak English as the teacher plays the part of a native speaker. Here the teacher is regarded not as a language teacher but as an English maths specialist. The teacher does not try to correct any mistakes: she does not even think to reprimand the pupils for speaking French. What is important in this case is that they focus on a maths problem to solve it. The language, be it French or English, is not the issue. It is simply a necessary tool to reach a solution. Maths is a language in itself; and it is the outcome which is most important. Pupils do not ask themselves 'How would I say this in English?' They simply think in maths. Mental operations (counting, etc.) learnt early in the mother tongue are instinctively carried out in the same way in a second-language context. Routine timesaving contributes to maintaining such habits. This is probably why these pupils constantly have to switch from one language to another.

In a CLIL class, great responsibility falls on the teacher, and the atmosphere in the classroom is even more important than in a simple maths class. If the teacher encourages the pupils to contribute spontaneously, however broken their English may be, they will feel less exposed and will not judge their fellow pupils' efforts negatively. Examples of good practice illustrate how a positive acquisitional bilingual learning climate can be created. They show how the stress connected with being accepted and not losing face before one's peers can be minimised. The whole mathematical process, including counting and thinking, can even become an exciting challenge in a foreign language.

Conclusion

In France, content teachers are in charge of CLIL classes. They have to teach the same curriculum in the second language, with the same objective of helping pupils to suceed, i.e. to pass the *baccalauréat*. Some pupils encounter difficulties both in language learning and in non-linguistic subject learning. This has to be taken into account.

A CLIL lesson has natural characteristics related to subject acquisition, language acquisition, and specific discourse experience. It seems obvious, even in a lesson where all the attention is focused on getting the content right, that pupils have many opportunities to use the second language to express themselves.

The above examples show how a CLIL class is based on quite complex networks of pedagogical objectives, communication and representation. The common denominator is the double focus: on the subject matter and on the language. However, it must be stressed that a CLIL lesson has its own way of making inter-actions in the second language more authentic, of giving sense to the use of the second language. Pupils in these examples learn to use specific maths discourse in a maths context without first being taught the different discursive parts. They experience and learn to use certain language functions similar or applicable to the thinking skills outlined in chapter 3: for example, necessary conditions (one needs to . . .), conjectures (it seems that . . .), hypothesis (if . . . then), etc. These forms might not be learnt otherwise, but are important cognitive tools for thinking and expressing this thinking in language.

What should be particularly stressed is that in a CLIL lesson the teacher takes time to remind the pupils of the objectives; to recapitulate what has been experienced; to be more attentive to pupils' potential difficulties; and to facilitate collaborative work. In other words, to build in pre-task planning, sensitivity to the cognitive process during the task and time for post-task reflection. Acquisition potential can be increased both in the language and in the subject matter as a result.

Maths teachers and pupils are concerned with verbal and mental clarity and the organisation of scientific discourse. We have seen that sometimes notions worked out in the second language provide pupils with a different perspective on a concept that helps comprehension. Mathematical terms in the second language may carry more connotations than they do in French. This can make it easier for pupils to remember. Pupils learn to associate different images with a different word. It is often believed that the first thing to do is to teach the subject terminology in the second language. We have seen that key lexical expressions are often quite similar: for example, cognates such as 'diameter', 'triangle', 'positive', 'equation', etc. When this is not the case, the expressions can be broken down or 'deconstructed'; for example, *médiatrice d'un segment* in French is 'perpendicular bisector' in English. 'Bisector' is quite similar to the French *bissectrice*. Pupils can understand and therefore use this image easily.

Both pupils and teachers can benefit from a CLIL perspective. A pupil who is better at English than maths gains a new interest and can improve because he will try to interact in English. His self-image, affirmed by his ability to speak English, can give him the will to take risks in maths. Pupils also get more feedback from a CLIL teacher than they would normally receive. There is certainly less stress in a CLIL class because everyone must co-operate. Clearly, these experiences impact on motivation in the ways outlined in chapter 3.

Teachers have to prepare CLIL lessons carefully. They must think of how to formulate questions clearly and how to give positive feedback. They have to conceive of ways of facilitating interaction in the second language and ways of encouraging pupils to participate naturally. They have to identify possible conceptual and language difficulties. Integration with another system helps the teachers gain perspective in their subject. All these demands facilitate pedagogic planning and implementation.

Issues and developments

The first major concern in France is the difficulty of achieving real language diversification (see Beatens Beardsmore 1993). Implementation of CLIL will not automatically guarantee that pupils are able to choose from different languages. This political aim is clearly stated in the French Circulaire 92–234 of 19 August 1992:

> *Les sections européennes devront s'intégrer à la politique menée en faveur de la diversification des langues vivantes en France. (European classes will have to play a role in the language diversity policy in France.)*

CLIL is sometimes taken as a typical case of bilingual immersion education (*Encyclopedia of Bilingualism and Bilingual Education* 1998). There is then a danger of restricting the language policy to two languages. A broader Languages Across the Curriculum perspective seems to be more open to this European ideal of language diversity.

The second challenge is to prevent CLIL classes from becoming another elite system restricted to well-off, clever pupils. The Alsace Region case study above shows that a CLIL perspective can be implemented throughout the educational system, from rural lower secondary schools to vocational schools and upper secondary schools. This requires political engagement and financial support.

The third challenge lies in the teaching resources. A CLIL perspective will not be achieved if nothing is done to develop initial and in-service CLIL-specific teacher training. In France, new measures will demand a certain level of language competence for intending CLIL teachers accompanied by national language certificates awarded by universities (it is important to take into consideration a broader definition of plurilingual competence (Coste et al. 1997)). The CLIL perspective would provide a good opportunity for integrating European teachers in national schools. European exchange programmes are very important in developing the CLIL perspective.

A fourth challenge concerns our capacity to 'Europeanise' our schools. The CLIL perspective should not be reduced to a simple question of improving language learning. It is much more than this. The French label 'European option', which is preferred to the 'NLD (Non-Linguistic Disciplines) class' label, really means that language contacts in schools are going to be less 'exotic' and exceptional and more general and natural. This will have a feedback effect on the traditional way of defining language competence.

Information and communication technologies will no doubt play their role in facilitating CLIL development. CLIL information can be found in the CLIL compendium website (http://www.mediakettu.jiop.fi/temp/clil/clilcompendium.htm). In France, websites dedicated to CLIL classes are growing rapidly. A promising idea is to use ICT to share experiences and develop data bases for different subjects (http://u2.u-strasbg/dilanet/classes européennes).

But the major step will probably be the integration of languages across the curriculum through transdisciplinary project methodology. This new way of teaching and learning is currently being experienced in France (see http://parcours-diversifies.scola.ac-paris.fr/PERETTI/TPE.htm). A good example of this approach is the WebQuest model developed in 1995 at San Diego State University by Bernie Dodge, outlined in 'Some thoughts about WebQuests' (http://edweb.sdsu.edu/webquest/webquest.html).

Pupils are invited to use ICT extensively. Languages can play a significant role in such a methodology. In the very near future, we will probably need a double perspective: a strict CLIL methodology devoted to specific subjects and a broader Languages Across the Curriculum methodology with a transdisciplinary perspective.

References

Bange, P. (1992) *A propos de la communication et de l'apprentissage*. Paris: AILE.
Baetens Beardsmore, H. (1993). *European Models of Bilingual Education*, Clevedon: Multilingual Matters.
Blanc, M. and Hamers, J. F. (1983) *Bilingualité et bilinguisme*, Brussels: Pierre Mardaga.
Conseil de l'Europe (1997) *Cadre de Référence Européen*, Strasbourg: Conseil de l'Europe.
Coste, D. et al. (1997) *Compétence plurilingue et pluriculturelle*, Strasbourg: Conseil de l'Europe.

Encyclopedia of Bilingualism and Bilingual Education (1998) Clevedon: Multilingual Matters.

Lüdi, G. (1987) *Devenir bilingue – parler bilingue*, Tübingen: Niemeyer.

Petit, J. (1993) 'L'Alsace à la reconquête de son bilinguisme', *Nouveaux Cahiers d'Allemand*, December.

Springer, C. (1996) *La Didactique des langues*, Paris: Ophrys.

—— (1999a) 'Quelques pistes de réflexion pour un cadre référentiel et des objectifs d'évaluation', in D. Marsh and B. Marsland (1999) *CLIL Initiatives for the Millennium*, University of Jyväskylä: Continuing Education Centre.

Websites

European classes in France: different links (institution, schools, . . .)
http://u2.u-strasbg/dilanet/classes européennes
Ministère de l'Education Nationale
http://www.education.gouv.fr
http://www.education.fr/
IUFM d'Alsace
http://www.alsace.iufm.fr/iufm00.htm
CLIL Compendium
http://www.mediakettu.jiop.fi/temp/clil/clilcompendium.htm
Transdisciplinary project in France
http://parcours-diversifies.scola.ac-paris.fr/PERETTI/TPE.htm
The WebQuest model developed in 1995 at San Diego State University
http://edweb.sdsu.edu/webquest/webquest.html
French University Language Certification (CLES)
http://u2.u-strasbg.fr/dilanet/dlacles
Common European Framework
http://culture.coe.fr/lang/eedu2.4.html

5 Belgium

Piet Van de Craen

Introduction

Belgium is officially a trilingual country (Dutch, French and German are recognised). It has three communities, the German-speaking, the French-speaking and the Dutch-speaking. It has three regions, the Walloon region, the Flemish region and the region of Brussels Capital, and it has no fewer than seven governments. These are in random order (1) the federal one, (2) the government of the German-speaking community, (3) the government of the French-speaking community, (4) the government of the Flemish community, (5) the government of the Walloon region, (6) the Brussels government and (7) the Council of the region of Brussels Capital. Given the fact that the area of Belgium is about 30000 sq. km, there is one government per 4.286 sq. km. I believe this to be a world record! The French-speaking and the Dutch-speaking regions have adopted the principle of linguistic territoriality, i.e. French and Dutch are the sole official languages in these official monolingual regions. The German-speaking region is bilingual (German–French), as is the Brussels region (French–Dutch). This situation means that in the bilingual areas, one would expect societal multilingualism to coincide with individual plurilingualism. Societal multilingualism is defined as occuring in societies legally accepting two or more languages, while individual plurilingualism refers to the actual knowledge of these languages by its citizens.

In societies where more than one language is spoken, that is often seen as encouraging bilingual education. However, this was hardly the case in Belgium. The reasons for this are historical and political. Nevertheless, by the end of the 1990s things did start to change slowly. In order to understand developments in Belgium, I shall first give some historical background. I shall then set out to show how Modern Languages Across the Curriculum has emerged in recent times.

Background

Historically speaking, East and West Flanders, a fiefdom of the king of France, adopted *de facto* societal multilingualism from the Middle Ages onwards. In Brabant and Limbourg, a fiefdom of the German emperor, French became important when the dukes of Burgundy made Brussels their northern capital in the fifteenth century. One of the best illustrations that societal multilingualism entails individual plurilingualism is the – probably apocryphal – anecdote about the Emperor Charles V, who spoke Italian to the ladies, Spanish at court, French to diplomats, German to soldiers and Dutch to servants and horses! However, individual pluralism was not the rule (see Armstrong 1965).

Individual plurilingualism in Belgium become established from the Middle Ages, was boosted in the seventeenth century through the prestige of Louis XIV's France, and caused the beginning of a language shift in Brussels in the nineteenth and early twentieth century. This process, referred to as Frenchification, came to an end in the early 1960s with the linguistic laws of 1962–63. In fact, the legislation promoted societal multilingualism but discouraged (early) individual plurilingualism. Since the introduction of the legislation, the teaching of foreign languages in Belgium has been strictly regulated. In Flanders and Wallonia, the second language cannot be taught before form 5, when the children are 11 years old. In Brussels, the second language, either French or Dutch, cannot be taught legally before form 3, when children are 8 (see, for instance, McRae 1986; Murphy 1988). In principle, there are no exceptions to these regulations unless the minister of education explicitly exempts the school authority from following them, for instance for 'experimental language pedagogical reasons'. Hence, any multilingual initiative needs ministerial approval. In the last decades of the twentieth century an increasing interest in individual plurilingualism has come about, mainly because of the internationalisation of Brussels.

What happened in Wallonia was completely different. The linguistic changes in this area echoed what happened in France. As in France, many dialects lost ground after the French Revolution and the French standardisation process gained momentum. As in France, foreign language teaching was never at the forefront of activities in school. Until the 1990s, few Francophone Belgian citizens mastered a foreign language. However, this is changing rapidly.

Modern Languages Across the Curriculum

In this section the first Belgium bilingual programme is discussed. It was introduced in the nineteenth century. Its rationale and principles are described. Next, today's official multilingual schools are examined. Among them are the *Foyer* Project and the Walloon initiatives related to immersion programmes. The European schools in Belgium and the various international schools in Brussels and elsewhere are not discussed in this chapter (see Baetens Beardsmore and Swain 1985; Baetens Beardsmore 1993).

Schools of transmutation

The first official bilingual system came into being in Brussels in 1881. In primary schools, French was the sole medium of instruction, but most pupils spoke Dutch; an enlightened alderman by the name of Karel Buls decided to make life easier for the large number of Dutch-speaking pupils. He suggested that the mother tongue should be the first language of instruction and that a shift to French should be made later. The system was called *transmutation* and functioned as shown in table 5.1.

The first bilingual programme ever in Belgium failed because a number of what now can be considered as sociolinguistic prerequisites were not fulfilled. As Van Velthoven (1987) writes, this system could only work under certain conditions: first, 'an honest classification of the pupils according to their mother tongue', second, 'a bilingual teaching force', third, a preparatory kindergarten programme, fourth, appropriate teacher training programmes, fifth, 'respect for both languages' and sixth, 'provision of relevant information to parents' (ibid.: 35). In fact, none of these conditions were fulfilled. The system became an issue in a heated political debate dividing pro- and anti-Dutch adherents. Finally, the transmutation schools disappeared at the beginning of the First World War in 1914.

Another reason why the system failed was the uneven language situation at the time. Standard Dutch as known today was hardly spoken in Brussels, which made the gap between the dialect of the lower classes and French, considered as culturally refined, even greater. Finally, although the instigators of the transmutation system strove towards a bilingual society, it resulted *de facto* in the strengthening of the frenchification process in Brussels, since Dutch cultural life was looked down upon and, at the time, incapable of competing with the predominantly French culture. Bilingual programmes are hardly efficient under such circumstances.

The Foyer Project

It is important to note that between 1914 and the 1980s, educational multi-lingualism was non-existent in Belgium. Dutch-speaking schools taught in Dutch and French-speaking schools in French. This did not prevent them from devoting considerable time to the traditional teaching of foreign languages. In 1981, the *Foyer*, i.e. 'a socio-pedagogical centre for the reception and guidance of immigrants and their children in Brussels' (Leman 1990: 10), started multilingual programmes in a number of Brussels schools. This time immigrant children of Spanish, Italian

Table 5.1 The language system in the transmutation schools in Brussels at the end of the nineteenth century (cf. Van Velthoven 1987)

Grade		Language of instruction	Pedagogical aim
1	(6–8-year-olds)	Dutch	Instruction in the mother-tongue, which is considered vital
2	(8–10-year-olds)	Dutch and French	To make the transition to French following parental demands
3	(10–12-year-olds)	French	Instruction in French, which is considered more important; Dutch taught as a foreign language

and Turkish origin were the target audience, although from the outset native pupils were not excluded.

The project's objectives went far beyond those of the transmutation schools. It was intended to have an impact on children and their families as well as teachers and the school. References were therefore made to (1) the complexities of a multilingual society, (2) trilingualism by the end of the primary school, (3) enhanced social opportunities should parents decide to return to education, (4) the quality of education and (5) the increasing participation in social life and society of otherwise excluded groups (see Leman 1990). The *Foyer* Project is a social project: it considers language as the key to social integration. Significantly, in the beginning the project was referred to as a *bicultural* rather than a bilingual one.

The prototype *Foyer* model for the first three forms is summarised in table 5.2.

While a number of slight changes have taken place, the prototype model is still valid in principle. The *Foyer* initiative continues to this day despite a number of practical and organisational problems. It has been evaluated many times. Standards in Italian, Spanish and Turkish as well as standards in Dutch together with subject knowledge were examined (Spoelders et al. 1990; Danesi 1991; Jaspaert and Lemmens 1990; Snoeck 1990). In all cases, the results are more than satisfactory: the linguistic proficiency of these children as well as their subject-matter knowledge is better than in control children. Moreover, after primary school fewer pupils attend vocational schools: an important boost for social integration via the job market.

While these pupils are educated to become at least bilingual in Dutch and their native language, in most cases Dutch is their third or fourth language. Because these Dutch-speaking schools are in a French-dominated environment the children's knowledge of French is far greater than that of pupils following traditional curricula. This seems to be a clear case of 'additive' multilingualism (cf. Lambert

Table 5.2 The prototype *Foyer* model of multilingual education in Dutch-speaking schools in Brussels

Kindergarten	Curriculum organisation
First to third year	50% in native language 50% in Dutch

Primary school	Curriculum organisation
First year (6-year-olds)	60% in native language *plus* mathematics 30% in Dutch but taught separately 10% integration activities, i.e. together with native or other children
Second year (7-year-olds)	50% in native language but no mathematics 20% in Dutch but taught separately 30% integration activities plus mathematics
Third year (8-year-olds)	90% in presented in Dutch for all groups together 3–4 hours a week in the mother tongue 2 hours a week in French

1980; Baetens Beardsmore 1986; Baker and Prys Jones 1998). As a result, as far as the *Foyer* schools are concerned it is appropriate to speak of multilingual rather than of bilingual education.

The *Foyer* Project gives rise to a number of observations related to language pedagogy as well as to the interaction between language policies and attitudes in a language-sensitive area such as Brussels. As far as language pedagogy is concerned, the project is one of a long list of successful European endeavours using the target language as a vehicle for learning. It is interesting to see how this project has helped to shape attitudes towards this kind of learning over the years (see Van de Craen and Pérez-Vidal 2001). While at the beginning of the project the aim was helping to integrate immigrants' children by giving them the opportunity to become multilingual, as time moved on ideas on integration gave way to the European ideal of multilingualism, i.e. that each citizen is supposed to be able to express her/himself in two foreign languages (cf. White Paper 1995). In this way the project's importance increased tremendously over the years.

As far as language policies and attitudes are concerned, matters have also changed – if not greatly. Language policy in Brussels' Dutch- and French-speaking schools has, up to now, been rather defensive. Dutch- and French-speaking schools have been reluctant to introduce other than traditional language learning methods. Immersion and content and language-integrated learning have been looked at with some suspicion because it is still believed that the introduction of the other language might unbalance the linguistic equilibrium. This is not surprising in an area where language censuses have been forbidden by law since 1947 (cf. McRae 1986).

Recently, a number of factors have influenced attitudes towards foreign language teaching and learning, which may eventually lead to more openness towards multilingual education. Today, many feel that traditional language learning methods seem to fail despite the large number of hours devoted to language learning in the curricula. We see this from the historical and theoretical perspectives outlined in chapters 2 and 3. A report written by the Dutch-speaking school inspectors in 1995 shows that language proficiency in French, English and German falls short of expectations. At the same time, social demand for foreign languages has been steadily increasing since the 1980s. It seems to be time to try another approach. In this debate the *Foyer* experience should play a larger role than before: what works for immigrant children works for native children too.

The Walloon immersion schools

In 1997 the Walloon minister of education was quoted as saying that she expected every citizen of Wallonia to be able to speak at least one foreign language in five years' time. She was addressing the traditional lack of foreign language proficiency in Wallonia. While her words provoked smiles among language professionals, the minister did not stop there. In July 1998 she issued the Onkelinx Decree (named after her), permitting primary schools, at their request and with ministerial consent, to organise the curriculum in two languages. Apart from the mother tongue,

French, subject matter can be taught in Dutch, German or English except in the Brussels area, where Dutch is the only option. Strictly speaking, this is a violation of linguistic legislation, but, as noted above, the minister of education can exempt schools for specific reasons. In the school year 2000–2001, sixteen schools throughout Wallonia asked and obtained permission to organise what is officially called 'enseignement du type immersif', i.e. immersion-*like* education. The latter term was chosen to differentiate this kind of immersion from the Canadian type, where Anglophone pupils were supposed to spend at least one year in a French-speaking classroom. In Wallonia, both languages are introduced at the same time, so that sort of requirement is unnecessary (see Braun et al. 2001). However, in Wallonia the term 'immersion' seems to prevail in references to this type of education. Of the 16 schools, 11 have Dutch as a second language, 3 have English and 2 have German. The reluctance of Brussels is illustrated by the number of Francophone schools participating – one. Table 5.3 shows how the curricula are organised.

One of the acute problems of this organisation is the availability of teachers. Native speakers of Dutch can apply and can be employed on condition that they pass an examination in French, as stipulated by legislation in 1963.

Although no large body of research is yet available, a number of evaluation studies have been carried out. One study examined the oldest and most famous bilingual school in Liège, the Lycée de Waha. Since 1989, the school has held immersion classes in French and English. The results are summarised here. (1) Linguistic performances of third-year kindergarten and first-form pupils do not differ from those of controls. First-form immersion results were even slightly better than for controls. (2) After two years of immersion, there are no traces of linguistic interference from English in French. (3) Proficiency in English is comparable to that of English children of the same age. The researchers note that 4–5-year-old children seemed slow to catch on but that this does not jeopardise immersion itself. These results motivated the school to continue its immersion approach. Later school results confirmed better overall results for French and mathematics compared to controls (see de Groot 2001).

Table 5.3 The organisation of curricula in Wallonian French-speaking schools following the Onkelinx Decree (1998)

Kindergarten	Curriculum organisation
Third year of kindergarten	Between 50% and 73% of the activities take place in the second language

Primary school	Curriculum organisation
From grade 1 to grade 3 (i.e. 6–9-year-olds)	Minimum 50%/maximum 75% of the subject matter taught in L2 with the exception of French, gymnastics, ethics and/or religion
From grade 4 to grade 6 (i.e. 10–12-year-olds)	Minimum 25%/maximum 65% of the subject matter taught in L2 with the exception of French, gymnastics, ethics and/or religion

Apart from these positive results, it is reported that 'immersion' pupils show more initiative and better memory capacity. They show a high degree of intellectual activity and they are easily motivated to study a third or fourth language. They are conscious of the cultural and linguistic diversity of their community and they are better at evaluating themeslves. Although it has not yet been systematically studied, the role of the parents is equally important. It is suggested that this success story is the result of the cooperation between the school authority, the teachers and the parents (de Groot 2001).

Braun et al. (2001) examined the pupils' Dutch oral proficiency in the third year of kindergarten, i.e. after one year of Dutch, by means of proficiency tests. The conclusion is that their performance was very satisfactory. Moreover, as could be expected, their proficiency in French is not influenced negatively.

De Groot (2001) conducted a study in the sixteen bilingual schools in order to investigate the reasons for implementing bilingual education. One of the most important factors was the geographical location of the schools near to the linguistic border and the German border or German-speaking areas such as Luxembourg. Furthermore, the social demand for languages expressed by the parents was great. The conviction that bilingual education is an added value and the importance of (language) pedagogical innovation were also mentioned.

Parents' reactions were quite positive: 70 per cent are clearly in favour, and 20 per cent were reluctant at first but became enthusiastic as progress manifested itself. Only 10 per cent needed regular reassurance. The school authorities did not hesitate to express their satisfaction: 'it is the most natural way to learn languages', 'it is a definite enrichment' and 'I am delighted with this kind of education' are some of the reactions de Groot (2001) mentions.

One group, the teachers, expressed scepticism, with 50 per cent remaining doubtful about the value of immersion programmes. The reason for this is not of a pedagogical nature but fear of unemployment. They fear having to compete with Dutch-, German- and English-speaking teachers and that, consequently,

Table 5.4 Overall results for mathematics and French compared to controls at the Lycée de Waha, 2000

Subjects	Immersion pupils' overall results (%)	Controls (%)
At the end of the second form (6 years of age)		(46 schools from the area of Liège)
Mathematics	84.4	76.5
French	78.5	77.8
At the end of the fifth form (9 years of age)		(Overall results from Wallonian schools)
Mathematics	69.4	34.4
French	69.6	56.2

their jobs will be at risk. However, teachers do not question the added value of immersion or bilingual education as such.

De Groot (2001) also examined the organisational problems that accompany educational change in general and bilingual education in particular. First, there is the problem of finding native speakers. Second, there is the fact that only a limited amount of teaching material is available. Third, there is the need for some form of monitoring.

It is clear that bilingual education in Wallonia has changed the participating schools. On the one hand, there is lot of enthusiasm and praise for the results. On the other hand, some anxiety is expressed about the organisation. It is difficult to avoid underestimating the change in mentality in these schools since the new curricula were introduced. Whereas before, the language of the other – Dutch and German – could not be used in schools, suddenly it became a vehicle for learning. This engendered openness and enthusiasm on a scale that no other curriculum change could have achieved. Wallonian schools following immersion programmes give an impression of vigour and energy, and this is hard to find in other schools today.

Conclusion

From this historical perspective, we can identify three main attempts at bilingual or multilingual education. These are summarised in table 5.5.

The ideological or sociolinguistic background of multilingual education in Belgium has been discussed. It shows the ways in which societal evolution and education go hand in hand as reflected in the objectives of bilingual education. It is apt to call it 'multilingual' because in Belgium no one really believes that knowledge of two languages is sufficient for success at work or elsewhere. And it is in this context that Modern Languages Across the Curriculum will have an increasing role to play in these early years of the twenty-first century.

Table 5.5 The aims of three bilingual education initiatives in Belgium

Bilingual programme	Nature	Aim
Transmutation (1881)	Dutch lessons in French-speaking primary schools	To facilitate Dutch pupils' learning environment, which was French
Foyer (1981)	Mother-tongue teaching (Italian, Spanish, Turkish)	To facilitate immigrant children's learning environment, which is Dutch
Walloon immersion (1998)	Immersion	To help native speakers become multilingual European citizens

References

Armstrong, C. (1965) 'The language question in the Low Countries: the use of French and Dutch by the Dukes of Burgundy and their administration', in J. Hale (ed.) *Europe in the Late Middle Ages*, Evanston: Northwestern University Press.

Baetens Beardsmore, H. (1986) *Bilingualism: Basic Principles*, Clevedon: Multilingual Matters.

—— (1993) *European Models of Bilingual Education*, Clevedon: Multilingual Matters.

Baetens Beardsmore, H. and Swain, M. (1985) 'Designing bilingual education: aspects of immersion and "European School" Models', *Journal of Multilingual and Multicultural Development* 6 (1), 1–15.

Baker, C. and Prys Jones, S. (1998) *Encyclopedia of Bilingualism and Bilingual Education*, Clevedon: Multilingual matters.

Braun, A., De Vriendt, M. J. and De Vriendt, S. (2001) 'L'Apprentissage d'une langue nouvelle par immersion: description et évaluation de performances d'élèves de 3ième maternelle'. Unpublished manuscript.

Craen, P. Van de and Pérez-Vidal, C. (eds) (2001) *The Multilingual Challenge/Le Défi multilingue*, Barcelona: Printulibro.

Danesi, M. (1991) 'Mother tongue literacy and the shaping of knowledge: the experience of the Italian children', in M. Byram and J. Leman (eds) *Bicultural and Trilingual Education*, Clevedon: Multilingual Matters.

Groot, B. de 2001. 'Meertalig onderwijs in Waalse basisischolen'. Unpublished manuscript.

Jaspaert, K. and Lemmens, G. (1990) 'Linguistic evaluation of Dutch as a third language', in M. Byram and J. Leman (eds) *Bicultural and Trilingual Education*, Clevedon: Multilingual Matters.

Lambert, W. (1980) 'The social psychology of language', in H. Giles, W. Robinson and P. Smith (eds) *Language: Social Psychological Perspectives*, Oxford: Pergamon.

Leman, J. (1990) 'Multilingualism as norm, monolingualism as exception: the Foyer Model in Brussels', in M. Byram and J. Leman (eds) *Bicultural and Trilingual Education*, Clevedon: Multilingual Matters.

McRae, K. (1986) *Belgium*, Waterloo, Ontario: Wilfrid Laurier University Press.

Murphy, A. 1988. *The Regional Dynamics of Language Differentiation in Belgium*, Chicago: University of Chicago, Geography Research paper no. 227.

Snoeck, K. (1990) 'Language and the teaching of Mathematics to Turkish children', in M. Byram and J. Leman (eds) *Bicultural and Trilingual Education*, Clevedon: Multilingual Matters.

Spoelders, M., Leman, J. and Smeekens, L. (1990) 'The Brussels Foyer bicultural education project: socio-cultural background and psycho-educational language assessment', in G. Extra and T. Vallen (eds) (1984) *Ethnic Minorities and Dutch as a Second Language*, Dordrecht: Foris.

Velthoven, H. Van (1987) 'The process of language shift in Brussels: historical background and mechanism', in E. Witte and H. Baetens Beardsmore (eds) *The Interdisciplinary Study of Urban Bilingualism in Brussels*, Clevedon: Multilingual Matters.

White Paper (1995) *Teaching and Learning: Towards a Cognitive Society*, Brussels: European Commission.

6 Germany

Dieter Wolff

Introduction

Foreign language teaching has a long tradition in Germany. Theories on how to teach modern languages most efficiently were developed in the nineteenth century. At the beginning of the twentieth century, methodological approaches based largely on grammar and translation were replaced by a new approach – the so-called 'direct method'. As explained in chapter 2, this approach was based on such principles as use of authentic materials, focus on content and not on language, and the exclusive use of the foreign language in the classroom. Although the direct method was very popular among language teaching theoreticians until the beginning of the Second World War, practising teachers, in general, preferred to teach modern languages in a fairly traditional way, focusing on grammar and on vocabulary learning and relying on text-books and other materials specially prepared for the classroom.

After the Second World War, the audio-lingual and later the audio-visual approach became the most influential theoretical paradigms in Germany as in the rest of the world. Based on structuralist and behaviourist thinking, this approach aimed at developing spoken language, leaving out grammar by making students learn ready-made chunks of language (so-called patterns) by heart. The language laboratory was seen as a valuable tool in these rote-learning exercises, in which students were expected to memorise the structural patterns of the foreign language by substituting words in sentences or by transforming sentence structures (pattern drills).

It was not until the 1970s that this approach was replaced by the so-called communicative approach. Communicative Language Teaching in Germany did not grow out of new developments in linguistic pragmatics, speech-act theory and sociolinguistics, as in Britain, but rather was based on philosophical theories like those elaborated by Jürgen Habermas, who claimed that developing communicative competence would lead to new forms of human interaction free of constraints and repression. Communicative competence soon became a key issue both in mother tongue teaching and in the foreign language classroom.

Communicative competence, as discussed in chapter 3, was understood in Germany as the ability to handle the pragmatic functions of language efficiently, i.e. the ability to choose the right speech acts for communication purposes and to make correct choices with respect to register and language form. Oral communication was regarded as the main classroom activity, and learners were expected to learn the language inductively by using the language. Authenticity of interaction and authenticity of materials were two other concepts which played an important role in the theoretical discussion.

Communicative Language Teaching is still the mainstream language teaching paradigm in Germany, but, during the last twenty-five years, a fairly conventional type of Communicative Language Teaching has evolved: it is highly dependent on audio-lingual and cognitive principles but also includes communication. Most teachers have developed their own eclectic approach, which includes communicative interaction between teachers and pupils but also relies on grammar teaching, rule learning and conventional vocabulary work. Text-books are still very common; they are graded according to topic areas but also according to grammatical difficulty. On the whole, foreign language teaching in Germany is fairly traditional, even when it is based on communicative principles.

Until fairly recently, the results of foreign language teaching in Germany were judged positively. People believed that the German students' standards in foreign languages were high and that they were well equipped to compete successfully in the European job market. In the light of the new language policy of the European Union the situation has changed. Our education authorities are beginning to understand that it is not enough to aim at becoming very competent in English alone and to neglect other foreign languages. They are beginning to realise that the multilingual abilities which the European Union demands of its citizens cannot be reduced to knowledge of one foreign language and that school leavers must be qualified in at least two more languages. They are beginning to realise too that English cannot be regarded as a foreign language any more but that knowledge of English has become a key qualification which everybody must have, and that we can speak of multilingualism only when one has mastered at least one other foreign language. On the whole, they are beginning to appreciate that our present approaches to foreign language teaching and learning are not enough to reach the goals set by the EU and by the treaties of Maastricht and Amsterdam.

More efficient approaches to language teaching and learning have been under discussion for some time now. Apart from Modern Languages Across the Curriculum, or Content and Language Integrated Learning (CLIL), which I will discuss in more detail in the following sections, there are, for example, approaches which are concerned with finding solutions to problems arising in the education of the children of the large migrant population. Although Germany is officially a monolingual country (but acknowledges two minority languages, Danish and Sorbic), a large number of different languages are spoken in the country, ranging from Serbo-Croatian to Russian, from Turkish to Italian, from Greek to Spanish. Children from these migrant families speak only a little German when they enter school and therefore have enormous difficulties in following the normal school curriculum and – later on – in learning foreign languages.

Unlike in other Western European countries like Britain or France, where such children are given specific instruction in order to learn how to read and write in their mother tongue (heritage language programmes), several *Länder* (states) of the Federal Republic have introduced so-called language encounter programmes in which children of different nationalities (including German children) 'discover' the other languages spoken in their classrooms. It is typical of language encounters, which are primary school programmes, that they do not follow any linguistic curriculum but that they take place across the general primary school curriculum: teachers are expected to make children aware of the other languages wherever possible and thus to develop a consciousness of languages and cultures which is considered useful in the process of language learning at a later stage. Although these encounter programmes are being replaced now in most *Länder* by early language teaching programmes, they should be seen as a fairly successful way of preparing children with different mother tongues for a common foreign language programme.

Other new approaches are comparatively rare. There is some discussion with respect to learner autonomy in foreign language learning, but in general, teachers have a fairly negative attitude towards it: they are afraid of losing control in the classroom, and they fear that children's language competence will not develop adequately in such a learning environment. On the whole, there is a movement towards more process-orientation in the classroom; the learning strategies discussed in chapter 3 are beginning to play a greater role; language awareness and self-evaluation are key-words, at least in the theoretical discussion.

Modern Languages Across the Curriculum

Bilingualer Sachfachunterricht, the phrase used in Germany for what is called 'Modern Languages Across the Curriculum' in this book, is considered an innovative approach to teaching in general and to foreign language teaching in particular. It is an offshoot of the approach developed in the Franco-German schools, which were founded after the friendship treaty between France and Germany had been signed in the 1960s. It was also influenced by the European school model which has been implemented in most cities of the European Union where European institutions are located. One common principle in all these schools is that a language which is not the students' mother tongue and not the language of the environment, is used to teach one or more curricular content subjects. This is the reason why the phrase 'Content and Language Integrated Learning' (CLIL) is also used in the German context to refer to this approach.

German CLIL schools are, in general, secondary schools in which one foreign language is used to teach up to three content subjects. Whereas Franco-German schools and European schools are elitist schools, however, in which upper-middle-class children's competence in other languages is being promoted, German CLIL schools are open – at least theoretically – to all children. The democratic nature of CLIL is probably one of the most innovative aspects of the German approach.

In the first fifteen years of their existence, CLIL schools in Germany were predominantly schools in which French was the language of instruction – this was due mainly to the influence of the Franco-German schools. However, from the 1980s onwards, more and more schools offered CLIL branches in which English was used to teach content subjects. Today, there are more than 400 CLIL schools in Germany. Three-quarters of them use English as the language of instruction, while most of the others are French CLIL schools; there are also some schools which use languages like Italian, Polish and Russian. About 150 CLIL schools are situated in North Rhine-Westphalia, the most densely populated *Land* of the Federal Republic.

The organisation of CLIL in the German school system is fairly complicated. This is not due to CLIL but to the fact that each *Land* is autonomous in educational matters and so can develop its own model. In the following, I will describe the two most important models, in North Rhine-Westphalia and the other in Rhineland-Palatinate.

CLIL in North Rhine-Westphalia is organised according to the following pattern. When children begin their secondary education at the age of 10, they have the right to opt for a CLIL education. They do not enter a CLIL class right away, however, but take a preparatory language course in the CLIL language of the school, which lasts for two school years. Usually this preparatory course consists of 2–3 additional language lessons per week in which the students are expected to develop a higher degree of general language competence, but also some basic ESP proficiency in the content subjects. In grade 7, when the children are 12, content education in a foreign language is introduced. As in normal classes, content subjects are taught for two hours a week; foreign language lessons continue as well, so learners are exposed to the foreign language 6–7 hours a week. Although schools try to organise their time-tables in such a way that one teacher teaches both the language lessons and the content lessons (which is possible in principle because teachers in Germany have usually been trained in two subjects), this is not always feasible. In general, neither the language nor the content teachers in North Rhine-Westphalia CLIL schools are native speakers of the CLIL language.

In Rhineland-Palatinate the first two years of secondary school are similarly organised. Students enter a kind of pre-course in order to develop a higher competence in the target language than under normal conditions. In the seventh form, when the CLIL course begins, students work with two teachers in the content class: one is a native speaker of the target language, and the other is usually German and a specialist in the content subject. Content subject teaching thus takes place not only in the target language but also in the students' mother tongue. The reason for this is that the central authorities hope to ensure that students who are being instructed simultaneously in their mother tongue and in the target language will know as much at the end of their course about the content subject as those who are only instructed in their mother tongue. They are afraid that instruction only in the target language will lead to less content knowledge in the end. Exposure to the foreign language is, of course, not as great in this model as in the one discussed earlier.

In both models a second content subject is introduced in the ninth form, when the pupils are 14. In a number of schools a third content subject will become part of the programme in the eleventh form. Most schools try to organise content subject instruction up to the students' final examination (the *Abitur*). In North Rhine-Westphalia the content subjects taught in the foreign language are also examined in the foreign language in the final exam; in Rhineland-Palatinate they are examined in German.

The most popular content subjects in all *Länder* of the Federal Republic are History and Geography. Politics is also a favourite, but even content subjects like Social Sciences, Biology and Sports are taught in a foreign language. There are some statistics available now as to the relationship between the major CLIL languages and the content subjects. Forty-two per cent of the CLIL courses in French are Geography courses, 40 per cent are History courses, 8 per cent are courses in Politics, 6 per cent in Social Sciences and 0.5 per cent in Sports. When English is the CLIL language, 41 per cent of the courses are Geography courses, 26 per cent are History courses, 11 per cent are courses in Politics, 4 per cent in Social Sciences, 4 per cent in Biology and 2 per cent in Sports. English is also used in a number of other content subjects like Economics, Physics and Religious Instruction. It is interesting to note that other content subjects, for example Mathematics and Chemistry, do not feature at all among the CLIL subjects. This can be explained by the beliefs of both teachers and education administrations as to the suitability of certain content subjects in a CLIL context. Mathematics, like other natural sciences, is, in general, regarded as too difficult to be taught in another language, although there is no empirical proof for that view. The strong preference for the Social Sciences can also be explained by the subject combinations students in teacher training courses choose. History and French is a very popular combination, as is English and Geography. On the other hand, Mathematics and a foreign language is a rather unpopular choice. And as CLIL programmes depend on teachers who have studied a language and a content subject, the students' choices of their subjects also influence the content subjects in CLIL.

CLIL as an innovative educational concept can only be put into practice on a larger scale if there is a sufficient number of teachers who can teach content subjects through a foreign language, i.e. who are not only qualified subject and foreign language teachers but who are also familiar with CLIL. Although in Germany we have teachers who already have a basic training both in a content subject and in a language as they have to study two subjects in a teacher training programme, we have not gone very far yet in the training of 'real' CLIL teachers. Until recently, there has neither been any pre-service nor any in-service training. Most CLIL teachers learn the CLIL-specific aspects of their profession in the field, i.e. while they are teaching in CLIL classes. Some German universities now offer additional pre-service teacher training programmes for students who want to qualify as CLIL teachers. The Wuppertal University programme consists of a course in bilingualism and bilingual education, a course in English or French for specific purposes, a course in learning strategies and a course in materials development. It also includes six weeks' teaching practice in a CLIL school and a placement of three months at a school in the target language country. Some in-service teacher training centres now also offer specific training seminars for intending CLIL teachers.

It should be clear from the above that CLIL is an approach which, although not widespread, is implemented quite well in Germany. It is estimated that about 20000 students study content subjects in a foreign language in German schools. For the time being CLIL can be found only in secondary schools, but I will show in the fourth section that primary school CLIL has also been successfully tried out in a number of schools. I will also show that a new approach to CLIL, so-called modular CLIL, will enable all secondary school students to benefit from the integration of language and content in the near future.

Methodologies and curricula

As in other European countries, teaching and learning processes in institutional contexts in Germany are based on curricular guidelines. The state of the art with respect to CLIL curriculum development varies between the *Länder* of the Federal Republic. In many *Länder*, no specific curricula for CLIL exist; teachers do what they think is best within the general CLIL framework. On the other hand, in North Rhine-Westphalia specific curricula have been devised for all subjects, from which the schools can select content subjects for CLIL. The fact that curriculum development is so advanced in this *Land* is related to the popularity of the approach. Although the North Rhine-Westphalia curricula are, in general, very similar to the corresponding mother tongue curricula, they differ in that they focus more on relating the mandatory content of the original content subject curriculum to content important for the target language culture, giving the latter more prominence within the CLIL curriculum. They also underline the importance of learning techniques and study skills both in the content subject and in the language. An important feature is the focus on language for specific purposes, which is not considered as a corpus of technical vocabulary but rather as a language in its own right with specific grammatical, lexical, textual and practical aspects. This fairly modern approach to language for specific purposes necessitates new language content, which is outlined very generally in the curriculum. One principle is inherent in all curricula: students who have taken the CLIL route must have the same knowledge of the content subject at the end of their school career as students who have studied the content subjects in their mother tongue. This principle does not make it possible to introduce a large amount of different content in the CLIL classroom, although in practice many teachers do focus more on topics relevant for the target language cultures.

In spite of what is being recommended in the curricular guidelines, the pedagogical approach predominant in CLIL classrooms is still quite traditional. This is true of all aspects of teaching and learning, of methodology, of content and materials, of the use of IT and other technologies, but also of the assessment of students, both in the language and in the content subject.

The methodological approach in most German CLIL classrooms is based on the traditional language and content-subject methodologies teachers are acquainted with. However, teachers cannot use special textbooks (which do not exist); they have to base their teaching on authentic or target culture text-book materials, which they try to modify in order to adapt them to the students' proficiency level in the foreign language (I will come back to materials development later). In general, one suitable text is chosen by the teacher for each lesson and each specific content subject topic. Before working through the text with their students, teachers discuss possible language problems, thus making the process of comprehending the text easier. New words are introduced; technical vocabulary is explained and then integrated in the appropriate semantic field. Complex grammatical structures are explained and grammatical rules are formed. Then the text is read aloud by students. In the next phase the teacher tries to ensure that the students have understood the text by asking questions about its content. A detailed discussion in the foreign language on the contents of the text follows. The students' homework consists of writing a short text on a specific topic related to the text and/or learning the newly introduced vocabulary. At the beginning of the next lesson aspects of the text are discussed again, and the new vocabulary is used. Then a new text is introduced. This kind of methodological approach is typical of traditional German classrooms, both language and content subject classrooms.

This approach does offer possibilities for developing activities in the pre-, during and post-task framework outlined in chapter 3. However, a growing number of CLIL/MLAC teachers are also trying to introduce project work, independent learning, and learning strategies into classroom pedagogy. They have realised that there is great pedagogical potential in a CLIL learning environment. Although in general these teachers base their teaching on written materials from various sources, they also have their pupils work on these materials more independently in small groups by giving them tasks to solve and by encouraging them to use other materials at their disposal. These materials can be language materials (dictionaries, grammars) but also content subject materials (authentic materials from other sources, for example reviews, text-books, the Internet). Usually, students work for several hours on specific aspects of a topic (project work): the results will then be presented by each group to the whole class. Of course, such a classroom, which can be thought of as a kind of 'work-shop' or research laboratory, is a much better environment both for language and content learning than a traditional classroom.

Another methodological feature plays a more important role in this classroom than in traditional classrooms. Teachers who work within this modern paradigm have recognised the importance of 'procedural knowledge' for CLIL; in classroom work they insist, for example, on improving the students' reading and writing skills. These are abilities which are much more important than in ordinary classrooms, because most of the classroom work is based on reading and writing. The teachers also introduce the different learning techniques and thinking skills referred to in chapter 3 and try to help pupils understand that most of them can be used both in content and in language learning.

Materials are a sensitive and controversial issue in the German MLAC/CLIL approach. Many CLIL teachers complain that there are no materials available. Although some materials have been developed by writers of schoolbooks – mainly collections of texts focusing on one specific topic (for example deserts or the rain forest in Geography), most publishers are not really interested in producing materials on a large scale, the market being too small and too diversified. Other teachers adapt materials from the target language country, using, for example, French History or English Geography books. Problems arise because the target language text-books only partly reflect the German content curriculum, and because, at least at the start, the texts are too difficult for German learners. A third group of teachers are looking for their own materials, making use of all kinds of sources: the Internet, television, radio, print media, etc. Materials development is an issue in which the pedagogical institutes of the different *Länder* try to help. The data bases prepared by some of them show that in the future sufficient materials will be available on the Internet for most content subjects and the major languages.

The use of new technologies in the CLIL classroom is another issue under discussion. Most teachers are still fairly conservative, and are probably also reluctant to use IT in their classrooms, although most German schools are now sufficiently well equipped. Only a few CLIL teachers make use of the resources function of the new technologies in classroom work, using the Internet, data bases or CD-ROMs themselves, or having their students use these tools to enrich the materials available for project work. There can be no doubt, however, that a new generation of teachers will recognise the importance of these tools and will make use of them to a much larger extent in the CLIL classroom.

The last important issue in this context is students' assessment in the CLIL classroom. Within the general framework of the German education system, in which frequent learner assessment plays an important role, the evaluation of the students' progress both in the content subject and in the foreign language is quite problematic. The question arises of whether students should be assessed according to their language competence or according to their results in the content subject. There can be no doubt that this question is important also in conventional language teaching: many teachers are confronted almost daily with the problem of how to grade an essay which is brilliantly written but the content of which is poor. But in MLAC/CLIL, the consequences are further-reaching because they concern two different school subjects at the same time. Should a student whose English or French is brilliant but whose knowledge in the content subject is less than average get a better mark in the content subject because he or she can express herself more fluently than another student whose content knowledge is better than that of the first student but whose linguistic competence is less developed? In general, within the German CLIL framework, content knowledge should determine the student's assessment in the content subject, and language proficiency in the language subject. But very often it is difficult to separate the two areas. The assessment issue has not been solved in the present context; it may be solved only if the approach to assessment in general is changed.

Issues and developments

There can be no doubt that MLAC/CLIL in Germany must be perceived as a well-developed approach which has gone beyond the early stages and might be seen as a new and promising model of teaching and learning content and language in an institutional context. It is not yet a mainstream approach, however, and is therefore still open to changes and developments. In this last section, I would like to sketch out two possible modifications which have been discussed quite extensively in recent years and which are now being tried out successfully. These new developments are modular CLIL and primary school CLIL.

Until recently, it was perfectly possible to open a CLIL centre in a German secondary school. The situation has changed because of problems in government funding: new CLIL centres are becoming fairly rare. Instead, education authorities all over Germany are proposing a new model for CLIL, which is based on the so-called modular principle. In introducing a modular approach, authorities hope to bring elements of content and language integrated learning into all secondary schools. All teachers who are both language and content teachers are expected to do part of their content teaching in the foreign language. They are expected to develop specific teaching sequences (projects) dealing with a topic which lends itself to instruction in a foreign language; for example in History a project on the French Revolution in French, or on early industrialisation in England in English. Ideally, in content teaching teachers would switch between the mother tongue and the foreign language several times during a school year. The modular approach cannot, of course, be compared with 'traditional' CLIL. Neither is there any linguistic preparation for the CLIL course, nor will learners be able to build up a specific register for the content subject in the foreign language. The results of modular CLIL with respect to language proficiency will not be as good as the results of traditional CLIL. On the other hand, modular CLIL is probably more efficient than traditional language teaching, as it bridges the gap for all students between language learning on the one hand and content learning on the other and thus also reduces the problem of content in foreign language learning. Moreover, modular CLIL is a particularly interesting model for vocational training.

The other new development is primary school CLIL. The question of whether it is possible to use a foreign language in the primary school classroom to teach content subjects came about when education authorities all over Germany decided to make a foreign language (which will be English in many *Länder*) compulsory in primary education. Most *Länder* opted for systematic language teaching, i.e. a traditional text-book-based language course beginning in the third form (when the children are 8 years old). However, this approach runs more or less counter to modern primary school pedagogy, which favours a holistic approach in which subjects are taught in a topic-orientated way. A specific topic, for example animals, is chosen and looked at from different angles, from the perspective of Science (types of animals and their specific features), from the perspective of Music (songs about animals), from the perspective of Art (drawing animals) or from the perspective of Language (stories about animals). A systematic approach to a foreign language would upset such a pattern. This is one reason why a growing number of practising primary school teachers suggest that it might be better to do parts of the topic-oriented teaching in a foreign language. To take up the example from above, this could mean that the topic is introduced by reading a story on animals in the foreign language. It would then be up to the teacher to decide which other aspects of the topic could be dealt with in the children's first language and which in the foreign language. In a number of primary schools in Berlin, this approach has been successfully tried out for several years now (see Zydatiß 2000). To say the least, the results show that primary school children are able to learn content through a foreign language. Quite a number of problems will have to be solved, however, before this approach can be implemented in a larger number of schools: one of the most important is, of course, learning to read and write both in the first and in a second language at more or less the same time.

Conclusion

At the end of this chapter, one point should be made very clear: MLAC/CLIL in Germany is not simply a new approach to foreign language teaching. Undeniably, one aim of CLIL in Germany is additive bilingualism. But on the other hand it should be kept in mind that the integration of language and content in German CLIL programmes is taken very seriously. CLIL is not simply a means to an end, in that CLIL students are exposed to the foreign language more frequently than others and thus develop a higher competence in this language. The new perspective on content which students develop when they learn content through another language is equally important.

Reference

Zydatiß, W. (2000) *Bilingualer Unterricht in der Grundschule: Entwurf eines Spracherwerbskonzepts für zweisprachige Immersionsprogramme*, Munich: Hueber.

7 Finland

David Marsh

Introduction

Finland is a large, but sparsely populated country with an inherently 'multilingual' history. Its present population of 5 million inhabitants inherits a linguistic history moulded by foreign occupation and other forms of intervention, and the fact that its major language, Finnish, is not an Indo-European language. About 94 per cent of the population has Finnish as the mother tongue, about 6 per cent, Swedish and less than 1 per cent, Sami. These languages are official languages of the country. English is the most widely used foreign language, followed by German.

Finland has a long tradition of placing considerable value on education. The learning of foreign languages has likewise carried special attention because historically this provided greater access to the learning of different subjects, and enabled people to have a broader understanding of the surrounding world.

There are certain milestones that reflect the longer history of education and the learning of languages in Finland that have direct bearing on the emergence of teaching and learning languages across the curriculum. One of the most important in recent times was the reform of comprehensive education in the 1960s, after which the entire school population was to start learning languages other than the mother tongue. This was a major breakthrough for proponents of language education because it gave access to foreign language learning for every child irrespective of socio-economic background or domicile. In the 1970s, this provision by which all students would have the opportunity to be linguistically confident in different languages was extended to vocational education, which, in comparison to many European countries, both then and now, represents quite a feat.

Whereas politically it could be argued that a languages-for-all policy was marked by the value of egalitarianism within this society which prides itself on being a meritocracy, pragmatically there were also views which link linguistic capability throughout the workforce to overall economic performance. In addition, it could be argued that the original OECD usage of the term 'information society' in 1975 also had some bearing on attitudes towards contemporary investment in language learning. If Finland was to be prepared for the information society, then it would need to ensure as high a degree of foreign language skill as possible throughout its workforce. By 1979, during a period in which Finland needed to examine its internationalisation strategies, the European Union also began to recognise the transition from post-industrial to information era. For some, it could be argued that the stage was set for even greater emphasis on development of human resources in terms of language and communication, and what followed over the next two decades validates this view.

During the 1980s, attention was given to practical means by which to 'internationalise' the educational system. Although many schools and colleges already had a tradition of international education, within Europe and beyond, the 1980s saw specific attention being given to the acquisition of practical skills. News of the Canadian 'immersion' programmes of the 1970s were of interest in the 1980s because research findings were emerging which validated the view that using a second/foreign language as the medium of instruction could bring substantial benefits.

Finland already had a number of foreign-language-medium schools in the country (English, French, German and Russian). This situation meant that the means by which language learning was developed in these very special educational environments could be scrutinised in situ. One key issue related to whether it might be possible to take the apparent advantages of 'learning through a second/ foreign language' from these 'foreign language' schools and incorporate these benefits into mainstream education for the benefit of ordinary young people.

In 1989, a working committee at the Ministry of Education recommended that it should be possible to introduce some form of this type of learning in ordinary schools. This was followed by a change in the law in 1991 that allowed foreign languages to be used as the *medium of instruction*. The 1991–96 National Development Plan for Education in Finland states that 'language teaching, cross-cultural understanding, foreign language content instruction, and other forms of instruction which are important from the point of view of increased international contacts and internationalisation of the working life, are systematically supported and developed at all levels of the Finnish educational system'. In addition, the report stated that by the year 2000, all upper secondary level students should be able to pursue studies or work experience abroad.

Alongside the top-down legal changes established at governmental level, there was also a growing 'grassroots' concern, particularly among parents and young people, that additional language development was a pre-requisite for success in future study and work. This may have been partly due to the fact that Finland was facing heavy social pressure because of the rapid internationalisation of its economy, and a corresponding economic depression resulting from major external global political and economic events.

This grassroots interest in means by which to enhance language learning has been an important element in the widespread interest shown in learning language across the curriculum which started in the 1980s and continues through to this day. One view voiced, which may be more particular to Finland than some other countries, was that foreign language learning had often been so theoretical that it had detracted from an individual's ability to use the specific language in real-life encounters. In other words, there was a sense that whereas citizens had considerable knowledge of the grammar and lexis of certain languages, it was necessary to convert these into 'hands-on' skills. This follows the semanticisation trends explained in chapter 2.

In 1996, when Finland joined the European Union, some would argue that it was well advanced to 'take a qualitative step forward in order to bind . . . the fields of education, training and youth . . . as closely as possible into the evolution of society and the world' (see O'Dwyer 1997) . In this same year the phrase Content and Language Integrated Learning (CLIL) was adopted by a Finnish-Dutch consortium to describe the diverse types of educational approach in which the 'learning of second/foreign languages has a joint curricular role' (see also Marsh and Marsland 1997). During 1996–2001, this term has become widely used throughout the EU to describe 'language-sensitive methodologies' and is included under the 'Modern Languages Across the Curriculum' title (see Marsh and Lange 2000).

A major review of foreign language teaching policy (Piri 2001) states that 'throughout the thirty year period (1970s–2000), the leading goal of the national language teaching policy has been diversification of the language teaching provision and language study'. One part of this diversification has been in the development of CLIL (see Räsänen and Marsh 1994; Marsh, Ennser and Sygmund 1999). The author of this review also comments that language policy and language teaching have been clearly integrated during the period covered. Integration occurred in many ways in Finnish educational development during the last decades, and it could be argued that integration of language and non-language subjects is a reflection of broader change within education.

The background to CLIL in Finland can be summarised according to three basic elements (see Marsh 2000 for an extended discussion):

Philosophy
Adapting and introducing approaches found in certain countries, areas (often border regions), and schools, into mainstream (government-funded) education to boost egalitarianism and prepare the future workforce for predicted post-millennial communication expectations and demands.

Educational perspective
Belief that language learning can be enhanced through learning by doing as in learn as you use, use as you learn, not learn now, use later. In professional circles, CLIL was viewed as a 1990s development and extension of communicative language teaching and its functional-notional approaches introduced into foreign language learning in the mid-1970s.

Impetus for action
Action resulting from a combination of pressure which has been top-down (parliamentary approval, Ministry directives and change of education laws) and bottom-up from the grassroots (parental and student demand).

Modern Languages Across the Curriculum

Modern Languages Across the Curriculum is therefore taken as Content and Language Integrated Learning in Finland. The Finnish approach to CLIL can be thought of as 'eclectic': it draws on elements from a variety of methods and perspectives. There is a wide variety of approaches used, at different educational levels, for equally different reasons. The most recent national research carried out on CLIL activities was reported in 1996–97 (see Nikula and Marsh 1996, 1997). The findings are summarised below.

Major reasons for implementing CLIL

As of 1998, Finland appeared to have about twenty different types of CLIL active in the school and college system. These fall into three broad categories, according to predominant aim:

- Boosting self-confidence and interest in the target language(s), by providing a 'feel good' and 'can do' experience for learners. Outcomes here are often focused on development of self-esteem and awareness of language as communication.
- Activating existing language(s) knowledge and converting this knowledge into skills. Outcomes as above, but accompanied by provision of skills in using language as a 'tool', alongside cognitive benefits and increased curricular achievement.
- Providing high competence in both mother tongue and target language(s). Outcomes as above, but with a desired high degree of functional bilingualism.

In total, those schools implementing or about to implement CLIL in 1996–97 amounted to:

About 8 per cent of primary schools
About 11 per cent of lower secondary schools
About 24 per cent of upper secondary schools.

Those schools most likely to implement CLIL were in municipalities rather than country locations, and the major start-up period was 1995–96. The most popular target language was English (80 per cent at primary level, 90 per cent at secondary level), followed by Finnish as a target language in Swedish-speaking schools, and Swedish vice versa. The other 'foreign' target languages were German, French and Russian.

Many of the schools surveyed in 1996 expected to increase their involvement during the ensuing years, and it is likely that the proportion of schools presently involved with CLIL is higher. One noticeable feature of development of CLIL related to choice of target language, with some administrators expressing the view that languages other than English might be considered in the future.

The eight most popular subjects in order by educational level were:

Primary
Environmental studies, music, mathematics, drawing, physical education, handiwork, religion, history.

Lower secondary
Home economics, biology, geography, history, mathematics, physics, physical education, chemistry.

Upper secondary
History, geography, biology, chemistry, psychology, mathematics, physics, religion.

In most schools, less than 20 per cent of pupils were involved with CLIL, and in some cases this involved very low exposure (5–15 per cent of total curriculum time). Very few schools, apart from those few with special language status, offer high exposure to CLIL (over 50 per cent of teaching time), or if they do, then this is not for a prolonged period. Within the classroom, about one-third of all CLIL-active schools used the target language from 50 per cent to 90 per cent of total learning time. This means that more than one language would be used, either in written or spoken form, in the classroom or in interlinked activities.

The reasons for starting CLIL were mainly linked to individual initiatives taken by teachers who wanted to experiment with this type of methodology within the school. It is interesting that the development of target language skills as a sole reason for implementing CLIL was ranked quite low as a reason for CLIL in the mid-1990s. Internationalisation, building of learner self-confidence and other non-linguistic reasons appeared to feature more highly. Involvement with CLIL was often directly linked to a school's internationalisation activities, and very often it was an instrumental part of forms of mobility, either physical or virtual, and other forms of networking and exchange. In more than half of the schools cited, CLIL was explicitly included in the curricula.

Another interesting feature concerns the use of selection criteria for CLIL student intakes. In most cases examined in the mid-1990s, specific selection criteria were not used (about 75 per cent) on the grounds that this was neither desirable nor necessary for the types of CLIL implemented. About 60 per cent of all schools had required or offered languages or methodologies training for teachers involved with CLIL. In some 30 per cent of primary schools the main CLIL teachers had specialised in the target language at university level, but this figure drops to 20 per cent at lower secondary level, and possibly as low as 5 per cent at upper secondary level.

Training in CLIL became available during the mid-1990s in the form of in-service teacher development programmes which were heavily supported by the state from 1996 to 1998. Some of these programmes soon became prototypes for European-based in-service training (see Marsh and Marsland 1999a, 1999b).

Initial (pre-service) programmes on CLIL methodologies did not develop during this period; although a number of teacher training institutions did offer special modules within programmes on teaching and learning through a foreign language (for example, the Universities of Oulu, Northern Finland and Jyväsklä, Central Finland).

Finally, we turn to schools' assessment of their experience with CLIL. This was predominantly positive, with overall outcomes and aims the same for CLIL streams as for those studying through the mother tongue. Only anecdotal comment has been available to date because of the lack of long-term research on the impact of CLIL in Finnish education. But what this shows is that whereas small-scale CLIL activity appears to bring positive results, some of the larger-scale approaches (high exposure) could be more problematic. Parental views ranged from the highly positive at primary level to the more sceptical, if not concerned, at upper secondary level. This was attributed at the time of the 1996 report to the importance of the national matriculation examinations which all secondary level students sit at the end of their schooling, and which generally involved answering scripts in one of the Finnish national languages (see Pohjanvirta et al. 1998). The key development issues reported by schools in the country were as follows:

- coping with parental and learner demand and expectations;
- nurturing the mother tongue alongside the target language(s);
- embedding CLIL in the school policy and not as a 'cosmetic' add-on value;
- encouraging teacher teamwork;
- integrating curricula;
- identifying and developing suitable materials;
- assessing teacher competencies in CLIL;
- learner selection processes;
- managing heterogeneity in student groups;
- managing extra teacher and learner workload;
- securing suitable in-service professional development programmes and consultancy;
- professional networking within Finland and abroad;
- identifying external support systems and resources;
- providing 'stepping stone' facilities in order that learners could continue with CLIL throughout their basic education;
- finding resources to conduct research to test assumptions about the value of CLIL;
- determining which subjects, or modules within subjects, might be most suitable for CLIL;
- examining how to introduce a target language other than English for CLIL.

(Marsh and Lange 1999)

Methodologies and curricula

Because of the eclectic approach to CLIL found in Finland, there are many ways in which the approach can be realised. This realisation will depend heavily on the predominant reason for implementing the approach. The list of 'focuses' given in the introduction to part 2 of this book can also be found in Finland (see Marsh, Maljers and Hartiala 2001). These include the Culture Dimension; the Environment Dimension; the Language Dimension; the Content Dimension and the Learning Dimension.

At kindergarten, CLIL may involve specific forms of play in the target language that could be as much as 50 per cent of any normal day. At primary level it may be in the form of 'language showers' in which all children in the school are exposed to very short (as little as ten minutes at a time) activities in the target language over one or two years prior to formal language learning in that language. At lower secondary level one or more modules (or topics) may be taught through the target language in intensive periods. Whereas at upper secondary level whole subjects may be taught exclusively in the target language over the whole school year.

The principles of CLIL in Finland evolved steadily over the 1990s (see Fruhauf et al. 1996), and the result is that there is no single Finnish model which is typical of any specific educational level. The fact that schools, and regions, have considerable autonomy in setting curricular objectives has facilitated this ability to select, experiment with and nurture that approach which best seems to suit the environment in which any specific school is located. Such variety of 'types' could not, for instance, be found in a country in which detailed national curricula were centrally developed and administered. So what is the future likely to be? The following is a list of possible 'scenarios' of how Modern Languages Across the Curriculum could develop in Finland.

Basic education (children from 7 to 15 years)
Grades 1–2: Language showers in which a language teacher visits different classes on a weekly basis to carry out 15–30-minute activity sessions using the target language. Sometimes this may involve drama, singing or some other form of 'fun' activity.

Grades 3–6: Up to 20 per cent of the whole curriculum in one or more target languages in the form of modules on specific theme units such as pets, families and local flora and fauna, which would then be integrated into certain subjects such as biology and geography. These modules would be highly interactive, using cooperative-type methodologies extensively. Translanguaging (in which more than one language is used in the classroom or learning context) to occur in order to achieve the best possible learner outcomes.

Grades 7–9: Up to 20 per cent of the whole curriculum taught in one target language in the form of either modules or subjects (geography, biology).

This may be done wholly, or partly, in conjunction with schools in other countries through the use of ICT and exchange visits.

Upper secondary and vocational education (young people from 15 to 19 years)
Grades 1–3: Selected subjects, or modules within subjects, taught in the target language through to Grade 3, the final year, when the language of instruction reverts to a national language in view of the final examination process.

(Vocational): Selected modules, or whole programmes taught through the target language.

Professional education (adults)
At degree level and non-degree level, selected subjects, but frequently whole programmes, taught through the target language

In terms of impact on the classroom, certain features have appeared to be common-place. Many of these could be viewed as integral parts of good teaching practice in terms of greater use of:

- visuality and illustrativeness;
- redundancy (saying the same thing in different ways);
- learner-centred orientation;
- use of interactional methodologies;
- simplified instruction;
- use of written text;
- comprehension checks;
- predictable routines;
- slower speed of instruction.

Issues and developments

The major issues of immediate concern in Finland have been as follows:

- the impact of CLIL on mother tongue development;
- the relationship between early language learning (as through CLIL in kinder-garten or early primary level) on both mother tongue and target language;
- adaptation of formal language curricula to suit learners with experience of CLIL in the target language;
- measuring the competencies required of teachers at all levels who teach extensively through CLIL;
- consolidating experience within Finland on CLIL so as to clarify region-specific characteristics.

Specific issues addressed in 1997–98 remain valid to the present because they often involve long-term analysis or development that will be necessary for CLIL to mature within mainstream education (see Marsh, Marsland and Maljers 1998). Some of the localised development issues for achieving success reported in 1997 and 1999 are as follows (see Nikula and Marsh 1997):

- The reason for the introduction of CLIL in any school, or municipality, needs to be clearly specified in terms of aims and focus;
- 'Trans-languaging' is to be encouraged according to relevance and need;
- Student selection should not discriminate against 'poor' achievers because of the success of CLIL in bringing these learners back into language learning;
- Guidelines need to be drawn up which identify CLIL teacher competence, which is more than mere target language competence;
- Teaching methodologies, particularly those which are subject-specific, need clarification in terms of 'language-sensitive' methods;
- Materials need to be developed which are culturally orientated towards Finland and Finnish curricula. CLIL should not be allowed to be a vehicle by which to adopt uncritically materials which may work against national educational aims;
- Pre-service (initial) teacher education programmes need to be available to produce CLIL qualified teacher graduates;
- Quality assurance systems need to be designed which validate the application of specific types of implementation;
- The integration of language(s) teaching, including that of the mother tongue, is to be synchronised with CLIL curricula;
- Even if CLIL appears to suit the development of a major 'lingua franca' such as the English language, the potential of this approach in introducing alternative target languages needs to be explored, even if these are introduced after initial use of a widely used language;
- Issues of assessment need to be clarified with respect to those learners who have high exposure to CLIL in any respective subject or curriculum.

Conclusion

The motto of the European Year of Languages 2001 was 'Languages open Doors.' In Finland, a number of references have been made to how MLAC/CLIL can be used to unleash potential and open the way for young people to have greater opportunities for success in their later lives by building firm linguistic foundations and the ability to learn other languages and also strengthen the mother tongue as a means of communication. This approach to language teaching and learning has been viewed, in most applications throughout the country, not so much as providing the 'house of language' as in full bilingual capability, but as providing the key to the doors of various 'language houses'.

References

Fruhauf, G., Coyle, D. and Ingeborg, C. (eds) (1996) *Teaching Content through a Foreign Language: Practice and Perspectives in European Bilingual Education*, The Hague: European Platform for Dutch Education.

Marsh, D. (2000) *Aspects of the Finnish Experience of CLIL 1980–99: Languages and Learning Cross-border Co-operation*, Helsinki: National Board of Education.

Marsh, D. and Lange, G. (eds) (1999) *Implementing Content and Language Integrated Learning: A Research-Driven Foundation Reader*, TIE-CLIL, Jyväskylä: University of Jyväskylä.

Marsh, D. and Lange, G. (2000) *Using Languages to Learn and Learning to Use Languages*, TIE-CLIL, Jyväskylä and Milan: University of Jyväskylä and Ministero della Pubblica Istruzione.

Marsh, D. and Marsland, B. (eds) (1997) *CLIL Initiative for the Millennium*, CEILINK, Jyväskylä: University of Jyväskylä.

Marsh, D. and Marsland, B. (eds) (1999a) *Fremdsprachlicher Fachunterricht: Ein Fernkurs zur Lehrerfortbildung*, DIESeLL, Jyväskylä: University of Jyväskylä.

Marsh, D. and Marsland, B. (eds) (1999b) *Distance In-Service Education for Enhancing Second Language Learning*, DIESeLL, Jyväskylä: University of Jyväskylä.

Marsh, D., Ennser, C. and Sygmund, D. (1999) *Pursuing Plurilingualism*, Jyväskylä: University of Jyväskylä.

Marsh, D., Maljers, A., and Hartiala, A.-K. (2001) *Profiling European CLIL Classrooms*, Jyväskylä and The Hague: University of Jyväskylä and European Platform for Dutch Education.

Marsh, D., Marsland, B. and Maljers, A. (eds) (1998) *Future Scenarios in Content and Language Integrated Learning*, EuroCLIC, The Hague: European Platform for Dutch Education.

Nikula, T. and Marsh, D. (1996) *Language and Content Integrated Instruction in the Finnish Primary and Secondary Sectors: A National Survey*, Helsinki: National Board of Education.

Nikula, T. and Marsh, D. (1997) *Language and Content Integrated Learning in the Primary and Secondary Sectors*, Helsinki: National Board of Education.

O'Dwyer, T. (1997) *A Knowledge-based Europe*, DG22: European Commission.

Piri, R. (2001) *Foreign Language Teaching Policy in Finland: National and International Context*, Centre for Applied Languages Studies: University of Jyväskylä.

Pohjanvirta, Z., Blumchen, A., Lindström, A., Mustajokl, A., Nurmimen, E., Mustaparta, A-K., Lindroos, K., Marsh, D., Roman, A. and Tommila, L. (1998) *The Matriculation Examination in Foreign LanguageS: Working Group Report 21 (98)*, Finland: Ministry of Education.

Räsänen, A. and Marsh, D. (1994) *Content Instruction through a Foreign Language: Research and Field Reports*, Jyväskylä: University of Jyväskylä.

8 Italy

Carmel Mary Coonan

Introduction

The situation of foreign language teaching in mainstream schools in Italy has changed dramatically over the last 30–40 years. Change began at the start of the 1970s when Italy became receptive to research in language teaching methodology carried out internationally. Prior to this, teachers of a foreign language were not even required to have a degree in the language they taught and followed essentially a grammar–translation method where knowledge of the language – in communicative procedural terms – was not in fact required or even essential.

Gradual expansion

In the 1970s and 1980s the teaching of foreign languages was gradually introduced to all school levels through a variety of means:

*   Primary school: through the new law on primary school programmes (1985), the teaching of a foreign language was introduced from the third year upwards (from 8 years of age). Since then,[1] there has been a major campaign to introduce foreign languages into the greatest number of classes possible. In 1998 75 per cent of all pupils at junior school level studied a foreign language. Eighty-one per cent of these study English (MPI: 1999). Prior to the law of 1985 and 1990, and in preparation for it, the national project ILSSE (1985) and the IANUA project (1994) (involving thousands of pupils in all) set out to explore the methodological implications and solutions for the early teaching of a foreign language and teacher training requirements.
*   Middle school: the new reform of the *scuola media* 1979 assigned great importance to the concept of language education and to the role of the foreign language (until then taught like Latin or Greek) within it. The foreign language was to contribute, along with Italian and the other subjects of the curriculum, towards the development of the expressive and communicative abilities of the students; thus, focus on performance (knowing how to communicate and express oneself) rather than linguistic knowledge became the aim.
*   Secondary school: a characteristic feature of high-school education in Italy is that foreign languages were traditionally taught, by law, in *licei linguistici*,

which are private institutions. However, the realisation that this situation is detrimental to all those pupils who do not opt to attend a *liceo linguistico* led to the gradual introduction of foreign languages in other high-school types as well. This was done in the form of autonomous school-driven experimental projects. There were maxi-projects, (e.g., Brocca), which concerned the overall curriculum (foreign language included) and mini-projects, which covered the introduction of a foreign language only. All such projects ceased to be experimental in the 1980s and became an integral part of the normal school curriculum.

Parallel to the expansion of foreign languages in the school curriculum, a need developed to think in terms of the training and education of teachers to teach them at the different school levels and within different school types. In view of the fact that an institutional structure for initial teacher training did not exist,[2] an in-service ministerial project called *Progetto Speciale Lingue Straniere* was established (1976) to train the teachers, throughout all the provinces of the peninsula, in language teaching methodology. Furthermore, language teacher associations were formed,[3] university departments began to open up to the science of Glottodidactics[4] and, for the first time, the state examination for language teachers included questions related to language teaching methodology (see Bertin and Perini 2001).

The present day

Various factors in Italy today are contributing to further expansion and qualitative development of foreign language teaching in mainstream schools:

New law on school autonomy

The new law on school autonomy introduced flexibility – in terms of both structure and curriculum content – which provided considerable changes for developments in the teaching of foreign languages. For example:

Curriculum change: there has been a change from a three-tier system to a two-tier system,[5] which has brought with it innovation in the curriculum.[6] The curriculum is now divided into a nationally driven core curriculum (80 per cent of the total time) and a locally driven curriculum (20 per cent of the total time). The national curriculum provides indications as to core content and objectives. The local curriculum is managed by the school to respond to its own specific demands and characteristics. Furthermore, the school is free to establish its own extracurricular activities. To date,[7] only the curriculum details for the *scuola di base* have been published (February 2001);[8] they will apply from the academic year 2001–2002.

Other innovations involve provision for the learning of *two* foreign languages – termed 'modern European languages' – one of which must be English. The learning of the first modern European language begins in the first *biennio* (from 6 years of age). The second modern European language begins in the second *biennio* (from age 11). Although the curriculum details for the *scuola secondaria* have not yet been published, it has already been officially stated that the two foreign languages begun in the *scuola di base* must continue to be studied in the *scuola secondaria*. Teaching time is expressed in terms of the number of hours allowed for the subject. The *Sintesi Aggiornata del Gruppo di Lavoro* indicates the number of hours to be allocated to both the first and the second foreign language during the school year.[9]

Modularity: the concept of the 'class' as a permanently fixed working unit organised according to age has been superseded by the concept of 'modularity', whereby teaching–learning work units may be combined and recombined according to the competencies that exist and/or competencies to be developed. The hours assigned overall for foreign languages can therefore be arranged according to what is suitable for the school and for the pupils. The relationship between outcome levels and the number of hours of study (rather than the whole 'school year') and the flexibility acquired in timetabling (e.g., adding extra hours to foreign language study within the local 'quota') and group organisation allow for the establishment of continuity between the *scuola di base* and the *scuola secondaria*. In the past, the question of continuity between school levels has represented an insurmountable problem, with the schools inevitably beginning from scratch with their language programme with each new intake.

Progetto Lingue 2000

A further indication of the strong moves currently underway in Italy to bring the situation of foreign language teaching and learning into line with the rest of Europe and, in particular, with the directives of the European Commission and the Council of Europe is *Progetto Lingue* 2000. The project, which involved several thousand teachers nation-wide, had the aim of bringing about innovation in the field of teaching and learning in order to encourage the acquisition of communicative competence in foreign languages by students in all schools throughout the country – from nursery school to the last class of high school. Certain innovative features characterise the project:

- students are formed into groups of no more than fifteen according to competence level;
- the total annual amount of hours is subdivided into short learning modules which are distributed throughout the year;
- new technologies are used to encourage independent learning and individualised instruction;
- outcome competencies are related to the scales of the European Framework of Reference;
- certification by foreign agencies is made possible.

The project is being systematically monitored at local, regional and national level to gauge the effectiveness and utility of the work underway. This is the background against which we should view the situation with regard to Modern Languages Across the Curriculum.

Modern Languages across the Curriculum

Recently, there has been a sharp increase in interest in the possibilities offered by the integration of content and the foreign language for enhancing foreign language learning. Such a combination is referred to here as CLIL (see Nikula 1997). Although numerous examples of this type of teaching have existed in mainstream schooling (outside of Special Statute regions)[10] for over a decade, the recent reform on school autonomy[11] actually allows the foreign language to be used for the school curriculum.[12] This policy has understandably led to a surge of interest in the field and to the establishment of other experiments.

Government projects

At the beginning of the 1990s, there were three government projects which incorporated the use of one or two foreign languages for the teaching and learning of 'non-language' subjects. The projects were developed as a result of the Treaty of Maastricht. They were *Liceo Classico Europeo*, *Liceo Linguistico Europeo* and *Liceo Internazionale*.

*   *Liceo Classico Europeo*: this project involves the *licei classici* or high schools, which offer a specialisation in Classics and did not normally offer a modern foreign language in the curriculum.[13] The project includes the introduction of two foreign languages, a greater European dimension to content and an overall aim of promoting a European awareness. An important feature is the use of one of the foreign languages to teach, from the first year (from 14 years of age), any of the other subjects on the curriculum except Italian, History of Art and Classics.[14]
*   *Liceo Internazionale*: there are twelve *licei internazionali*. A special feature of them is that they allow foreign languages other than English to be used to teach non-language subjects to pupils aged 14 and over.
*   *Liceo Linguistico Europeo*: there are 95 *licei linguistici europei* and, as in the examples above, the project aims to promote greater European awareness. Of the three languages studied, one is used for the teaching–learning of one or two non-language disciplines. Many of the schools now opt to start such teaching at 14 years of age (instead of 16) (see table 8.1).

With regard to the *Liceo Linguistico Europeo*, the figures in table 8.2 show the extent of teaching curriculum subjects through a foreign language.[15]

A series of seminars have been organised by the Ministry for all three types of *liceo* to introduce the necessary structural and curricular changes that the new law reform on school autonomy necessarily entails. Over and above these projects, it is clear that many other schools are moving rapidly in the direction of some

same school (see table 8.3). The project is in three phases: a series of seminars on the theoretical and methodological aspects of CLIL; introduction in the schools from September 2001 to May 2002; a final seminar for the presentation of results.

'Independent' schools

Other schools have acted independently. These are to be found, with only one exception, in the Friuli-Venezia-Giulia region situated in the north-east of Italy bordering on Slovenia and Austria. The schools are normally very independent in setting their own pace of reform. However, they have established a *Rete* CLIC network,[19] to co-ordinate efforts, share experiences and resources. The *Rete* is also a project, as it has set out a developed work programme of training and monitoring.

Table 8.4 shows the range of curriculum subjects taught through the foreign language at the schools in the *Rete* CLIC.

Methodologies and curricula

The general picture

From the above, it is possible to see that the increased interest in MLAC/CLIL in Italy is manifesting itself in diverse ways to accommodate different objectives, different situations, different ideas, all set within the general framework of this approach to second languages, namely that of Content and Language Integrated Learning. Indeed, the developing situation indicates that the 'traditional' view of CLIL – that of a subject taught in the L2 throughout year-long courses – is giving way to a multi-faceted situation. I now turn to these various aspects.

The focus

Experience in Italy shows that practice locates itself on a continuum between a content-driven focus with language enhancement and a language-driven focus with content enhancement:[20]

Table 8.4 Subjects taught in the schools in the *Rete* CLIC

Languages	Subjects
English French German Spanish	Law, Law and Economics, Mathematics, Science, Philosophy, Latin, Chemistry, Religion, Mechanics, Electronics, Construction Theory, Business Studies, History, Geography, Computer Science, Physical Education, Word Processing Studies*

Note
The variety of the subjects is due to the diverse school types involved and their particular specialisations, for example, commerce, business, industry, technology.

1   Content-driven – in this focus we find:
    (a) the teaching of the subject in the L2. There are, however, varying degrees of weight given to the L2 within any one lesson.
    (b) the teaching of the subject in the L1. During the course, however, teaching units or longer modules are prepared for the teaching of the subject matter through the L2. The content of the modules represents the curricular subject objectives. Teaching is conducted by the subject teacher alone or together with the foreign language teacher.

2   Language-driven – in this focus we find:
    (a) interdisciplinary or pluri-disciplinary modules that are carried out by the foreign language teacher separately or together with one or more subject teachers. Whatever the case, the module is developed and elaborated upon the basis of inter-teacher planning. The module carries a strong orientation towards language.

The teacher

Who are the teachers who adopt the MLAC/CLIL approaches? What kind of collaboration is there? Overall, the Italian CLIL teacher is a non-native speaker of the language s/he teaches through. The presence of native-speaker teachers is higher in the government projects, especially the *Liceo Internazionale* and the *Liceo Classico Europeo*.[21] Teachers organise their teaching in one of two ways. Either the non-language content teacher works together with the foreign language teacher – they are both present during the lessons; or the non-language content teacher works alone but prepares and elaborates his/her teaching activity in tandem with the foreign language teacher. They are not actually together in the classroom, however. Similarly, the foreign language teacher may work together with the non-language subject teacher to plan units or modules that s/he may choose to deliver on his/her own.

The students

The experiences reported above mainly concern students in upper secondary schools. Some CLIL teaching begins with the *triennio* (16–19 years of age) (the *Liceo Linguistico Europeo* and some of the 'independent' schools), and some with students in the *biennio* (14–16) (the *Liceo Internazionale* and the *Liceo Classico Europeo*). There is a tendency in some CLIL projects to bring the introduction of CLIL forward, moving it from the *triennio* alone to the *biennio* (this is sometimes the case with the *Liceo Linguistico Europeo*). However, the ministerial circular of 2001 (*Progetto Lingue* 2000) specifies that experimentation can begin in the middle school.

The weighting of the L2

The teaching of a subject in the foreign language does not necessarily imply that the foreign language is the sole language used. Responses to a questionnaire given to teachers in the government projects (hence those who teach a subject through the foreign language) (Pavese and Zecca 2001) show that only a third of the respondents indicate that the foreign language is used for more than 85 per cent of the lesson time.[22] For the remaining two-thirds of the respondents, only about half of the lesson is conducted in the foreign language. Furthermore, less than half the respondents actually present the content entirely and solely in the foreign language. The preferred style is to present the content in the L1 and then switch over to the L2. This is done for reasons connected with the difficulty of the content and the low language competence of the students.[23] Pavese and Zecca hypothesise that the imbalance in favour of the L1 could be attributed to the fact that teachers – the foreign language teacher and the non-language subject teacher – are both present in the classroom. Such a situation demarcates quite clearly the language roles of the two teachers and, thus, the weighting of the two languages in the lesson. It may also be due to the fact that the teacher can use an Italian text-book rather than one written in the foreign language.[24] Moreover, more than two-thirds of the respondents say that they allow the students to use the L1 mainly when asked to present complex content (76 per cent) but also for asking questions (15.4 per cent), for interacting with peers (11.5 per cent) and for interacting with the Italian (subject) teacher (3.8 per cent). This 'concession' obviously influences the balance of the L1 and L2 in the lesson.

Classroom practicalities

What is a MLAC/CLIL lesson like? Given the situation above we can expect considerable diversity in the way lessons are conducted. The diversity will concern various features, but an important one concerns the weight given to the L2 as opposed to the L1, and the way the two alternate. Of course, the more the orientation is towards monolingual delivery, the more demanding it is for the teacher, who has to draw on a variety of resources to make delivery as clear and as comprehensible as possible. It is demanding for the students as well, for they have to follow the lesson and to participate using the language effectively.

The following illustration is from a Physics lesson conducted entirely in English by a non-native-speaker Physics teacher with students of 17–18 years of age.[25] It is a lesson that exemplifies just one of the many forms of MLAC/CLIL that exist at the moment in Italy. Hence it cannot be considered to represent a typical lesson – rather, a typical lesson for the teacher who chooses a monolingual L2 approach to teaching the subject.

The teacher and the lesson

STRUCTURING THE LESSON

At the beginning of the lesson the teacher adopts a series of strategies that serve to set the scene – affectively and structurally.

Affectively: his first linguistic moves consist of a greeting, using an informal register:

T: Good morning, guys!

And then jokingly pretending to scold students:

S: Good morning. Excuse me, teacher, may I go out?
T: Ooh! Every time I enter the class there is always someone who wants to go out!

The whole move, which the teacher regularly makes in his other lessons too ('Hi, guys. Did you have a nice weekend?/Good morning, boys and girls. Today is cold, isn't it?'), sets a friendly tone to the lesson, important for generating motivation and a readiness to co-operate.

Structurally: the teacher immediately proceeds to inform the students what he is going to do with them during the lesson and the order in which he will do this. Notice that this indication is oral as well as presented in written form.

T: Today I'll introduce the argument about magnetism. Do you know what a magnetic field is?
S: Yes, perhaps. A sort of magnet that attracts objects made of iron such as paper clips.
T: Yes, now I will give you some photocopies with the main points of the lesson. . . . I divide the lesson into two parts. The first part is the explanation of the topic plus the experiment; at the end we'll correct the exercises I gave you last week. Any problems?

The teacher then signals the end of the 'preamble' by announcing:

T: Ok, I will begin my lesson, good!

The structuring role of the teacher, which has the effect of contributing towards the overall comprehensibility of the lesson, continues throughout the lesson with him guiding the students' attention to what he is saying through such expressions as:

You notice how this instrument . . .
Look at . . .

You see that if . . .
Now, . . .
So, a compass . . .
I give you another example.

DEALING WITH THE CONTENT

The content of the lesson is presented entirely in the second language – English – both orally and through written material (text-book, hand-outs and photo-copies). The content is broken up into small chunks. These chunks are more digestible because of their short length. Firstly, the written parts the students are asked to consult are short and the oral presentation is broken down into bits by the teacher encouraging an interactional format. The interactions serve to break up the teacher's monologue. The teacher also frequently carries out comprehension checks ('Is it clear now? Any doubt?'); asks students questions; and gets the students to do something ('Do you want to try Chiara?'). The students themselves also interrupt the teacher to ask questions or make comments:

S: So, taking off the coil from the bolt which is linked to the battery there is no more magnetic field, is there?
S: Wonderful!
S: It's fantastic! Look, Marco!
S: But, should we do a report about a magnetic field?

THE APPROACH

The teacher integrates the theoretical with the experiential following a bottom-up approach. In other words, the input begins with the students watching the teacher carry out an experiment with magnets. They are also encouraged to try parts of the experiment themselves. It is during the experiments that the teacher explains the properties of magnetism. The teacher also explains the reason why the experiments are important, thereby contributing to the students' learning strategies and cognitive awareness, as outlined in chapter 3:

T: I want to make these experiments with you because the topics are difficult and I want you to be able to do hypotheses and not to solve or guess a problem by chance as I often notice.

This is a Physics lesson, and it may be that the nature of the discipline lends itself to such a practical approach. However, in this example, the main linguistic actor is still the teacher. Compared to the single student, he speaks more frequently and his utterances are much longer. Those of the students are generally much shorter.

Conditions could be created for student linguistic participation by dispensing tasks for the students to carry out in small groups.[26] In this way, not only would the students have to carry out the task, but they would also have to discuss the way they would present the results of the task (discussion in L2) as well as present the data (in L2) either orally or in written form.

The student and the lesson

It is important to note that, although the students all share the same mother tongue (Italian), they take it as normal that they speak in the foreign language.[27] On those few occasions that the students use Italian (mostly 'off-talk', chattering to a friend) the teacher checks them immediately:

T: Have you ever seen a compass needle?
S: Sta scherzando, vero Prof?
T: In English, please?
S: You are joking, teacher!!

Focus on language

In this particular lesson, the teacher is a Physics teacher. There is no foreign-language teacher present, nor is there any indication that the teacher develops his work in tandem with the foreign-language teacher. Furthermore, there are no examples of written work or any other activity that focuses even indirectly on functional language development (e.g., matching words for definitions, semantic maps for clustering words through associations, work on genre (writing reports of experiments), etc.). It seems to be the case that where there is the presence, direct or indirect, of a foreign-language teacher, there is a tendency to focus more on the students' attention to linguistic form(s). In the survey carried out by Pavese and Zecca (2001), more than half of the teachers deal with grammatical problems during their lessons (59.6 per cent) and explicitly explain L2 lexis (94.2 per cent):

> Il lessico specialistico viene introdotto per la maggior parte del tempo con gli esempi, . . . sempre contestualizzando sotto forma di spiegazioni adeguate, esemplificazioni . . . mediante traduzione e sinonimi.[28]

Students' language errors are corrected in 78.8 per cent of cases; these are mostly where the message is difficult to understand (although there are some who hold a normative view regarding errors). The issue of focus on form is an important one. According to Swain (1990) one of the features that characterise immersion programmes is the lack of focus on form, which she relates to the low competence levels in speaking and writing on the part of the students. She calls for the need to intervene not so much with corrections but with strategies that force the student to notice the formal/functional inadequacy of his/her utterance for what s/he wishes to express.

Issues and developments

There are numerous issues arising from the Italian experience of MLAC/CLIL that require attention. They include problems like the availability of texts in the foreign language for use in the class and the availability of non-language-subject teachers competent in the foreign language. However, three issues are especially pressing: student outcomes; assessment; and teacher education.

Student outcomes

Regarding the practice of MLAC/CLIL in the classrooms – either for teaching a subject or for the 'softer' approach of teaching themes through modules – insufficient attention is sometimes paid to linguistic objectives, especially to the *final* linguistic objectives. In most cases, language objectives to be pursued during the programmes are not fixed. However, CLIL approaches are adopted for the potential they offer for greater competence in the foreign language: competence in a micro-language; capacity to conduct higher-order thinking efficiently in the L2; competence in writing or interaction skills. Greater awareness of the potential to develop these competencies would allow teachers to establish expectations and nurture development more purposefully. So, linguistically speaking, what can we expect from CLIL teaching? What do we want from CLIL teaching? To answer these questions, we need a clear specification of immediate, intermediate and final objectives of a complete cycle of CLIL for a given group of pupils or students. Language teachers need to work with the other subject teachers in order to incorporate language elements into their syllabuses.

Assessment

Directly related to the above is the question of assessment. Adequate assessment can only take place if objectives have been fixed. Assessment against these objectives will allow the teacher to gauge not only the language development of his/her students but also the success of the programme itself. With regard to the student, there are important options: whether foreign language competence is to be assessed through the subject/content matter; whether content matter is to be assessed concomitantly with the foreign language; whether the foreign language is to be assessed quite separately.

Scales and descriptors need to be available that will allow for a criterion-referenced rather than norm-referenced assessment. The levels and descriptors offered by the Common European Framework of Reference are useful in this case, as they can provide the starting point for the elaboration of additional scales and descriptors within the overall framework, suitable for the specific characteristics of CLIL learning.

Related to the issue of assessment is that of the quality of the models of approach themselves. The Italian situation offers different models of CLIL – some more established than others. In order to understand the efficacy of the different models and also their feasibility within the newly reformed Italian school system, a programme of monitoring and evaluation is needed.

Teacher education

There is no institutional teacher education in MLAC/CLIL in Italy. Attempts are currently underway in some regions[29] to introduce initial training within the *Scuole di Specializzazione*. The main existing form of training is in-service, carried out on a small scale in the form of 1–3 day-long courses. These are organised by the teachers themselves within the schools involved in CLIL or by other authorities who are directly involved in organising CLIL teaching (IRRSAE, *Inspectorates*, Ministry of Education for *Progetto Lingue* 2000).

Conclusion

We have seen that experimentation with MLAC/CLIL approaches to second language learning and teaching in Italy need to be set within a developing awareness of the importance of learning second languages. There are a number of projects which now encourage language learning and raise the possibility of teaching curriculum content through foreign languages. What is most important for us is to address the issues of organisation and practice which these experiments have raised. There are questions of curriculum design and content and assessment. Finally, there is a need for teachers to develop their methodological approaches in the light of what we know about the linguistic processes and pedagogic procedures of language learning set within a Modern Languages Across the Curriculum perspective.

Notes

1 Law 148/1990 and the ministerial decree of 28 June 1991 provided further indications as to how the foreign language was to be taught in the primary school.
2 Such a structure – the regional inter-university *Scuole di Specializzazione* – was instituted in 1999.
3 The language teacher associations which historically have contributed to debate and development in the field are: ANILS (Associazione Nazionale Insegnanti di Lingue Straniere) and LEND (Lingua e Nuova Didattica).
4 The first *cattedra* in language teaching methodology was established in 1979 at the Istituto di Linguistica e Didattica delle Lingue at the Università Ca' Foscari of Venice.
5 The present system is: *scuola elementare*; *scuola media*; *scuola superiore*; the new system – to be introduced gradually from September 2001 – is: *scuola di base* (*biennio, triennio, biennio*); *scuola secondaria* (*biennio, triennio*).
6 Law of 30 February 2000.
7 March 2001.
8 Commissione per il Programma di riordino dei cicli, *Sintesi Aggiornata del Gruppo di Lavoro*.
9 The Synthesis Report indicates 120 hours for the second foreign language and 420 hours overall for the first foreign language. Furthermore, reference is made to

specific outcome levels (those of the *Common European Framework*) in competencies: first foreign language: oral competence and reading A2; written: A1; second foreign language: A1 in all competencies.

10 The Special Statute regions where forms of bilingual education are underway are the Valle d'Aosta and Alto-Adige (the province of Bolzano). See Van de Craen and Wolff (1997).

11 Law of 8 March 1998, article 4, sub-section 3.

12 "Within teaching autonomy formative courses can be arranged that involve several subjects and activities as well as teachings conducted in a foreign language on the basis of international agreements."

13 The project has been developed for the particular structure of the Convitti or Educandati femminili (e.g., longer hours, boarding facilities, intake of students from abroad).

14 The subjects that require no special permission to be taught through a foreign language are History and Geography. Requests to teach subjects other than these through one of the foreign languages on the curriculum must be presented and discussed by the *collegio dei docenti*.

15 Data provided by Inspector Miceli at the Ministry of Education. The information refers to 2000.

16 IRRSAE are regional institutions charged with dealing with in-service teacher training and with experimentation.

17 The co-ordinator of the project is the Sovrintendenza Scolastica di Milano, Ispettrice Langé.

18 http://www.ase.org.uk/sworld.html.

19 The co-ordination of the *Rete* passes from school to school every year.

20 MET (1998) makes this distinction.

21 See Pavese and Zecca (2001) for their questionnaire sent to twenty-five mainstream high schools (*Licei Classici Europei* and *Licei Internazionali*).

22 The questionnaire was sent out as part of the activities of the *TIE-CLIL* project.

23 From the results reported it is not clear whether the same content is dealt with again in the other language or whether there is an extension/expansion of the content through the second language.

24 The need for text-books in the foreign language suitable for teaching what the Italian programmes stipulate represents an urgent problem for those who teach a subject as opposed to single themes.

25 One of four transcribed lessons in an unpublished degree dissertation by Dott. ssa Ivana Spinello.

26 The model described by Willis (1996) is useful.

27 The students are in their second year of learning Physics through English.

28 'The specialist vocabulary is mostly introduced through examples . . . it is contextualised in the form of suitable explanations, exemplifications . . . by means of translation and synonyms.'

29 Venice, Pavia, Milan.

References

Annali della Pubblica Istruzione (1985) *Il Progetto ILSSE e l'insegnamento della lingua straniera nella scuola elementare*, Florence: Le Monnier.

Bertin, B. and Perini, M. (2001) 'L'insegnante di lingue straniere nella realtà delle scuole: dal POF alle FO', *SELM* 1.

Coonan, C. M. (1997) 'Language teacher training and bilingual education in Italy', in P. Van de Craen and D. Wolff (eds) *Language Teacher Training and Bilingual Education*,

Report prepared for the TNP Evaluation Conference Lille, III, Université Charles de Gaulle, July 1997 (The Continuing Education Centre, University of Jyväskylä).

—— (1998) 'Content and language integrated learning (CLIL) in Italy: present situation and possible developments', in D. Marsh, B. Marsland and A. Maljers (eds) *Future Scenarios in Content and Integrated Language Learning*, Jyväskylä: The Continuing Education Centre, University of Jyväskylä and The Netherlands: European Platform for Dutch Education.

Council of Europe (2001) *Common European Framework of Reference: Learning, Teaching, Assessment*, Cambridge: CUP.

Craen, P. Van de and Wolff, D. (1997) *Language Teacher Training and Bilingual Education Subject Report*, Lille: University of Lille.

Freddi, G. (1994) *La lingua straniera alle elementari*, 2 vols, London: Longman.

Met, M. (1998) 'Curriculum decision-making in content based language teaching', in J. Cenoz and F. Genesee (eds) *Beyond Bilingualism: Multilingualism and Multilingual Education*, Clevedon: Multilingual Matters.

Ministero della Pubblica Istruzione (1999) 'Liceo linguistico europeo', official mimeo.

Nikula, T. (1997) 'Terminological considerations in teaching content through a foreign language', in D. Marsh, B. Marsland and T. Nikula (eds) *Aspects of Implementing Plurilingual Education: Seminars and Field Notes*, The Continuing Education Centre, University of Jyväskylä.

Pavese, M. and Zecca, M. (2001) 'La lingua straniera come lingua veicolare: un'indagine sulle prime esperienze in Italia', *SILTA* 1.

Swain, M. (1990) 'Manipulating and complementing content teaching to maximise second language learning', in *Foreign/Second Language Pedagogy Research*, Clevedon: Multilingual Matters.

Willis, J. (1996) *A Framework for Task-based Learning*, London: Longman.

9   Spain

Carmen Pérez-Vidal

Introduction

In this chapter, I shall begin with a brief summary of the historical–political context for second language learning in Spain. In Spain, we use the CLIL rubric for Modern Languages Across the Curriculum. I shall consider the first experiences of CLIL. Next, I shall discuss the impact of CLIL on foreign language education in Spain and look at the results of CLIL programmes. After that, I offer an example of a particular CLIL programme as a Spanish case study involving mixed-ability secondary school pupils in mainstream education. Finally, some thoughts for future directions are included.

Background

Following the Civil War (1936–39), Spanish was declared the only official language of the territory of Spain; neither Basque, Catalan, nor Galician could be used in public, although clandestine use continued in many homes. During the 1940s and 1950s, Spanish was the only language used in education. Starting in the 1960s, some use of the regional languages began to appear in the schools as central control of education weakened. Demographic change in the second half of the twentieth century was another key factor influencing language use in Spain. The relocation of workers from other parts of Spain to the more industrialised areas of Catalonia and the Basque country played a significant role in decreasing the percentage of speakers of the regional languages. With the coming of democracy in 1978, and the passing of the Statutes of Autonomy (*Boletín Oficial del Estado* – BOE 1981,101), which created a number of 'Autonomous Communities' within Spain, a process of decentralisation at many levels began, and regional languages were again granted official status.

Modern Languages Across the Curriculum

In this section, I want to look at the approach of integrating second language and curriculum subject content in terms of how this has occurred in the context of regional second languages. I then consider the approach from the perspective of so-called 'foreign' languages *per se*.

Regional second languages

Through the laws of linguistic normalisation in the early 1980s, the Autonomous Communities regained local control over the linguistic policies affecting the educational system and the media. However, people did not want two separate communities within each Autonomous Community, but rather one country where all citizens could become fully integrated and able to take part in all areas of public life. Such integration would not be possible without acquiring the local language. So, beginning in the early 1980s, these socio-political developments impelled different types of immersion programmes, in the Basque Country, Catalonia, and Galicia.[1] These programmes were models of second-language teaching using CLIL methodology delivered to children of a majority language and culture (Serra 1997: 15). Different authorities set up different combinations of programmes according to a range of options. Table 9.1 contains examples of the context of L1 and L2 in different areas of Spain and the type of language teaching possible there.

The percentage of each model type varies from region to region and according to the socio-political objectives of different regions. The 'variable' and

Table 9.1 Immersion programme models in Spain

Modality	Basque Country	Catalonia
Monolingual Spanish Regional language taught as language subject 4–5 hours a week	Model A	Minimal Catalanisation (before the linguistic normalisation law)
Variable Spanish and regional language tuition in varying degrees	Model B[a]	'Medium Catalanisation'/ 'immersion model' or: 'Progressive' or 'Static' bilingual[b]
Monolingual regional Spanish as language subject 4–5 hours a week	Model D	'Maximum Catalanisation' or 'normalisation' model

Sources: Basque Country definitions – Cenoz and Perales (2001); Catalonia definitions – Pradilla (2001), citing Alsina et al. (1983) and Vila (1995).

Notes
a Basque is taught for approximately 50 per cent of the class time, although this varies from school to school (Artamendi 1994). These schools are intended for students who are native speakers of Spanish and want to be bilingual in Basque and Spanish. It is a model which can be compared with other European models (Baetens Beardsmore 1993) and with models of partial immersion in Canada, in which French and English are the languages of tuition for majority-group English-speaking students (Genesee 1987; Cummins 1997).
b As the name implies, progressive bilingual schools introduce Catalan gradually as the medium of instruction, whereas static bilingual schools split the curriculum between Spanish and Catalan (Vila 1995).

'monolingual' regional language schools share specific objectives – total competence in both official languages in the long term – and an 'instrumental' (see Serra 1997) methodological approach (i.e. CLIL), using the regional language as the medium of instruction for content subjects.

Initially, most immersion programmes were of the variable type, with fewer monolingual regional language schools. The trend is being steadily reversed. In the Basque Country, the different programme types coexist, with Models B and D progressively becoming more popular. In Catalonia, the prevailing model in the last decade was the maximum normalisation model, with the explicit objective of avoiding a split educational system – a situation that could lead to social disharmony.

In Galicia, the situation has evolved at a rather slower pace (see Artigal 1993; Xunta 1995). The law for language normalisation provides for a mixture of Galician and Spanish in the primary grades, and it is often left to the discretion of the individual teacher to decide, rather than implement a full immersion programme. Regulations within each school involve the normalisation of the language through a Commission for the Normalisation of Galician, which will ensure that the use of the language spreads and improves.

Given the diversity of student/pupil populations, how we define language teaching methods for each of these types of schools depends on the model and the profile of the students. For a student whose first language is Spanish, studying in a school in which the medium of instruction is the regional language (e.g., Basque Model D), the methodological approach is CLIL. The same would apply if a student whose L1 is a regional or other language were to study in a Spanish monolingual school.[2] However, when the language (Spanish or a regional language) is taught as a subject, instruction tends to focus on grammar and literature, and many teachers adopt traditional language instructional approaches with relatively formal syllabi, similar to the traditional methodology most often adopted in foreign languages.

Foreign languages

After becoming a member of the European Community in 1986, Spain had to set itself several objectives to meet its new social demands and educational goals. Students had to become competent in one or more languages in addition to Spanish and, in some cases, as mentioned above, their own regional language, which put even more strain on time and budgets. These changes have raised social awareness about the linguistic needs of a modern society. Both schools and educational authorities have taken steps to promote multilingualism.

The regulations of the Spanish Education Reform Law (LOGSE, passed in 1990 and fully implemented in 1998) include a clear commitment to move towards a multilingual society. Three of its features are particularly significant:

1   A call for a Languages Across the Curriculum approach, in which foreign language modules ('credits') are used to teach non-language subjects. CLIL

methodology in the form of project-work and task-based approaches in foreign language classes is suggested, based on the hypothesis that procedures can be transferred from one language to another.

2 An earlier introduction of languages (at 8 rather than 11).
3 An optional second foreign language as early as primary school.

The progressive decentralisation of the past twenty years has led to a great variety of scenarios in the present use of CLIL in the teaching of foreign languages in Spain. Even if not all the regional authorities support CLIL in the same way or at the same rate, there is a general interest in it. Contributions to CLIL from the private sector should not be ignored (see Navés and Muñoz 1999). However, in this context I now want to consider the characteristics of CLIL in Spain, in terms of its dissemination and implementation as part of the state initiative.

Current CLIL programmes dealing with foreign languages

In this section, I shall discuss MLAC/CLIL programmes which affect several regional authorities and then those designed and run by the single regional authorities.

Programmes that affect several regional authorities

The Bilingual and Bicultural Project: The Spanish Ministry of Education, Culture and Sports and the British Council agreed on The Bilingual and Bicultural Project in 1996. This project involves 42 state infant and primary schools and 10580 children aged between 3 and 8. The target language is English. The project involves 135 British teachers in schools working jointly with 620 Spanish teachers and suggests moves towards an official bilingual curriculum. The subjects taught in English are Social and Natural Sciences, PE and Arts and Crafts. This project was agreed on when the centrally based Ministry of Education was still in charge of educational policy in the regional authorities of Aragon, Asturias, the Balearic Islands, Cantabria, Castilla-La Mancha, Castilla-León, Extremadura, Madrid, Murcia, and the cities of Ceuta and Melilla on the north coast of Morocco. These communities have now taken on the project.

Comenius Programmes: Since 1995, Spanish primary and secondary schools have been participating extensively in this European programme. In Comenius, three schools from three different countries establish a link with the aim of working together on a common educational project. Although Comenius is not a CLIL programme in itself, the communication needs created by the collaboration have encouraged many Spanish schools to use a multilingual approach to learning, so that Comenius has naturally led to the use of CLIL.

Programmes designed and run by single regional authorities

Here are examples of CLIL in some of the regional areas:

CLIL in Aragon: The Spanish–French bilingual branches were established in March 1999 in eight state secondary schools, and the programme is expected to last until at least June 2005. It is the result of a bilateral agreement between The Department of Education and Culture of Aragon and the French Ministry of Foreign Affairs. In this programme, which involves 465 students and 25 teachers, students can opt for an additional subject in French, which covers the same curricular topics as the corresponding Spanish subject. The subjects offered are Social Studies, Arts and Crafts, Music and PE. Similar programmes are being run in the Communities of Andalusia, Galicia and Murcia.

CLIL in the Basque Country: From 1996 to 2000, three CLIL programmes were developed in state schools. First, there are a programme involving 8–12-year-old pupils in four primary schools and another involving 12–16-year-old students in four secondary schools. In the year 2000–2001 three new programmes were created in which one or several subjects are taught in English. At present there are forty primary schools with 8–12-year-old pupils in which the usual English lessons are taught with activities corresponding to other areas.

Second, there was a programme involving 12–16-year-old students in six secondary schools. The subject areas vary a great deal depending on the school. The subjects chosen – which include Social Studies, Natural Science, Maths, Arts and Crafts, Drama and PE – are those in which students know the basic concepts and terms in Basque and Spanish, and are either highly motivating or highly relevant. Materials are the same as those used in Spanish-medium schools, and the emphasis is on literacy skills.

Third, there is the Trilingual Baccalaureate, which is a two-year post-compulsory secondary course in which Basque, Spanish and English are the means of instruction for a variety of subjects corresponding to the scientific, technological and humanistic branches of the course. The 26 students taking part in this last programme were selected using proficiency tests in English and Basque in order to guarantee a certain degree of uniformity in their linguistic skills.

CLIL in Catalonia: As early as 1988, the Department of Education of Catalonia started to promote programmes that aimed at the early introduction of French and English as foreign languages in the already bilingual Catalan–Spanish primary classroom. In these programmes, Arts and Crafts were taught in French, while a multidisciplinary approach was adopted in the case of English. These programmes involved a total of 260 schools and 52000 pupils and lasted until 1999.

In 1999, the Orator Project was launched. It aims to improve the teaching and learning of foreign languages in state primary and secondary schools by promoting various kinds of innovations, in which CLIL plays a major role. Although the project does not favour any foreign language in particular, the medium of instruction opted for by the majority of schools is English in the first place and French in the second. At the present, 15 schools and 910 students are taking part in CLIL programmes within the Orator framework. The schools involved in the project receive financial and training support from the Department of Education over a two-year period, after which new schools are incorporated. It is hoped, however, that schools will carry on with the innovations even after their funding period ends. The project will be in effect until 2004.

A total of sixty Catalan schools are also taking part in a number of international programmes that require the use of at least one foreign language as the means of instruction to a greater or lesser extent.[3] These programmes are Science Across Europe (30 schools; 3000 students), Linguapax (15 schools; 900 students), International Baccalaureate (4 schools; 240 students), Globe (8 schools; 240 students), and Eurosésame (9 schools; 240 students).

Although these accounts clearly show a variety of approaches to CLIL in Spain, some common patterns do emerge. Since the early days in Catalonia in 1988, the central and regional authorities have shown a growing interest in CLIL that has become reality in the different programmes described above. However, CLIL programmes are experimental projects. Consequently, the number of schools presently involved in them is still relatively small. CLIL is viewed by schools as a means of providing students with some extra exposure to the target language and as a means of enhancing the profile of the school. The procedure for the selection of schools to take part is similar in the different Regional Authorities. Once the initiative is launched by the administration, the schools interested in participating present a project and are selected according to the quality of their proposal.

As might be expected, the predominant language of instruction in these programmes is English, while French is the second most popular language. There is a wide variety of subjects taught in a foreign language. In primary education, there is a preference for more practical subjects such as Physical Education or Arts and Crafts, while Social Studies is the preferred subject for CLIL among the more academic subjects. In secondary education, there is a greater variety in the selection of subjects, which depends to a large extent on the particular conditions of each school.

All programmes provide for some linguistic and pedagogic training for content teachers. The pedagogic training usually takes the form of preparatory courses and weekly seminar meetings. In Aragon, an annual symposium on bilingual education is organised. In Catalonia, meetings between language teachers and content teachers are held. In the Basque Country teachers also receive support in the form of ready-made materials designed by consultant teachers and teacher trainers. Language improvement is catered for by language courses within the regional authority throughout the school year. Grants are also awarded for courses in Great Britain or France.

Teacher education

As teacher education is one of the key factors determining the gap between theory and actual MLAC/CLIL practice, a consistent programme of teacher education that prepares teachers to assimilate and adapt to the new circumstances described in this chapter needs to be implemented in Spain (see Pérez-Vidal 1999). The task of implementing changes in the school systems after the restoration of the regional authorities was certainly gigantic, for language competence as well as for methodology. In 1980, few teachers spoke the language of their regional authority. This has improved a lot, with extensive government-sponsored language training programmes for teachers.

In the area of foreign languages, primary teachers have the advantage of an overall understanding of the different subjects in the primary curriculum, a good base in didactics, and now, as a result of increasing specialisation in their initial training, adequate levels of competence in target languages. Thus, they are well equipped for implementing Modern Languages Across the Curriculum. For secondary-school teachers, it is the reverse: an 'academic' tradition emphasises the importance of theoretical/scientific knowledge in their academic discipline, and educational theory and methodology and teaching practices are devalued and neglected. In addition, secondary teachers are specialists in one subject. The consequence of this is that language teachers often lack deep knowledge of the subject matter, and the language command of the content teachers is insufficient for a whole lesson in the target language. What is worse, when teachers do have a double qualification (e.g., content and foreign language), this fact is not recognised and they must opt for only one of them. As a consequence, innovations like CLIL are often viewed as something exotic that will surely lead to the lowering of standards in the content areas.

Further issues

Evaluation of the academic results of the immersion programmes has been very positive and provides a sound motivation for extending the use of CLIL methodology. Reports from Catalonia (Gabinet d'Estudis del Servei d'Ensenyament del Català 1983; Arnau and Artigal 1997; Boixaderas et al. 1991; Ribes 1993; and Serra 1997, among others) agree with results from the Basque Country (Cenoz and Perales 2001: 101–2, citing Jauréguierry 1993; Lasagabaster 1997), which corroborate those from Canadian immersion programmes (Genesee 1987; Swain and Lapkin 1982). At the same time, they extend these results to the case of native speakers of an indigenous minority language (Cenoz and Perales 2001). These results also reveal that immersion programmes have an additive effect on the overall linguistic competence of the children. This is of critical importance when we look at the panorama of increasing need to learn foreign languages at a time of falling education budgets. Some results even indicate (Sanz 2000) that when students in bilingual (i.e. CLIL) programmes are compared with those in monolingual programmes, they do better on national achievement tests: in their L1, in other academic subjects, *and* in foreign languages.[4]

As regards regional languages, studies indicate that proficiency in Basque increases with more instruction in Basque (Gabiña et al. 1986; Sierra and Olaziregi 1989; Sierra 1994). According to these reports, 2–4 hours per week are not sufficient to produce proficiency in a minority language. On the other hand, there seem to be no significant differences among the three immersion models mentioned in table 9.1 (A, B, and D) as regards proficiency in Spanish, provided Spanish is the language used at home. Apparently there is enough Spanish in the environment to compensate for this lack. Of great interest to the question of whether to extend the use of CLIL across the curriculum is that these programmes seem to favour competence in the first language while developing competence in the second.

In addition to the practical consideration that increased exposure and communicative use of a language help someone to learn it better, these programmes also implicitly connect the student to the culture(s) of the language. Considering the CLIL compendium (see Marsh, Maljers and Hartiala 2001), these sorts of programmes clearly have advantages in the dimensions of *Cultix* (culture), *Entix* (environment), and *Lantix* (language).[5] Just as the use of Catalan as the medium of instruction creates identification with Catalan culture, the use of CLIL in another language fosters a sense of understanding of that culture and of 'European Citizenship'.

So far, it remains to be seen what the effects of the current educational reform are going to be on the actual foreign language proficiency of our students. The official recommendation contained in the law indicates a CLIL approach, although this has not necessarily always been followed. The earlier introduction of the foreign language has not meant an increase in the number of hours, only that approximately the same number of hours are spread over a longer time-scale, which has decreased the intensity of instruction. The conclusions of previous and continued research show that in order to benefit from the early introduction of a foreign language, considerable and adequate exposure is required (Muñoz 1999; Pérez-Vidal et al. 2000; Singleton 1995). This exposure could be considerably increased by using a foreign language as the medium of instruction for content subjects. As time is precious in school curricula, particularly in bilingual communities, with two languages to teach already, we are interested in finding the most efficient type of programme for language tuition and the introduction of the idea of European citizenship at the same time.

Methodologies and curricula

CLIL for mixed ability secondary classrooms

What follows is a sample of how a CLIL programme was approached in a mixed-ability classroom where the target language was a 'foreign' language for the learners, who hardly had any contact with it once the lessons ended. In 1998, various educational initiatives prompted a state comprehensive secondary school on the outskirts of Barcelona to start a CLIL programme.[6] They offered an optional quarterly History course in English as a foreign language for 15–16-year-olds entitled 'A history of the 20th Century', which is now part of the Orator programme of the Departament d'Ensenyament de la Generalitat de Catalonia. This is how it is organised (see Cuscó, Escobar, and Roquet 2000):

- *Target students*: A group of students in the last year of compulsory education (age 15–16). Previously, these students had seven years of English instruction (approximately 630 hours).

- *Course type*: Three 60-minute lessons per week for eleven weeks.

- *Student selection criteria*: No selection. Students choose their own courses according to what is offered by the school. There is a wide range of interests and abilities.

- *Course content*:
  1. Reading tasks: Students read a range of historical texts and carry out different tasks, such as comprehension exercises, interpretation and analysis;
  2. Speaking tasks: Reading work is followed by group discussion, where ideas and information are exchanged. Conclusions are reached. Different tasks are designed to shape the discussion, for example, classifying activities, group work. Role-play, poster design, etc. There are also plenary discussions;
  3. Project work: Students also form *expert* teams to carry out a research project on a particular period of the twentieth century. Data are collected from various sources: books, articles, software, the Internet. A written report is produced, and an oral presentation given. The whole of the twentieth century is covered.

A team of teachers planned, implemented, evaluated, and redesigned the course as part of an action-research project. Their discussions led to the identification of a set of eight guiding principles, which constitute the key components for a successful implementation of CLIL aimed at mixed-ability students with a moderate command of the language. These guiding principles are briefly presented below and illustrated with examples taken from the lessons. In addition, a selection of the most successful teaching and learning strategies for each principle is given.

1 Enhancing student Involvement

CLIL courses attract students who may feel slightly discouraged by previous foreign language learning experiences, or who simply lack enthusiasm for the target language, although they may have some interest in the subject. However, the extra effort required of students in order to process new content and a foreign language at the same time can only be expected if they are really eager to learn what is being taught. For this reason, handing over part of the responsibility for the success of the course to the students proved to be a very valuable strategy. Also, the way the topics were approached was shown to be essential for the success of the CLIL unit.

- The topics and tasks for the activities finally used in the classroom were agreed on between the teacher and the students from a list of different possibilities.
- Reading texts were used as a starting point for discussion, going from particular cases to more general topics such as racism, women's rights and war and peace. Some examples: Mrs Rose Parker's incident on an Alabama bus (the fight for equal rights throughout the twentieth century); the story of a suffragette (women's rights); photos of the effects of the Second World War on civilians (Second World War); the bombing of Guernica (Spanish Civil War) or Gandhi's disobedience campaign (the end of colonial empires).
- Project work: this was the basis for the research project and presentations referred to in table 9.2.
- Role-reversal: during the presentations students took over the role of the teacher and became a source of input for their classmates. They also eagerly took on tasks such as controlling discipline or setting homework without having been asked to do so.
- Teams were asked to write a set of questions to guide and test their classmates' understanding of the most important facts throughout the presentation. The list of questions produced by all groups was used by the teacher to generate items for the final test.

2 Facilitating comprehension

In order to facilitate comprehension, it is necessary to select materials and design reading and listening tasks with care. It was observed that while general reference books were difficult for the students to understand, texts written for older native-speaker children and adolescents were a source of valuable material. Once the documents had been chosen, comprehension was encouraged through varied comprehension tasks, similar to the ones usually employed in the foreign language classroom.

Comprehension of the teacher's explanations is also essential. Although they are not the only source of input, explanations play an important role in the CLIL classroom. Students make a greater effort to understand subject-matter concepts in a foreign language than in an ordinary classroom context. Consequently teacher explanations need to be kept brief. The recommendations for the teacher specify that plenty of linguistic, paralinguistic and non-linguistic strategies are necessary to aid understanding.

- Different types of reading tasks were used in line with the cognitive skills outlined in chapter 3: (1) pre-reading tasks, such as true/false or multiple-choice quizzes, predicting the content of the text from key-words or from pictures; (2) during-tasks to be completed while reading, such as jigsaw-reading and categorising activities; and (3) post-reading tasks, such as answering comprehension questions or vocabulary work.

- Where students were already familiar with a particular topic (e.g., the Spanish Civil War), a worthwhile strategy was to ask them to prepare questions in groups about a particular aspect of it and build up the explanation and understanding around those questions.

3 Promoting student–student interaction and co-operative work

The benefits of pair and small group work have been highlighted by research from very different sources (Long and Porter 1985; Varonis and Gass 1983; Pica 1987; Donato 1994; Griggs 1997; Nussbaum 1999). As discussed in chapter 3, applied linguistic studies have shown the capacity of learners to negotiate meaning in face-to-face interaction and how this 'negotiated meaning' leads to higher degrees of comprehensibility of the input. Other studies of student–student interaction show how this entails higher levels of student involvement and a wider use of exploratory language. Studies carried out under Vygotskian perspectives, again discussed in chapter 3, show how more proficient peers can help less proficient ones to do things that they still cannot do on their own. With the use of pair and small-group work, students become the input providers for their own classmates. Finally, if pair and small-group work is to be successful, students need training in the use of production and reception strategies.

SAMPLE TEACHING STRATEGIES

- Group work was extensively used.
- Well-known language practice activities such as role-play or for/against discussions were a great help when applied to the understanding of some historical facts.
- Students received training in the use of reception and production learning strategies as referred to in chapter 3, such as marking lack of understanding, asking for clarification, repeating, stressing the problematic word or paraphrasing.

4 Systematic work on the academic skills and strategies characteristic of the subject matter

Skills such as the interpretation of visual aids (maps, diagrams, charts, photos), the use of flow-charts and time lines to organise information, the formation of ideas of simultaneity and change, the establishment of cause and effect relationships, and other skills cannot be taken for granted. They need to be modelled and practised in the classroom if they are to be efficiently applied by the students to their own piece of research.

SAMPLE TEACHING STRATEGIES

- Students learnt to assign different events to social, political, economic, or cultural categories. They were encouraged to establish links among the different categories.
- The teacher and the class jointly constructed a time line of the period from the end of the First World War to the end of the Second World War. Later, the students were asked to produce a time line for the period studied in their own research project.
- Students sorted captions describing the characteristics of the socialist and the capitalist models of economy and matched them with the corresponding part of an explanatory diagram.

5 Systematic work on communication skills for academic purposes

Even in the L1 classroom, communication skills for academic purposes cannot be taken for granted (see Benejam and Quinquer 2000). Raising awareness of them and providing hints for successful communication are absolutely essential in the CLIL classroom. Students cannot possibly succeed without careful guidance on the part of the teacher. In oral presentations, basic skills such as selecting content, clear delivery, fluency and the ability to hold the attention of the audience all need to be developed. The CLIL classroom is a privileged place in which students can extend the skills and abilities they normally exercise in the conventional language classroom in different contexts.

SAMPLE TEACHING STRATEGIES

- Students were guided in the selection and organisation of content to be included in the research project. Support was provided with the language.
- A session was devoted to a discussion of different strategies for keeping the listeners' attention in formal presentations.
- Students were required to use visual aids (posters, leaflets, and transparencies) to highlight the main points of their presentations.

6 Access to information and communication technology (ICT)

ICT has become indispensable in all fields of human activity. Similarly, in education, it is an essential element for learning and teaching. The Internet is a privileged learning tool, and accessing it is a goal in itself. Possessing the necessary Internet skills allows students to access a whole world of information and communication possibilities both inside and outside school. The CLIL classroom cannot ignore these facts and must incorporate the use of different tools (word processors, CD-ROMs, the Internet) for different purposes (e.g., searching for information, drafting, and editing).

SAMPLE TEACHING STRATEGIES

- As computers were not available in the regular classroom, from the third week on students spent at least one session per week in the computer room finding information on the web or on the available CD-ROMs and drafting and editing their texts on a word processor.

7 *Accepting code-switching as a normal feature of the CLIL classroom*

A CLIL classroom is, by its very nature, a multilingual environment, where students usually share at least one common language. It is natural, then, for students to use all the linguistic resources at hand, including their knowledge of the mother tongue when they are confronted with highly demanding tasks. The use of an L1 when they were trying to solve problems posed by the foreign language (e.g., when decoding a text about decolonisation, or collaborating on writing a list of the major inventions of a decade) created favourable conditions for metalinguistic reflection and language acquisition (Guasch 1999). The use of the target language was, nevertheless, encouraged in the classroom by attaching great value to the students' attempts to use it to communicate and by tape-recording students' oral productions. This technique has shown itself to encourage target language use among students (see Escobar 2000).

SAMPLE TEACHING STRATEGIES

- Communication and understanding were given priority over target language use at all costs.
- Students tape-recorded some of the oral tasks. Once the recording was finished, they listened to themselves and discussed ways to improve their productions. This included the identification of frequent words and expressions uttered in L1, which were later translated into L2 with the help of the teacher.

8 *Joint assessment of content and communication skills*

Although it may seem redundant to argue that assessment of CLIL programmes should focus on content as well as on language, this needs to be emphasised. This problematic issue can best be addressed if evaluation is approached in a global way, where the same task yields relevant information about both types of competence. However, when designing the assessment tasks, it is important to be aware of the learners' linguistic limitations so that their performance is not negatively affected. Knowledge of simple facts can be tested with traditional multiple-choice questions written with the help of the students. Skills and abilities are better assessed throughout the process of elaboration of their research project and in the final presentation of the report.

SAMPLE TEACHING STRATEGIES

- Process features were assessed by means of observation of students' work in the classroom.
- Students were assessed on both content and delivery in the oral presentation of their project report. Assessment criteria were discussed with the students so that they were aware of the criteria for excellence that would be applied.
- A multiple-choice test was administered at the end of the term to test recognition of important information. Many of the items on this test came from the list of questions compiled by the students.

While some of the principles identified above derive from well-established language-teaching practice and others bear a close relationship with the teaching of History, the majority of them combine language and content in such a way that each area is used to support the other. Similarly, in CLIL, content and language are combined, with priority given to the content syllabus. The question arises as to whether the guidelines outlined above, with their emphasis on attention to the development of linguistic competence in mainstream compulsory education, should be confined to the foreign language curriculum or rather embrace first languages as well, in a global approach towards additive multilingualism. CLIL may well indeed be a good reason to rethink our approach to any kind of teaching situation.

Conclusion

In conclusion, it should be possible to help learners and teachers adapt what we have learnt from second-language immersion programmes to Modern Languages Across the Curriculum or Content and Language Integrated Learning in foreign languages. It should be perfectly possible to apply it to the Spanish context. If such views were accepted, then all efforts could be directed towards the implementation of these programmes. The approach has certainly been used successfully in other countries (see Van de Craen and Pérez-Vidal 2001; Fruhauf, Coyle, and Christ 1996), where pupils demonstrate improved linguistic skills.

In Spain, measures need to be taken in order to enhance CLIL programmes so as not to lose pace with national and international trends and developments. These measures need to include linguistic training for content teachers, and teachers should be officially recognised and rewarded with a double qualification in content and language. Co-operation between language and content teachers also needs to be fostered. Finally, co-ordination between the different levels of compulsory education needs to be promoted to ensure the desired continuity of programmes. In this way, we shall be guaranteeing our students proficiency in several languages, which is a requisite for full integration in modern Europe.

Notes

1   For detailed information on the sociolinguistic situation in bilingual communities, as well as the background to the bilingual programmes and a complete analysis of linguistic minorities and migrated speech communities in Spain see Turell 1994, and 2001a.
2   Although this report depends mainly on data from speakers of Spanish or the languages of Spain's Autonomous communities, there is a growing segment of the population who are immigrants from outside Europe and whose first language is a non-European community language. Clearly these students are learning in a CLIL methodology.
3   The following figures correspond to schools and students in current programmes.
4   This confirms Genesee's (1987) results, Cummins' (1997) Interdependence Hypothesis, and Baetens Beardsmore's (1997) proposals.
5   *Cultix* refers to the Culture Dimension of CLIL, which aims to build intercultural knowledge and understanding, develop intercultural communication skills, and help students to learn about specific neighbouring countries/regions and/or minority groups. *Entix* refers to the Environmental Dimension, which prepares students for internationalisation, specifically EU integration, helps them access International Certification, and enhances the school profile. *Lantix* refers to the language Dimension, which aims to improve overall target language competence, develop oral communication skills, deepen awareness of both mother tongue and target language, and develop plurilingual interests and attitudes.
6   The Lluis de Requesens School is located in Molins de Rei (Barcelona).

References

Arnau, J. and Artigal, J. M. (eds) (1997) *Els programes d'immersió: una Perspectiva Europea. Immersion Programmes: A European Perspective*, Barcelona: Universitat de Barcelona.

Artamendi, J. A. (1994) 'Rendimiento de bilingües en Test de Aptitudes según lengua/s de presentación', in I. Idiazabal and A. Kaifer (eds) *Eficacia educativa y enseñanza bilingüe en el País Vasco*, Gasteiz: IVAP.

Artigal, J. M. (1993) 'Catalan and Basque immersion programmes', in H. Baetens Beardsmore (ed.) *European Models of Bilingual Education*, Clevedon: Multilingual Matters.

Baetens Beardsmore, H. (1993) *European Models of Bilingual Education*, Clevedon: Multilingual Matters.

—— (1997) 'Bilingualism across Europe', ELC Launching Conference, unpublished paper.

Benejam, P. and Quinquer, D. (2000) 'La construcción del conocimiento social y las habilidades cognitivolingüísticas', in J. Jorba, I. Gómez, and A. Prat (eds) *Hablar y escribir para aprender*, Barcelona: Síntesis.

Boixaderas, R., Canal, I., and Fernández, E. (1991) 'Avaluació dels nivells de llengua catalana, castellana i matemàtiques en alumnes que han seguit el programa d'immersió lingüística i en alumnes que no l'han seguit', Unpublished mimeograph, SEDEC.

Cenoz, J. and Pesales, J. (2001) 'The Basque-speaking communities', in M. T. Turell (ed.) *Multilingualism in Spain*, Clevedon: Multilingual Matters.

Craen, P. Van de and Pérez-Vidal, C. (2001) *The Multilingual Challenge/Le Défi multilingue*, Barcelona: Printulibro.

Cummins, J. (1997) 'Theory in multilingual education: the status of the threshold and interdependence hypothesis', Paper given at the Seminar on Multilingual Europeans and Minority Languages, University of San Sebastian, EEC Summer Course.

Cuscó, I., Escobar, C., and Roquet, M. (2000) 'A history of the 20th century: un crèdit AICLE per 3r d'ESO', unpublished.

Donato, R. (1994) 'Collective scaffolding in second language learning', in J. Lantolf and G. Appel (eds) *Vygotskian Approaches to Second Language Research*, Norwood: Ablex.

Escobar, C. (2000) *El portafolio oral como instrumento de evaluación formativa en el aula de lengua extranjera*, Doctoral dissertation, Bellaterra: Publicacions de la Universitat Autònoma de Barcelona.

Fruhauf, G., Coyle, D., and Christ, I. (eds) (1996) *Teaching Content in a Foreign Language: Practice and Perspectives in European Bilingual Education*, Alkmaar: European Platform for Dutch Education.

Gabiña, J. J., Gorostidi, R., Iruretagoiena, R., Olaziregi, I., and Sierra, J. (1986) *EIFE 1 Euskararen irakaskuntza: aktoreen eragina*, Gasteiz: Hezjuntza, Unibersitate eta Ikerketa Saila.

Gabinet d'Estudis del Servei d'Ensenyament del Català (1983) *Quatre anys de català a l'escola*, Barcelona: Departament d'Ensenyament Generalitat de Catalunya.

Genesee, F. (1987) *Learning Through Two Languages: Studies of Immersion and Bilingual Education*, Cambridge, MA: Newbury House.

Griggs, P. (1997) 'Metalinguistic work and the development of language use in communicative pairwork activities involving second language learners', in L. Díaz and C. Pérez-Vidal (eds) *Views on the Acquisition and Use of a Second Language: Eurosla Proceedings*, Barcelona: Universitat Pompeu Fabra.

Guasch, O. (1999) 'De cómo hablando para escribir se aprende lengua', *Textos de Didáctica de la Lengua y la Literatura* 20, 50–60.

Jaúreguiberry, F. (1993) *Le Basque à l' école maternelle et élémentaire*, Pau: Université de Pau et des Pays de l' Adour.

Lasagabaster, D. (1997) 'Creatividad y conciencia metalingüística: incidencia en el aprendizaje del inglés como L3', unpublished Ph.D. thesis, University of the Basque Country/Euskal Herriko Unibertsitatea.

Long, M. H. and Porter, P. A. (1985) 'Group work, interlanguage talk and second language acquisition', *TESOL Quarterly* 19, 207–28.

Marsh, D., Maljers, A., and Hartiala, A.-K. (2001) *Profiling European CLIL Classrooms*, Jyväskylä and The Hague: University of Jyväskylä and European Platform for Dutch Education.

Muñoz, C. (1999) 'The effects of age on instructed foreign language acquisition', in S. Fernández, R. Valdeón, D. Garcia, A. Orjanguren, M. Urdiales and A. Antón (eds) *Essays in English Language Teaching. A Review of the Communicative Approach*, Oviedo: Servicio de Publicaciones, Universidad de Oviedo.

Navés, T. and Muñoz, C. (1999) 'Implementation of CLIL in Spain', in D. Marsh and G. Langé (eds) *Implementing Content and Language Integrated Learning: A Research driven TIE-CLIL Foundation Course Reader*, Jyväskylä: Universtiy of Jyväskylä.

Nussbaum, L. (1999) 'Emergence de la conscience linguistique en travail de groupe entre aprenants de la langue étrangère', *Langages* 134, 35–50.

Pérez-Vidal, C. (1999) 'Teacher education: the path towards CLIL', in D. Marsh and B. Marsland (eds) *CLIL Initiatives for the Millennium*, Jyväskylä: University of Jyväskylä.

Pérez–Vidal, C., Torras, M. R., Celaya, M. L. (2000) 'Age and EFL written performance by Catalan/Spanish bilinguals', *Spanish Applied Linguistics. A Forum for Theory and Research* 4(2), 267–90.

Pica, T. (1987) 'Second language acquisition, social interaction and the classroom', *Applied Linguistics* 8, 3–21.

Pradilla, M. A. (2001) 'The Catalan-speaking community', in M. T. Turell (ed.) *Multilingualism in Spain*, Clevedon: Multilingual Matters.

Ribes, D. (1993) '*Immersió al català*', unpublished Ph.D. thesis, University of Barcelona.

Sanz, C. (2000) 'Bilingualism and foreign language acquisition', *Applied Psycholinguistics* 21, 1, 23–44.

Serra, J. M. (1997) *Quaderns per a l'anàlisi, 9: Immersió Lingüística, rendiment acadèmic i clase social*, Barcelona: Horsori. Web page: http://www.redestb.es/personal/josus.

Sierra, J. (1994) 'Modelos de enseñanza bilingüe: sus resultados y su futuro', in M. Siguan (ed.) *Las lenguas en la escuela*, Gasteiz: Hezkuntza: Unibertsitate eta Ikerketa Saila.

Sierra, J. and Olaziregi, I. (1989) *EIFE-2 Euskararen Irakaskuntza: Faktoreen Eragina*, Gasteiz: Hezkuntza, Unibertsitate eta Ikerketa Saila.

Singleton, D. (1995) 'A critical look at the critical period', in D. Singleton and Z. Lengyel (eds) *The Age Factor in Second Language Acquisition*, Clevedon: Multilingual Matters.

Swain, M. and Lapkin, S. (1982) *Evaluating Bilingual Education: A Canadian Case Study*, Clevedon: Multilingual Matters.

Turell, M. T. (1994) 'Beyond Babel: across and within', in F. Sierrra Martínez, M. Pujol Berché and H. Den Boer (eds) *Las lenguas en la Europa Comunitaria, Diálogos Hispánicos 15*, Amsterdam: Ed. Rodopi, 23–40.

—— (2001a) 'Spain's multilingual make-up: beyond, within and across Babel', in M. T. Turell (ed.) *Multilingualism in Spain*, Clevedon: Multilingual Matters.

Varonis, E. M. and Gass, S. (1993) 'Non-native/native conversations: a model for negotiation of meaning', *Applied Linguistics* 6, 71–90.

Vila, I. (1995) *El Catala i el Castella en el sistema educatiu de Catalunya*, Barcelona: Horsori.

Vila, X. (1996) 'When classes are over: language choice and language contact in bilingual education in catalonia', unpublished Ph.d. thesis, Université Libre de Bruxelles.

Conclusions

Michael Grenfell

In the introduction to this part of the book, I wrote of the personal response that was represented in these practical case examples. The various contributors have chosen distinct formats to describe Modern Languages Across the Curriculum. However, such differences in accent are more than simple personal preference. Rather, they reflect cultural differences of theoretical understanding and practical implementation in modern languages learning and teaching. There are individual ways in which the methodological trends discussed in chapter 2 and the theoretical reasons explored in chapter 3 have impacted on the policy and practice of various nation states. Interpretation, adaptation and application will always be shaped by cultural factors, as well as perceived priorities, opportunities and threats. There are also wishes and needs: what would happen in an ideal world and what must happen in order to comply with official policies. Questions of who decides practice and how to support developments are also raised. However, despite differences in cultural horizons, the various case examples demonstrate a remarkable uniformity in terms of issues and concerns. I want to address these briefly by returning to the dimensions listed in the introduction to this part.

Firstly, it is clear that all countries have, to a greater or lesser extent, developed language teaching practice in line with developments in linguistic theory and methodology. The notion of competence as a psychological condition and social practice is clearly accepted by different countries, which have moved to treat languages as a pragmatic skill as well as an object of academic study. In Germany, we see the move from grammar–translation to the Direct Method, to the Audio-visual and Audio-lingual Methods, and finally Communicative Language Teaching. We also see how this move has always been incomplete, with vestiges of 'old' practice remaining present in the 'new' practical approach. There are differences in timeline, but countries seem to pass through these stages in their progress to a modern form of language teaching and learning. Oral skills are stressed in this modern approach; although interesting questions are raised about the role of reading and writing in developing speaking and listening. Moreover, there is the issue of target language and its mix with native language. Traditionally, Communicative Language Teaching has stressed the maximisation of target language. However, we have seen different percentages achieved in various classrooms in our case examples. In these cases, it is important to ask where the native and target language is used and for what pedagogic purpose. We have also seen an example of a modular approach to MLAC/CLIL, where history is taught in the language of the topic country.

Various languages are the subject of Modern Languages Across the Curriculum or Content and Languages Integrated Learning. In theory, any language can be taught through any subject. There is then the potential for plurilingualism, and we have seen mentioned such languages as Serbo-Croatian, Turkish, Russian, Greek and Japanese as well as the more common languages French, German, Spanish, Italian and English. Such plurilingualism implies a diversity of practice and a multitude of levels of competence. These case examples raise the concerns of assessment: of what, how and when? In other words, what does it mean to be competent in situations where content and language are integrated in this way? Clearly, there is a need to be working to a common framework, a point I shall return to in the conclusion to this book.

We have indeed seen a wide range of curricular subjects taught through the second language. Why is it that one country sees Mathematics as an ideal choice for this approach to content and language and another decides against it? One reason is expectations and the question: will content knowledge suffer if it is delivered in a second language? Both the French and German case examples show how this approach developed content in a different way, and provides different terminology and a distinct perspective on the subject covered. However, we can see that there is a preference for 'soft' social sciences subjects – History, Geography, etc. – rather than the 'hard' sciences. In one respect, it is understandable since the cultural dimensions of language make it possible to connect linguistic and cultural levels. However, the conceptual ideas behind the social sciences can be more sophisticated and the physical sciences provide concepts which are more 'clear-cut' and thus less ambiguous. This clarity could be highly advantageous when developing thinking skills in a second language. It should also not be forgotten that technical language and scientific knowledge are often important professionally in a world of international vocationalism. There are then academic and professional reasons, as well as pedagogic principles, for selecting content areas with care.

Intercultural and *intra*-cultural knowledge are synonymous with the plurilingual approach to language teaching outlined in these case examples. There are distinct levels: individual, regional, national and international. Countries recognise the need for intercultural understanding and communication within the European Union and see these as desirable for political, social and economic reasons. However, the cases of regional distinctiveness are everywhere apparent. In the cases of Spain and France, it is very clear that a prime motive for MLAC is the wish to integrate regional languages or dialects with the national language. Here and elsewhere, there is also the local proximity of another country which predisposes individuals to integrate the study of content with the language of that state in order to develop the necessary know-how, both linguistically and culturally. The question of regional identity and expression is possibly more pressing than the quest for European citizenship. This issue raises concerns about autonomy and integration. Finally, there is the presence of minority groupings within nation states and their linguistic and cultural integration. I shall return to these issues in the conclusion to this book. For the moment, it is clear that the cultural dimension of MLAC is complex and multifaceted. It is also a dimension which is highly sensitive to perspective and motivation.

These are environmental matters and raise questions of legitimation and recognition. We have to ask how it is that internationalism and integration are presented – in whose terms, and on behalf of whose interests? Are the terms of definition open to all? Is access available to all? In purely linguistic terms, such recognition implies international certification as an available option. What does exist – Institute of Linguists, International Baccalaureate, Alliance Française, Goethe-Institut – is quite old now and comes from particular institutions rather than international accord on academic certification. Yet, such certification also raises the question of individual profiles of scholastic institutions. The German case example raised the question whether MLAC was appropriate for primary schools and answered that it probably was. This issue, however, returns us to the questions of content, competence and the objectives of this approach to language teaching. In other words, what should a school at each individual phase range be offering in terms of language teaching, and hence MLAC/CLIL? And, by implication, how should this be recognised and certificated in a way which can be understood and accepted at an international level?

A major rationale for adopting Modern Languages Across the Curriculum is what it implies in terms of learning, and consequent pedagogic practice. The case examples allude to these learning dimensions for enhanced language learning. The Italian case example suggests, as chapter 3 did, that language structures thought. Therefore, a content-rich environment provides opportunities for deeper thinking skills common to language and subject discipline. The German case example describes how teaching is organised in terms of pre-, during and post-task activities as a way of matching the stage of learning with the required cognitive skills. Learning techniques or strategies are also alluded to in the German example, as well as those from Italy and Spain. New opportunities emerge for classroom organisation, including autonomy. Some teachers are clearly suspicious of relinquishing control over learning and teaching. Yet, group work is used more extensively according to the German and Italian examples, offering the possibility for more learner-initiated learning similar to the 'good language learner' practices described in chapter 3. What is clear is the diversity of practice across the examples. The Italian case also raises the motivation issues: that language and content imply affective responses, which impact on the learning process and outcome.

These case examples need to be read as synchronic descriptions of diachronic processes in that they can only ever give a snap-shot of change. It is where we are at the start of the new millennium. As such, the examples can be viewed individually or as a whole: of separate countries in a state of transition, and of an international movement in language teaching and learning. Our dimensions of learning and teaching can be understood in terms of culture, theory, practice, economics, policy, politics – as separate aspects – or all of these at one and the same time. They overlap and are distinct. They appear from the past and what was accrued there, but also project to the future. We can know something about the past; the future we can only predict. To conclude this conclusion, I would simply again raise the fact that there are different versions of MLAC, and for identifiable and understandable reasons. No one case is necessarily better than another since they are all highly contextually dependent. Nevertheless, they do highlight factors against which we can understand any application of this approach to language learning and teaching. Moreover, it may help us to decide what is most appropriate in our own case. The best way to view these approaches and issues is probably not simply to see them as 'strong' and 'weak' versions but as multifaceted, including a range of adaptations over a range of principles or theory and practice. To reiterate a point made earlier, such strands are best understood as continua rather than clear-cut alternatives. In part 3, we illustrate these possibilities with some practical materials in order to see how Modern Languages Across the Curriculum might look in practice.

Part 3

Modern Languages Across the Curriculum

In practice

10 Practical materials

*Michael Grenfell, Cheryl Hardy, Kim Brown,
Shirley Dobson and Rosanna Raimato*

Introduction

This chapter is an illustration of what practical materials may look like where Modern Languages Across the Curriculum is adopted in a school or college. We have seen in previous chapters how MLAC can be understood as a natural extension of second language learning and teaching and a consequence of the progress in methodology over the last century or so. We have also seen how such an approach can be justified from several different theoretical standpoints. Such theoretical bases include the sociological and cultural as well as the psychological and linguistic. Many of these features are illustrated within the case examples, which show how these trends have been actualised in various European countries. Context is all. We have seen European languages taught in first language national situations; cases where regional languages are taught in L1 contexts or where L1 is taught in regional contexts. Finally, there are non-European languages taught as second languages. Governing principles of practice, however, remain the same, and are always available for adaptation to individual situations.

Within this diversity of languages and language contexts, we concluded part 2 by highlighting the range of subjects that can be the medium for MLAC. Subject content itself can be seen as a continuum. On the one hand, the curriculum is broadened to offer a wider range of topics than might normally be available. On the other hand, there is the full delivery of a curriculum area such as Mathematics or Physics in a second language. Clearly, the latter case is true bilingualism and, to a certain extent, at this stage the language medium becomes almost incidental in the way it operates. Here, the curriculum content proceeds in L2 in much the same way as it would in L1. Obviously, this case entails advanced language and content skills for both teacher and student, and, therefore, tends to involve the later stages of education. Here, an MLAC Science or History lesson is much the same as any other Science or History lesson. As a consequence, in this part of the book, we have focused on those aspects of MLAC which serve to broaden and enrich the existing curriculum.

Examples follow of how different practitioners have adopted cross-curricular topics and themes in their own settings. We consider how MLAC can be used to develop more individual responses from students through work which encourages personal, affective, spiritual or aesthetic involvement in the content. We see how Art might be used as the basis of second language lessons. Finally, we include examples of where MLAC might be developed in a Business Studies setting. All of these examples are illustrated with exercises which pupils undertook as individual language activities and in longer-term project work. Rather than simply offer these practical materials as examples, we include some commentary from those who have worked with them in order to set the context and highlight the purpose behind each practitioner's approach.

Broadening the curriculum

KIM BROWN

I want to suggest a step-by-step approach so that we think of language teaching in increasingly broad terms. Firstly, we need to look at the learning needs and interests of pupils in language classes – what are the special demands that language learning makes on pupils, and how can we respond to these? We can then move beyond the language curriculum to consider activities and learning taking place in other subject areas in the school. The final step is to move to the world outside school for topics and issues that might help pupils to engage more fully with their language learning.

So what do we mean when we talk about cross-curricular teaching in modern language lessons? Firstly, we need to be clear about what it is not. It is not an argument against a strict focus on language. However, there is little point in trying to teach pupils cultural and structural aspects of the language they are learning, such as the distinction between *tu* and *vous* or *du* and *Sie*, if they do not know how to treat each other with care and mutual respect. In the same way, a lesson on language structure is lost if pupils are not interested in the topics which are offered to support their learning of the new language.

One difficulty that has arisen in Britain is that communicative language teaching has tended to be interpreted in a narrow fashion, in terms of transactions largely of a commercial nature, such as shopping and tourism, and has failed to motivate pupils to communicate with each other (see Grenfell 1994; Coyle 2000). Inspections of secondary language lessons have indicated concern about the dominance of teacher talk in lessons and the limited opportunities that pupils have to practise the language they are learning. Lessons are often taught as whole class activities and group work is much less common (see Dobson 1998). As a first step to getting pupils involved in their lessons, I have tried group work strategies based on lessons in humanities, and personal and social education, for example, where pupils are required to work together and to come to group decisions about the issues under discussion. Not only do they need to develop skills of co-operation and consensus building, but they also need to use their language skills in truly communicative ways.

Diamond-ranking activities (see figure 10.1), for example, offer pupils the opportunity to talk to each other as well as to understand differing perspectives on a common problem.

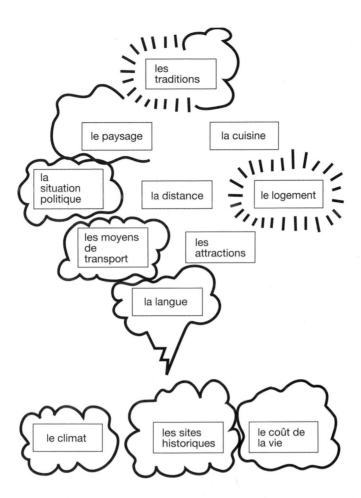

Figure 10.1 Diamond-ranking diagram. From Kim Brown and Margot Brown, *Pathfinder 27: New Contexts for Modern Language Learning* (CILT, 1996), Reproduced with permission from CILT.

In this activity, pupils are given twelve cards listing factors which influence people's decisions about their holiday destinations. As a group they have to agree on three cards to reject and then discuss and agree to a ranking of the other factors in order of importance. Immediately pupils ask for phrases to express suggestions, negotiation, acceptance of another's point of view and disagreement as well as help with explaining the reasons they have for the decisions they make. The nature of the task generates the language learning needs of the pupils. Transcripts of interactions between pupils can help teachers to see the value of this approach as pupils begin to learn from each other and to construct sentences around the cards they are working with.

Matching, sorting and sequencing tasks all offer good opportunities for interactive group work. Diamond-ranking activities work well, as do jigsaw photograph activities. In these activities, a large photograph or magazine picture is cut into several simple pieces. Pupils must then discuss in the target language where to place each piece of the jigsaw in order to reconstruct the picture. The content of the task and the skills required to complete it work together to draw pupils into the process of language learning. Cross-curricular teaching is a first step in helping to prepare pupils for their role as active citizens in society, and this involves teaching and learning in personal and social skills as well as their cognitive development.

The interactions in language classrooms provide important opportunities for teachers to help pupils develop a sense of co-operation and fairness in their treatment of others and a sense of responsibility towards their own learning. In my experience, arguments over the injustice of school uniform, for example, where girls felt they were given more limited choices than boys, led to a language activity on equal opportunities and human rights. This in turn led to reading and writing activities based on French newspaper articles about the controversy over Muslim pupils wearing the veil, the *hijab*, to school (Brown and Brown 1996, 1998). Again, a concern with pupils' personal development paved the way for a range of new resources and challenging content to support language learning.

Pupils give teachers valuable feedback on the topics they teach and on their way of teaching. I have found that new ideas such as using photographs in language lessons or doing activities such as surveys around the school can help to change pupils' negative perceptions of learning languages. I found, for example, that growing sunflowers with a disaffected Year 8 group of pupils changed attitudes and enhanced the learning of pupils in a number of areas such as basic numeracy and literacy, as well as the development of their affective skills in learning to care for their own young plants (Brown 2001).

In another environmental project, older pupils were encouraged to film and photograph their local communities and to look for aspects which limited and enhanced the daily life of target groups of residents, for example, elderly people or parents with pushchairs. Motivation and interest were high throughout this project, and pupils talked of their increased sense of responsibility for their own learning. As one pupil put it, it's 'a much more adult way of learning' (Brown 2001).

The concern with the lack of challenging resources in language lessons has been noted. The focus tends to be on domestic issues, daily routine and school life, for example, with which pupils are already familiar, and less on problem solving or tasks which make pupils *think*. One example from my own teaching was unexpectedly successful in engaging pupils' interest and helped me to think more about this question of challenge. The class of 12-year-olds had been learning to tell the time in French and I had set up a carousel lesson of activities designed to build up their confidence with numbers. The pupils generally worked well, but it soon became apparent that one activity was causing more than the usual levels of excitement. Pupils had been asked to use word cards to make sentences about

Figure 10.2 Pupils' sunflower work.

their daily routine – *Je me couche / à six heures, Je me lève / à cinq heures* – and to place these sentences under one of two headings: *c'est tôt, c'est tard*. The next step was for the group to decide why the people in their sentences had got up or gone to bed early or late. They were encouraged to try to give reasons in French and they had a support sheet of suggestions to guide them. This was where the heightened sense of animation and discussion came in. The pupils quickly understood that it was not simply a case of putting sentences beginning with *Je me lève* in one group and *Je me couche* in the other. They soon realised that the sentences could belong to either group and the decision depended on the inclusion of time phrases such as *du matin, de l'après-midi, du soir*. They realised that the context was central to the decisions they made, so that a young child who was tired might go to bed at five in the afternoon and that would be *early*, but for someone who had been at an all-night party, it would be *late*. Pupils began to ask for the French to express this ambiguity – *ça dépend* – and used it repeatedly to challenge decisions made by other members of their group. They were really having to *think* about what they were doing.

The activity challenged their understanding of the language, but it went further than the simple construction of sentences in French. It challenged their understanding of the concepts of late and early and of the factors that shaped their meaning. A significant aspect of the activity was that it drew directly on the pupils' own experiences. One pupil talked to me about her mum's job and how it affected the household, and pupils talked in groups about working patterns in their families, of brothers on shifts and dads working nights. The sense of engagement that these pupils experienced at both a conceptual level and at a personal level enhanced the relationships within their group, the interactions between pupils and teacher and their language learning.

There are many opportunities in the school year for language teachers to link up with teachers in other subjects in projects or display work. For example, a display put up by English teachers in my school on war poetry encouraged me to introduce the pupils in my language lessons to war poems in French. Rimbaud's *Dormeur du val* and many of Prévert's anti-war poems have worked well with secondary pupils who have begun to see the universality of the experiences they describe and to understand the links between the subject areas which make up their school curriculum. Through the introduction of these poems, pupils learnt a little more about cultural, political and historical aspects of the language they were learning. At the same time, I was reminded of my own language learning experiences and of those areas that had helped to make the subject special for me. In other words, by drawing on aspects of the subject that hold a special significance for me, I was able to enhance the experiences of the pupils in my lessons.

It may be that links with other subject areas are not immediately obvious to the language teacher. For example, a science project and display on the water cycle may not appear to support topic work in languages. And yet, pupils often spot these links. In a lesson on ordering drinks in a cafe, pupils asked about the French custom of drinking bottled mineral water, at that time a relatively unknown habit in the UK. The discussion led to topic work on the reasons why people in both countries chose to drink mineral water, and to a water-tasting competition, all conducted in French, to see if pupils could taste the difference between tap and bottled water. In addition, water was brought from the pump rooms in this spa town to taste. In this example, the work pupils were doing in their Science lessons and the opportunities provided by the town in which they lived enabled us to bring new dimensions to their language learning. Ordering a bottle of mineral water for a GCSE role-play examination becomes much more meaningful if you understand some of the cultural background to this act and if you have tried it yourself.

A final aspect of linking to activities in other curriculum areas is looking for resources that can support language learning. A map is an obvious example. Language teachers often teach pupils about travel and holidays in Europe, for example, but textbooks rarely offer good maps to help pupils visualise the journeys and locate the destinations being talked about. By talking to teachers of Geography or History, language teachers can discover resources they can use to enhance their lessons and different ways of teaching. There are specific techniques that Geography teachers use, for example, when looking at photographs with pupils. They encourage them to ask questions to the people in the photograph or to imagine what they are saying, or pupils might ask each other questions about the location of the photograph and the clues they have which enable them to make an informed guess about this. In other words, a visual prompt can provide the stimulus for structured language work which can work just as well in a foreign language as in the pupils' mother tongue. More and more photo-packs are being produced. Teachers in subject areas such as humanities, personal and social education and religious education may already have these in school. The accompanying booklets offer information and teaching strategies which language teachers can easily adapt for use in their lessons.

For example, one pack teaches primary pupils about life in a Tanzanian village and includes details of a typical school day (Manchester Development Education Project 1992) (see figure 10.3).

The topic is familiar to language teachers, but the context is new. For one activity, I produced a series of cards each describing one aspect of a school day in this village. The cards were distributed around the class, with care being taken not to give longer statements to pupils who were less confident about their language skills. Pupils were then asked to get out of their seats, to read and show each other their cards and to form a line to represent the events of the school day in the order in which they happened. The physical nature of this timeline activity helped pupils to appreciate the length of the day compared with their own and offered new opportunities for language learning. For example, pupils first read aloud the words on their cards. They were then challenged to learn these by heart and to recite the events again, wherever possible without looking at their cards. The following day, the class went through the events again and were delighted to find that they could reconstruct this story, often prompted in their mind's eye by the person who had spoken the words and by the position they had had in the timeline.

Figure 10.3 A school day in a Tanzanian village. Manchester Metropolitan University, Department Education Project, From *Living and Learning in a Tanzanian Village: A Child's Perspective* (1992).

In this example, resources from the humanities department and active learning strategies, not necessarily associated with language learning, brought new dimensions to pupils' language learning. The fact that they were learning about the experiences of young people in a community other than their own and using entirely familiar language to do this makes it possible to envisage other examples like this of cross-curricular teaching. Teachers might look at meals around the world, or family life in different countries. But if the contexts are different and offer language teachers exciting new approaches to their lessons, the issues that are raised are serious ones and need to be treated with care by teachers. In the case above, for example, it would be important to focus on the successes of the school community that is described as well as on the hardships the pupils face. The booklet accompanying the resources makes this clear, but it is up to individual teachers to engage with the issues to ensure that these are not misrepresented in the languages classroom.

Language teachers often teach about tourism in their lessons. The GCSE syllabus in the UK expects pupils to be able to make their way in a French- or German-speaking country; for example, by ordering food and drinks or booking into a hotel. Pupils may also be encouraged to write and talk about the tourist facilities and attractions in their home town or village, often produced as tourist information leaflets and guides. But it is much more unusual for language teachers to address political issues arising from tourism in their lessons. The pack of materials *Development Education through the Teaching of Spanish* (*Development Education Pack* 2001), offers an activity which illustrates the full potential of a cross-curricular approach to tourism in language lessons.

The aim is to raise pupils' awareness of the harmful effects that tourism can have on local communities, through a case study of attempts by an international company to buy National Park land in a small town not far from Mexico City to build a golf course (see figures 10.4 and 10.5). Pupils are given statement cards in Spanish representing the views of members of the different groups involved in the plans and protests: the politicians and the company members, the environmentalists, and the local people. Their task is to read the cards aloud to each other and to decide as a group who is most likely to have voiced the views

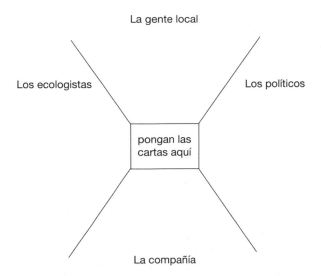

Figure 10.4 A cross-curricular approach to tourism (1). From *Development Education Pack: Development Education through the Teaching of Spanish: Vidas Méxicanas* (The Centre for Global Education, York St John College, 2001).

La compañía

Queremos construir un campo de golf.	Queremos dar trabajo a la gente de aquí.	No queremos dar dinero a los granjeros.
Queremos la paz para poder construir el campo de golf.	Lo queremos construir aquí porque la mano de obra es barata aquí.	Queremos tener beneficios económicos.

✂- -

La gente local

No queremos un campo de golf. Perderemos nuestras tierras.	Queremos parar las obras.	Queremos proteger los espíritus de nuestros antepasados.
Queremos decidir cómo utilizar nuestras tierras.	No al Club de Golf. Viva Zapata. La Lucha sigue.	Necesitamos ayuda con nuestro trabajo en el campo.

✂- -

Los ecologistas

No queremos que construyan un campo de golf en la Reserva Ecológica de Ajusco-Chichinautzin.	Queremos que el estado proteja los recursos naturales tanto como los valores culturales.	Los campos de golf gastan demasiado agua. Queremos que la gente local tenga este agua.
No queremos que usen insecticidas. Son malos para la tierra.	No queremos que suba tanto el valor de la tierra. La gente local no podrian comprarla.	No queremos que esto tenga un efecto malo para la fauna.

✂- -

Los políticos

Queremos atraer nuevos beneficios económicos a nuestras tierras.	No queremos que la gente de aquí se pongan en contra nuestra.	Estamos planeando sumistros de agua para todos. Queremos que el campo de golf se autofinancia
Queremos mejorar el nivel de vida para nosotros. Debemos trabajar todos juntos.	La gente nos ha votado. Queremos lo mejor para todos.	Queremos apoyar el progreso. La superstición y la ignorancia no caben en el futuro.

Figure 10.5 A cross-curricular approach to tourism (2). From *Development Education Pack: Development Education through the Teaching of Spanish: Vidas Méxicanas* (The Centre for Global Education, York St John College, 2001).

being expressed. These cards are then placed on the table in groups to represent the different points of view in this debate. This first step helps pupils to learn new language in the process of understanding it and using it. Further activities ask them to use the statement cards to write about the topic from different positions or to design slogans and protest posters. The activity and the language that it requires are highly structured and effective for supporting language learning in this way. There is also an important page of background information for teachers to ensure that they are aware of the aims of the activity, the different points of view in the controversy and of the added dimension that an activity like this adds to a language lesson about tourism.

This example is drawn from the experiences of Spanish-speaking people in Mexico. But there are many international and global events which take place in communities which do not necessarily speak the language being learnt by our pupils. These also have a lot to offer pupils in terms of engaging their interest and offering new contexts for language learning. Natural events such as earthquakes, volcanic eruptions, floods and drought, as well as political and social events such as war, protests, election campaigns and international sporting events, all provide language teachers with authentic texts and issues of topical interest to enhance language lessons. The rationale is not that these events affect French- or German- or Spanish-speaking people in their own communities but that these are the events which will appear in their newspapers and television reports just as they do in ours. It is this global dimension, and the broad teaching aim to engage pupils with world issues through their language learning activities, which distinguishes cross-curricular teaching from more traditional approaches to language learning.

Moving towards curriculum content

SHIRLEY DOBSON

The possibilities of using other curriculum content areas as a medium for modern languages teaching and learning are endless. The two following examples explore the areas of History and moral and spiritual themes. These latter are not synonymous with traditional Religious Education but refer to dimensions present in any teaching and learning context. The content in the examples uses grammar and vocabulary appropriate for intermediate French and German. In the first case, the theme of 'Citizenship' is explored. This area does include a specific religious source, but this is expanded upon to develop a whole range of related issues to which learners can make a personal response.

Le Bon Voisin

'The Town' is a familiar topic for language learners. The first stage in this unit of work is for the learners to write down in the target language the names of each building on a town plan. Next, they identify and write the names of the groups of people who use each location. The community is then considered alongside the groups within it who service it. A modern-day version of the Good

Samaritan story is given to pupils as a series of pictures to order and to match with narrative phrases. Next, pupils consider human characteristics and qualities by exploring the notion of 'the good neighbour' by reflecting on a vocabulary list (see figures 10.6 and 10.7). They select and then compare themselves with this range of qualities.

This exploration of characteristics then turns to the context of the town. Firstly, they compile a questionnaire to identify the qualities they would look for in a candidate for town mayor. Having decided this, they also draft a campaign speech and design a poster to support the election of this person.

This work highlights a number of language features as well as drawing out a personal response to the pupils' environment in relation to their own wants and needs,

Jugend gegen Hitler

My second example is more centrally connected with historical events. This topic, called 'Jugend gegen Hitler', demonstrates the way in which young German students risked their lives by distributing anti–Hitler leaflets in universities around Germany during the Second World War. The students formed a resistance group called the White Rose. The sequence of activities commences with pictures shown on an overhead projector (figure 10.9) based on the lives of Christoph Probst and Hans Scholl. Various questions are used to reconstruct an outline of their lives so that the pupils are drawn into the characters, particularly through the fact that they were executed at a very early age.
These questions which relate to the sketches can then be used:

1   Wieviele Personen waren in der Familie?
2   Wieviele Geschwister?
3   Wie heisst der Vater?
4   Wie heisst der ältere Bruder/Sohn?
5   Wie heisst die jüngste Tochter?
6   Wie hatte Sophie Geburtstag?
7   Wann ist sie geboren?
8   Wie alt war sie?
9   Was für Hobbys hatte Sophie?
10   Wo hat sie studiert?
11   Was hat sie studiert?
12   Welche Farbe hat die Rose?
13   Wohin sind die 3 Studenten gefahren?
14   Was haben sie mitgenommen?
15   Warum?
16   Was ist passiert?

The questions then lead to a gap-fill or Cloze activity to recreate the story of the lives of the three key figures (see figure 10.10).

Le bon voisin

Qui est le bon voisin? *A lire*

Un jeune homme demande à Jésus, 'Comment dois-je vivre?'

Jésus répond, 'Tu dois aimer le Seigneur et tes voisins.'

Le jeune homme demande, 'Qui est mon voisin?'

Et Jésus raconte une histoire.

La voici en version moderne.

Fais correspondre les phrases aux images. Fini? Lis l'histoire à haute voix avec un(e) partenaire.

Exemple

1 _C_ 2 ___ 3 ___ 4 ___ 5 ___ 6 ___ 7 ___ 8 ___

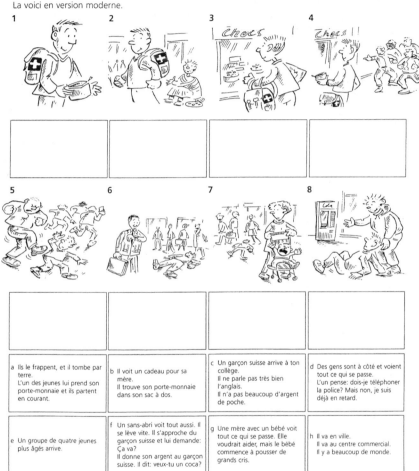

a Ils le frappent, et il tombe par terre.
L'un des jeunes lui prend son porte-monnaie et ils partent en courant.

b Il voit un cadeau pour sa mère.
Il trouve son porte-monnaie dans son sac à dos.

c Un garçon suisse arrive à ton collège.
Il ne parle pas très bien l'anglais.
Il n'a pas beaucoup d'argent de poche.

d Des gens sont à côté et voient tout ce qui se passe.
L'un pense: dois-je téléphoner la police? Mais non, je suis déjà en retard.

e Un groupe de quatre jeunes plus âgés arrive.

f Un sans-abri voit tout aussi. Il se lève vite. Il s'approche du garçon suisse et lui demande: Ça va?
Il donne son argent au garçon suisse. Il dit: veux-tu un coca?

g Une mère avec un bébé voit tout ce qui se passe. Elle voudrait aider, mais le bébé commence à pousser de grands cris.

h Il va en ville.
Il va au centre commercial.
Il y a beaucoup de monde.

Figure 10.6 The theme of citizenship explored in French (1). Extract from *Charis Français* units A1–A4, © The Stapleford Centre, The Old Lace Mill, Frederick Road, Stapleford, Nottingham NG9 8FN. www.stapleford-centre.org.

Le bon voisin

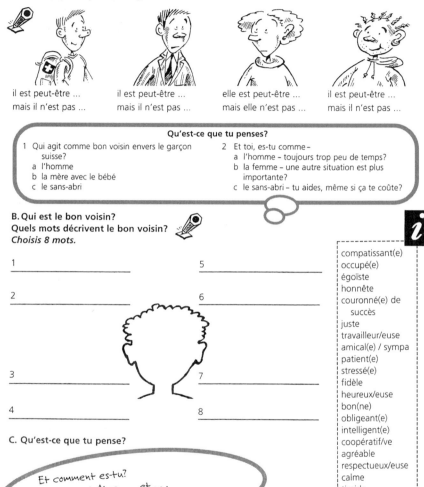

Etre bon voisin
A. Les gens de l'histoire de la feuille de travail 2a, comment sont-ils?
Qu'est-ce que tu penses? *Regarde la liste à droite.*

il est peut-être ...   il est peut-être ...   elle est peut-être ...   il est peut-être ...
mais il n'est pas ...   mais il n'est pas ...   mais elle n'est pas ...   mais il n'est pas ...

Qu'est-ce que tu penses?

1 Qui agit comme bon voisin envers le garçon
   suisse?
   a l'homme
   b la mère avec le bébé
   c le sans-abri

2 Et toi, es-tu comme –
   a l'homme – toujours trop peu de temps?
   b la femme – une autre situation est plus
      importante?
   c le sans-abri – tu aides, même si ça te coûte?

B. Qui est le bon voisin?
Quels mots décrivent le bon voisin?
Choisis 8 mots.

1 _____   5 _____

2 _____   6 _____

3 _____   7 _____

4 _____   8 _____

compatissant(e)
occupé(e)
égoïste
honnête
couronné(e) de
   succès
juste
travailleur/euse
amical(e) / sympa
patient(e)
stressé(e)
fidèle
heureux/euse
bon(ne)
obligeant(e)
intelligent(e)
coopératif/ve
agréable
respectueux/euse
calme
timide
fier(fière)
froid(e)
impatient(e)

C. Qu'est-ce que tu pense?

Et comment es-tu?
Je suis peut-être ... et ...
mais je ne suis pas ...

Figure 10.7 The theme of citizenship explored in French (2). Extract from *Charis Français*
units A1–A4, © The Stapleford Centre, The Old Lace Mill, Frederick Road,
Stapleford, Nottingham NG9 8FN. www.stapleford-centre.org.

Etre maire pour une journée!

A. Tu voudrais être maire.

> Comme maire, je voudrais être travailleuse et couronnée de succès.

> Comme maire, je voudrais être travailleur et couronné de succès.

Qu'est-ce que tu dis?

Comme maire, je voudrais être _____ et _____ .

Et je pense que, pour être bon maire, il faut être _____ et _____ .

B. *Tu es maire. Fais un poster: 'Mon rêve pour notre ville'.*

Décris la ville comme elle devrait être.
Qu'est-ce qu'il y a d'important dans la ville?

Mon rêve
pour notre
ville

une salle de sports
des poubelles
beaucoup d'autobus
des fleurs
des arbres
des zones piétonnes
des gens sympa
un syndicat d'initiative accueillant
des accès pour les personnes handicapées
du travail pour tout le monde
la sécurité
de bonnes écoles
des cours de récréation
des pistes cyclables
pas de graffiti
pas de drogue
pas de bruit
pas de racisme

Figure 10.8 The theme of citizenship explored in French (3). Extract from *Charis Français* units A1–A4, © The Stapleford Centre, The Old Lace Mill, Frederick Road, Stapleford, Nottingham NG9 8FN. www.stapleford-centre.org.

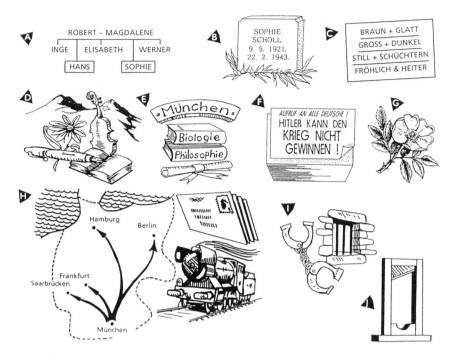

Figure 10.9 A History topic taught in German (1).
Extract from *Charis Deutsch, Einheit 1,* © ACT, 1996. The Stapleford Centre,
The Old Lace Mill, Frederick Road, Stapleford, Nottingham NG9 8FN.
www.stapleford-centre.org.

A listening text is then used to find out more about the White Rose resistance movement. Pupils work in small groups according to their ability on different aspects of the lives and activities of the White Rose group.

The aim is eventually to discover information from cassette and reading that gives an account of the lives of the White Rose students. Nazi propaganda is considered, as well as the anti-Hitler leaflets that the group distributed. This information leads to poster displays of journeys made and acts undertaken by these people at the time of the Second World War to oppose fascism. In this case, specific historical events are links with human values and the theme of choice. Both of these connect with other topics covered elsewhere in the curriculum: History, Citizenship, etc.

These are just two ideas, from a variety of other possibilities, that come from approaching the teaching of Modern Languages with an eye to opportunities for spiritual and moral development. The most important aspect of such an approach is to provide material which appeals to more of our students than a standard textbook. Material like this is more challenging, builds on their interest in other subjects and, by doing so, raises the profile of the foreign language in their eyes.

Zum Verständnis

A *Was bedeuten diese Wörter auf englisch?*
Wähl jeweils das richtige Wort und schreib es auf.

Beispiel   der Krieg = _war_

die Widerstandsgruppe = _____

verteilen = _____

das Flugblatt(¨er) = _____

verhaftet = _____

vervielfältigen = _____

verurteilt = _____

der Verräter/die Verräterin = _____

das Gefängnis = _____

das Schafott = _____

trial	prison	leaflet(s)
war	to distribute	sentenced
traitor	resistance group	executed
scaffold	arrested	to duplicate

hingerichtet = _____

der Prozeß = _____

B *Füll die Lücken mit den richtigen Wörtern aus dem Kästchen aus.*

Beispiel

Die Geschwister ____*Scholl*____ und ihre Freunde haben eine

_____ gegen Hitler gegründet. Die weiße

_____ war das Symbol der Gruppe. Sie haben

die _____ selbst auf der _____

getippt. Dann haben sie die Flugblätter _____

und verteilt. Die *Gestapo* hat die Gruppe monatelang gesucht

und dann endlich entdeckt. Die Mitglieder der Gruppe wurden

_____ und kamen ins _____

in München. Kurz danach gab es einen _____ .

Sie wurden _____ genannt. Sie wurden zum

Tod _____ und an demselben Tag wurden sie

zum _____ gebracht und hingerichtet.

Rose

vervielfältigt

Verräter

Widerstandsgruppe

Scholl

Schreibmaschine

Flugblätter

verurteilt

Gefängnis

Schafott

Prozeß

verhaftet

Figure 10.10 A History topic taught in German (2).
Extract from *Charis Deutsch, Einheit 1*, © ACT, 1996. The Stapleford Centre, The Old Lace Mill, Frederick Road, Stapleford, Nottingham NG9 8FN. www.stapleford-centre.org.

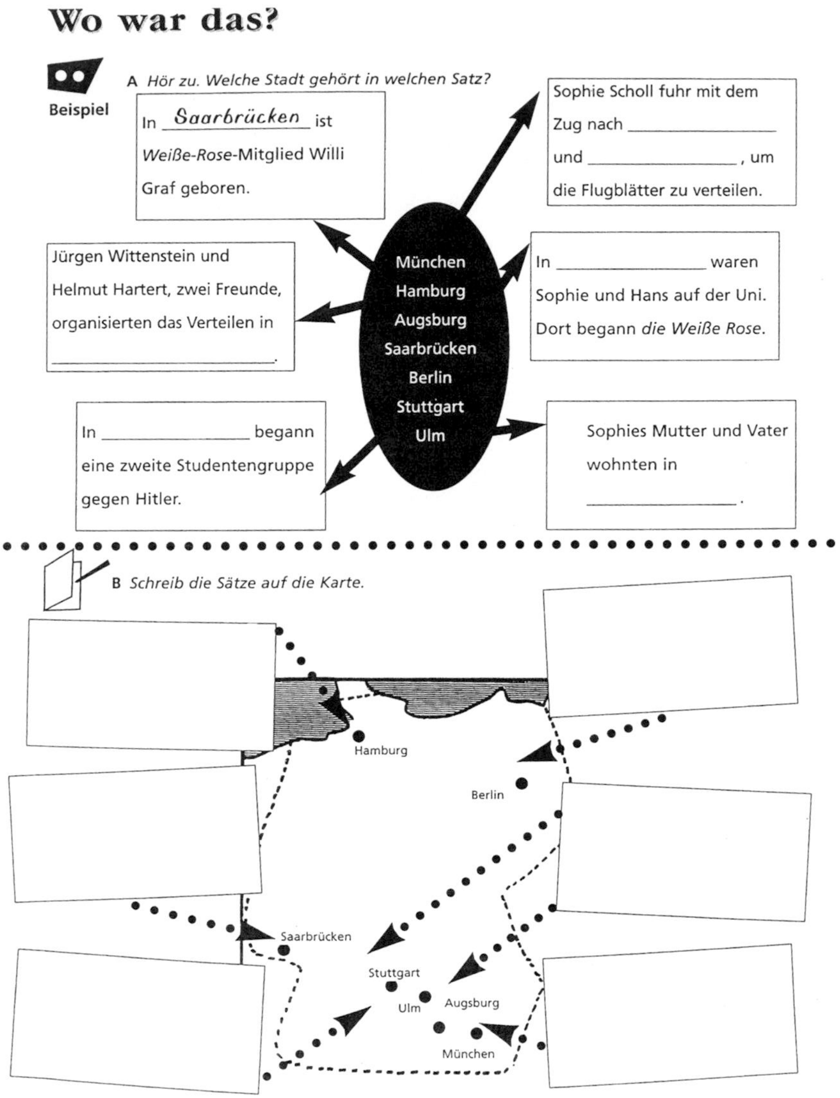

Wo war das?

A *Hör zu. Welche Stadt gehört in welchen Satz?*

Beispiel

In __Saarbrücken__ ist
Weiße-Rose-Mitglied Willi
Graf geboren.

Sophie Scholl fuhr mit dem
Zug nach _____
und _____ , um
die Flugblätter zu verteilen.

Jürgen Wittenstein und
Helmut Hartert, zwei Freunde,
organisierten das Verteilen in
_____ .

In _____ waren
Sophie und Hans auf der Uni.
Dort begann *die Weiße Rose*.

München
Hamburg
Augsburg
Saarbrücken
Berlin
Stuttgart
Ulm

In _____ begann
eine zweite Studentengruppe
gegen Hitler.

Sophies Mutter und Vater
wohnten in

_____ .

B *Schreib die Sätze auf die Karte.*

Hamburg

Berlin

Saarbrücken

Stuttgart

Ulm   Augsburg

München

Figure 10.11 A History topic taught in German (3).
Extract from *Charis Deutsch, Einheit 1,* © ACT, 1996. The Stapleford
Centre, The Old Lace Mill, Frederick Road, Stapleford, Nottingham
NG9 8FN. www.stapleford-centre.org.

It demonstrates that language learning offers a wider view of life than lists, words
and simplistic role-play situations. If students' motivation improves, then they
will be willing to tackle more demanding material where understanding meaning has a higher priority than recognising superficial grammatical structures.

Then, language learning is seen to be of value in considering some of the larger questions about life and what matters.

References

These materials come from Charis Resources, which offer photocopiable teacher books for both French and German across the age range 11–16. These are available from: The Stapleford Centre, The Old Lace Mill, Frederick Road, Stapleford, Nottingham, NG9 8FN. E-mail: admin@stapleford-centre.org.

Aesthetic and vocational topics

ROSANNA RAIMATO

The following materials were developed for teaching pupils aged 14–16 in a British language college. Current policy in Britain is to allow secondary schools to seek specialist subject status, for example, as a sports, technology, or performing arts college. The language college entails more instruction in second languages, a greater choice of languages and their integration 'across the curriculum'. This integration occurs through 'linked' teaching, where a subject is taught by a language teacher for an extra hour per week with the remaining lessons delivered by the specialist subject teacher. Subjects covered are Art, History, Business Studies, Geography and Physical Education.

Planning conferences and regular meetings throughout the year are held to design units of work. Subject specific content, style, key words, concepts and thinking skills are identified and then built into the associated language lessons. Tasks might include:

- describing figures and scenes from Italian Renaissance and twentieth-century German works of art;
- using computers to produce and present brochures about Spain for business travellers and providing advice about choosing appropriate hardware for Spanish business;
- finding out about the effects of tourism in Spain;
- investigating employment trends in Italy by communicating with Italian companies;
- producing publicity materials for marketing projects. The following examples offer a selection of materials used in Art and in Business Studies courses. Some of these are used in courses where pupils start a language from scratch alongside a curriculum subject. The first example shows how pupils 'get to know their language'.

Getting started

Today, you are going to 'get to know' the language you will be learning and how you are able to do so. Your tools are going to be a book of essential expressions and structure, the Internet (you find the sites!), your teacher, a dictionary, your partners and most importantly – your brain . . . (Work on your own at home or in a group at school.)

Task 1 Give yourself 20 minutes to find out how to say the following in your new language:

1	the numbers 1–10	2	the days of the week
3	5 school subjects	4	5 countries, including the UK
5	5 foods	6	5 drinks
7	5 sports	8	5 items of clothing
9	5 rooms in a house	10	5 methods of transport.

Task 2

Now choose one of the categories. You will have 10 minutes to practise how you think the words in that category are spoken in the new language – remember to use the 'tools' listed above. You must be able to say these words 'by heart' – you can share this out within the group or choose one person.

Task 3

You now need to think about what you learnt and how you managed to complete the tasks. Make a list of points to say: how you found the words and their pronunciation; how well you worked with others and why; how you learnt/helped someone to learn the words; what you could do to make it easier next time.

Art in Italian or German

The following is a plan for Art in Italian or German. It covers one year's work and is spread out over three terms.

Art and Italian

Term 1 (Autumn)

Theme: Meals
Language content: Introduction to Italian/German language and culture – emphasis on art and customs, as well as acquisition of basic language skills such as pronunciation and 'survival' vocabulary. The language used for describing art: colours, location, scale. Talking about food: ordering,

expressing likes and dislikes, phrases used at mealtimes. Vocabulary specific to the theme of meals, using Italian/German examples.

Term 2 (Spring)

Theme: Myself
Language content: Describing self and others in detail: physical descriptions, moods, interests, clothing. Communicating with others. Using Italian/German to research, find, understand and describe art specific to this theme by native artists. Presenting findings simply in the relevant language.

Term 3 (Summer)

Theme: Domestic Interiors
Language content: Vocabulary and phrases used to describe house and home: decoration, furnishings, rooms, household items. Welcoming guests, dealing with requests and problems. Exploring Italian and German architecture and art on the theme of domestic interiors.

The following three pupil worksheets show the tasks pupils are given to work through on the 'Meals' theme from Term 1 of Italian and Art.

Art and Italian 1

You are currently preparing a piece of art work depicting a meal. In our lesson today, you are going to use pictures and sketches of your own to start incorporating Italian words and phrases into your art, in order to describe it.

We have already looked at some food vocabulary, and at colours. What we need to do now is build on this so that you can express your own ideas and individualise your descriptions.

Today:

- Use the pieces that you have brought along to the lesson to put together a representation of a meal.
- Make a list of the vocabulary you will need to describe what is in the picture: the names of the foods, the colours, other objects shown.
- Use dictionaries and your teachers to help you complete your list by finding out the Italian words. Are they going to stay the same when you use them, or do you have to think about using plurals or changing the spelling of adjectives such as the colour words?
- Now you can begin either to label the objects and the foods or to try to incorporate the words into your picture.

For the next lesson:
We would like you to find out the names of Italian artists – and also to think about when they produced their work. The easiest periods to find out about are the Renaissance and this century. Can you find out the names of any of the styles they used or bring in prints or photographs of their work?

Having used dictionaries to find Italian vocabulary to describe the objects in their pictures, pupils go on to explore ways of describing the relative positions of the food objects.

Art and Italian 2

Prepositions
The prepositions we need to use for this task tell us about the position of different objects: accanto a – next to
vicino a – near
davanti a – in front of
dietro a – behind
di fronte a – opposite

examples: C è davanti a D Gianni è vicino a Sandra

Where we use names, there is no change in how we spell the prepositions – they stay the same as in the list above. However, where we use any other nouns in Italian, we must use the word for 'the' (the article). You will remember that this changes depending on whether on a word is masculine, feminine, or begins with a vowel. This is how it changes our prepositions:

Masculine	il	=	davanti AL
Feminine	la	=	davanti ALLA
Vowels	l'	=	davanti ALL

Examples: Il pane è davanti al burro La forchetta è vicino alla tazza
L'arancha è accanto all'acqua

Tasks:
You are going to make yourself an illustrated guide to these prepositions and the rules explained above.
Draw objects using the vocabulary we have looked at this term to do with meals.
You need to incorporate the correct phrases to state where all the objects are in relation to each other.
Ask for help and use the dictionaries and your exercise books to help with vocabulary.

In the third exercise, pupils put together the skills they have just acquired and use them to describe their final composition in Italian.

Art and Italian 3

You will need:
The 'Prepositions' sheet
The Glossario sheet

Some more prepositions:
sopra – on top of
sotto – under
fra – between
tra – between (or among)

Look at these sentences:
La tazza è sopra il piattino
Il piatto è sotto la forchetta
Il piatto è tra la forchetta e il coltello
Il bicchiere è fra il tovagliolo e la tazza

In order to make your final composition look accurate, think about:

* Perspective
* Shading
* Line
* Pattern
* Proportion
* Distance

Now add to your illustrated guide.

A similar approach might be made using the German structures shown in figure 10.12.

A further unit in Italian uses materials for a 'Portraits and Movement' project. This project emphasises adjectives and verbs. Pupils follow a unit of producing self-portraits in their Art course. In language lessons, they study portraits by Italian or German artists, which are described. Following work on describing themselves using photographs and styles borrowed from foreign artists, they move on to depicting and describing movement in art. The final outcomes are oral, using verbs and adverbs in Italian, and visual presentations, using pupils' own artwork. The following extracts indicate some of the tasks that pupils might undertake.

Hier sieht man	Here, you can see	
einen Mann (m.) eine Frau (f.) ein Kind (n.) einen Mann und eine Frau zwei Männer (pl.) zwei Frauen (pl.) zwei Kinder (pl.)		a man a woman a child a man and a woman two men two women two children
Der Mann/Die Frau Der erste/zweite Mann Die erste/zweite Frau Das erste/zweite Kind	The man/The woman The first/second man The first/second woman The first/second child	has a big nose. is tall and thin, etc.
hat eine große Nase. ist groß und schlank etc. **(Full physical description, please!)**		
Er/Sie trägt	He/She is wearing	a blue coat. red trousers. a black dress. white socks.
einen blauen Mantel. (m.) eine rote Hose. (f.) ein schwarzes Kleid. (n.) weisses Socken. (pl.)		
Er/Sie steht Sie stehen	He/She is standing They are standing	in front of a tree. alone.
vor einem Baum. allein.		
Er/Sie sitzt Sie sitzen	He/She is sitting They are sitting	on a chair.
auf einem Stuhl.		
Er/Sie liegt Sie liegen	He/She is lying They are lying	on a bed. on the ground.
auf einem Bett. auf dem Boden.		
Der Mann Die Frau Das Kind	The man The woman The child	looks strict/happy. is scared.
sieht streng/glücklich aus. hat Angst.		
Die Männer/Frauen/Kinder	The men/women/children	look peaceful/sad.
sehen ruhig/traurig aus.		

Figure 10.12 Describing pictures and paintings of people in German

Movement in Art Task 1 Starting a glossary
To begin with, think about what words, verbs and adverbs, you might need to use.
Verbs describe an action, for example, to run, to stand, to sleep, to wash. Adverbs describe how that action is carried out, for example, slowly, silently, peacefully, hurriedly.
You are going to make a glossary for this project.

- Make a list of the locations (for example, rooms) – at least five.
- Write down at least five verbs for actions associated with each location.
- Note at least three adverbs to describe these actions.

Movement in Art Task 2 Using verbs
You should now have a least a sketch or a scene you have found which you are going to describe. You should have listed the words you are going to use to describe the movement – the verbs and adverbs – appropriate to this scene.

You now need to prepare your description, then work on how to pronounce and learn the words in order to complete your presentation. Now try working out how you would describe these actions in Italian, using the verbs listed:

Studiare – to study	Cucinare – to cook
Vedere – to see	Ascoltare – to listen
Scrivere – to write	Parlare – to talk
Guardare – to watch	

Movement in Art Task 3 Adding adverbs
You can now complete the description of the action by adding the adverb, which describes the movement completely.

Using the dictionary, find out what these adverbs mean in English, then use them by adding appropriate phrases from those above, for example, Lei dorme profondamente = she sleeps deeply.

Tranquillamente	Rapidamente
Studiosamente	Lentamente
Chiaramente	Facilmente
Precisamente	Profondamente
Velocemente	

German and Business Studies

There are many basic tasks that link work in the second language with Business Studies contexts:

- using suitable forms of address;
- taking and/or listening to telephone messages;
- giving the gist of correspondence or other written material;
- writing letters – business letters, making arrangements for a visit;
- writing a CV;
- simple job applications;
- making presentations – work done, results, surveys, publicity, selling a product;
- specialised vocabulary – documents for payment, business letters, abbreviations;
- background information on business culture.

These can be extended to deal with tasks listed on German and Business Studies vocational syllabuses. For example,

- Describe businesses and customers.
- Make a sales presentation to a customer.
- Explore ways of processing payments.
- Produce and check payment documents.
- Plan for employment in business.
- Present the results of investigation into employment.
- Plan, design and produce promotional material.
- Provide customer service.

The important element of this particular approach is the way language work complements content covered in the specialist curriculum area. For example, a group of pupils following a Business Studies course visited Longleat Wildlife Park. This park has been set up in the grounds of a stately home and attracts many tourists coming to view the wild animals now living there. The Business Studies task was as follows:

Task

Whilst on your visit to Longleat carry out research to find out about the market and business environment within which Longleat Ltd operates. You should be interested in

- why Longleat is located where it is;
- how near it is to other businesses (find out about its competitors as well as any businesses which might provide goods or services to Longleat);
- how many people visit Longleat and how far they come from;
- how visitors get to Longleat;

- the size of the market that Longleat operates in (local, regional, national, international);
- the value of this market and Longleat's share and annual turnover;
- what marketing communications (advertsing and promotion) Longleat undertakes;
- the effectiveness of these marketing communications in improving its market position;
- Longleat's product range (produce a list of all the different things you can do at Longleat).

You will need mainly to use the research techniques of observation and questioning during your visit. Collect any written information you can as well as examples of Longleat's marketing materials.

This project was carried out in English for the Business Studies course. However, it was complemented with a simpler project in the second language.

Task
You are to produce publicity materials to market Longleat to a German audience:

- Decide on the target market and give reasons.
- Describe the area in German.
- Show how you would reach Longleat.
- Describe the facilities they offer.
- Feature specific areas of interest for your market audience.
- Give details of costs and optional extras.

Here we see how the German tasks build on and complement the content knowledge and skills developed in the curriculum subject. Thinking skills require specific content language and vice versa, as discussed in chapter 3.

Elsewhere, information technology and Spanish are linked. In one task, pupils produce a rough guide to Spain:

The Rough Guide to Spain
You have been invited by a leading holiday company to produce the essential tourist guide to part of Spain or a Spanish-speaking country. The guide that no tourist can live without! Unfortunately, the holiday company has invited many other companies to submit their ideas as well as you. You need to make sure that your guide wins the commission and beats off all the competition.

Produce a guide containing at least eight pages.
Your guide needs to be eye-catching, informative and accurate.
It also needs to include up-to-the-minute information and give details of useful websites for tourists to use before they leave on holiday, for example, 'Yes, Spain': http://www.sispain.org/english/index.html.

You must include:
The Spanish phrases you think no visitor to Spain could live without.
Local information about shops, opening hours, banks, currency.
Cultural information about eating times and habits and local specialities.
Details of restaurants, bars and cafes.
Things to do and see.
Accommodation.
Transport.
Information about climate, geography.
Anything else that would be useful

This project entails searching the Internet and selecting the most important information. As well as information retrieval, word-processing and design skills are called upon to create a brochure that is easy to use, appealing and informative.

Conclusion

There is certainly diversity of approach in Modern Languages Across the Curriculum. The above examples are an indication only of how it might be organised and taught. MLAC requires planning over the long, medium and short term. It also needs to be flexible in adapting itself to particular professional contexts. Such contexts are culturally and institutionally specific. Finally, there is the question of language task and technique. As discussed in the early chapters of this book, recent decades have seen the dominance of Communicative Language Teaching, and our case studies alluded to the impact this has had in particular countries and the current versions operating there. These are pedagogical concerns. The practical materials offered in this chapter demonstrate individual responses to the issues of developing communicative competence in meaningful settings. Here, we can see the tensions of grammar and structure sitting alongside the communicative imperative to make meaning in a content-rich environment. We also see the need to develop the links between thinking and language, together with associated learning strategies (see Grenfell and Harris 1999). The accent is on learning to learn, real meaning, personal response and involvement, developing cognitive skills. The materials in this section show a rich repertoire of activity for doing so.

References

Brown, K. (2001) 'A more adult way of learning', in G. Chambers (ed.) *Reflections on Motivation*, London: CILT.

Brown, K. and Brown, M. (1996) *Pathfinder 27: New Contexts for Modern Language Learning: Cross-curricular Approaches*, London: CILT.

—— (1998) *Changing Places: Cross-curricular Approaches to Teaching Languages*, London: CILT.

Charis Resources in French and German, The Stapleford Centre, The Old Lace Mill, Frederick Road, Stapleford, Nottingham.

Coyle, D. (2000) 'Meeting the challenge: developing the 3Cs curriculum', in S. Green (ed.) *New Perspectives on Teaching and Learning Modern Languages*, Clevedon: Multilingual Matters.

Development Education Pack (2001) *Development Education Pack: Development Education through the Teaching of Spanish: Vidas Méxicanas*, York: The Centre for Global Education, York St John College.

Dobson, A. (1998) *MFL Inspected Reflections on Inspection Findings 1996–7*, London: CILT.

Grenfell, M. (1994) 'Communication: sense and nonsense', in A. Swarbrick (ed.) *Teaching Modern Languages*, London: Routledge.

Grenfell, M. and Harris, V. (1999) *Modern Languages and Learning Strategies*, London: Routledge.

Manchester Development Education Project (1992) *Living and Learning in a Tanzanian Village: A Child's Perspective*, Manchester: Manchester Metropolitan University.

Part 4

Modern Languages Across the Curriculum

Teacher education

Introduction

Michael Grenfell

In parts 1–3 of this book, we dealt with the historical background and theoretical justifications for Modern Languages Across the Curriculum. We saw then how this approach to integrating content and language might look like in practice by looking at case examples from a range of European contexts. Part 3 showed the type of teaching materials which might be employed first to broaden the curriculum and then to lead on to to subject coverage in a recognised discipline area. We have seen issues of principle and practice in implementation, including national, regional and international variations, as well as common practical aims and objectives. Whatever the approach, language and subject content, Modern Languages Across the Curriculum has to be taught by a trained and committed teaching force. This part of the book deals with issues surrounding the training of such teachers. Clearly, there are differences across countries. However, the profile of the proficient MLAC teacher probably retains more similarities than differences. The first chapter in this part considers teacher *education* as distinct from teacher *training* in the diversity that is the European context. We see what MLAC teachers need to know: the basic components that make up MLAC teacher knowledge. These components include language-specific and content knowledge, as well as general pedagogic skills. This description gives rise to an 'agenda' for educating MLAC teachers; in short, the content and organisation of teacher education for this breed of teachers. Such an agenda has clear policy implications, and these are sketched out as a way of making clear what European teacher education might look like in terms of structure, experience and curricular content. There is also mention of the in-service needs of practising teachers; what support they need and how might it be provided in order to help them teach in this way. In the second chapter, we include materials and ideas which might be used with teachers in order to introduce them to Modern Languages Across the Curriculum and plan for its adoption in their individual teaching programmes.

11 Teacher education

Glenn Ole Hellekjaer and Aud Marit Simensen

Introduction

The terminology of ideas in education keeps changing. However, a change is normally not haphazard – it usually implies a new perspective. The core idea of this book has, through the years, been dealt with as, among other things, immersion, bilingual education, content-based language instruction, and content and language integrated learning, as discussed in the preceding chapters. The phrase used in the present book, Modern Languages Across the Curriculum (henceforth MLAC), implies a new perspective. In essence, this perspective suggests that education in modern languages may take place across the curriculum, i.e. in most, if not all, of the subjects of a school's curriculum, not only in the foreign languages on the timetable. This principle extends the responsibility for foreign language education to other agents than those traditionally involved at the individual school level. Such thinking is comparable to the movement Writing Across the Curriculum, which started in Britain in the 1970s.[1] Clearly, these perspectives have implications for teacher education.

The purpose of this chapter is to discuss teacher education from the point of view of Modern Languages Across the Curriculum. It takes as its point of departure essential differences between systems of teacher education in Europe. It then discusses the qualifications – in terms of language, subject content and pedagogy – that must be required of prospective MLAC teachers. It proposes components and modules of a teacher education programme appropriate for this type of teaching and considers a series of associated questions and problems. It suggests a higher degree of internationalisation in the study programmes of individual students and recommends trans-national co-operation on specific points. The chapter must be considered an outline only of ideas that may be adapted to the needs of individual institutions and differing national systems.

Teacher education

The concept 'teacher *education*' implies more than is traditionally included in the concept 'teacher *training*'. It encompasses both a subject-matter part and a peda-gogical part. The subject-matter element incorporates academic subjects such as

Mathematics, History and foreign languages or vocational subjects such as Health Care and Nursing. The pedagogical element normally comprises three basic components: educational theory, methodology and school teaching practice. In the following, we give priority to a discussion of teacher education in terms of a combination of academic subjects and the components of the pedagogy.

It is necessary to specify which level of the educational system we are preparing teachers to enter. Here, a distinction is made between three levels: the primary level, the lower secondary level and the upper secondary level. Teacher education for the pre-school level and for higher education might also be included. For obvious reasons, we cannot include all these levels in the discussion below. We will therefore limit ourselves to teacher education for the lower and the upper secondary levels of the school system. Teacher education may also involve initial education, in-service education or continuing education. Our focus in this chapter will be on initial education. However, the other types will also be considered, where relevant.

Diversity in current teacher education in Europe

Current teacher education in Europe varies from country to country. First, there are organisational differences. Two major approaches to educating teachers may be distinguished. In the first, the subject and pedagogy are integrated. This approach is normally called the *concurrent* type. In the second approach, the two elements are dealt with successively – the subject-matter part first and the pedagogical part afterwards. This approach is usually referred to as the *consecutive* type. To our knowledge, the latter approach is the more widespread for the levels of education we are dealing with here in many European countries. The present chapter therefore focuses on the *consecutive* approach.

Second, there is a difference with regard to the number and types of components required in the subject-content element of teacher education. In some countries, such as Germany and Norway, students with an academic degree from a university have normally studied two or more academic subjects appropriate for teaching in schools – so-called 'double degrees' (see Wolff 1999). It is when these subjects include a foreign language and one or more non-language subjects that there is a good point of departure for MLAC teaching.

Third, there are, of course, differences between countries regarding the pedagogical part of teacher education, such as the minimum level of understanding required in the discipline and the minimum time initial teacher trainees are expected to spend in schools doing teaching practice. However, provided all basic components are present, differences of size are probably not so significant.

Finally, there is a difference between countries as to the type of institutions that are responsible for teacher education, especially with regard to the pedagogical or methodological element. Such institutions range from the purely academic, such as universities and university colleges in countries like England, Finland and Sweden, to various types of post-secondary-level institutions in other countries in Europe (see Sander 1999).

What MLAC teachers need to know

Subject content and language

The supply of teachers capable of teaching, or willing to teach, a non-language subject through a foreign language is a key factor limiting the introduction of MLAC programmes. Contrary to what might be expected, this is the case even in countries where double degrees with a foreign language and a content subject are common. Consequently, the issue of which academic qualifications are needed is a pressing one when designing an MLAC teacher education programme.

MLAC teachers can be divided into three main categories. First, there are teachers with subject-matter degrees only, but who are capable of teaching through the foreign language. Second, there are teachers with double degrees in a foreign language and a non-linguistic subject. Finally, there are those teachers with language degrees only who teach in co-operation with other subject-matter teachers, or who teach separately formal foreign language (FL) classes to pupils receiving MLAC instruction elsewhere in their timetable. Possession of a double degree would seem the ideal for MLAC purposes, but it is clear that what is needed to be a MLAC teacher is common to all, whatever the language and subject background. So, what is required of a MLAC teacher?

One of the traditions in 'Language for Specific Purposes' (LSP) instruction is that courses should be based on an analysis of learner needs. This necessity is, of course, just as relevant for teacher education. One such needs-analysis for MLAC instruction exists: a survey of MLAC teacher needs in Estonia, Germany, and Finland (Räsänen et al. 1996). This survey gives a fairly good picture of what teachers feel they need in order to teach MLAC classes. Here, for relevance, we focus on the answers of the German MLAC teachers who had double degrees. These experienced teachers indicated the need for improvement in the following areas, ranked in order of importance (see Räsänen et al. 1996: 285):

- subject-specific vocabulary;
- language used in social interaction;
- discourse features (i.e. organization of spoken and written texts, conventions);
- fluent expression;
- general vocabulary;
- classroom management language.

In other words, even experienced MLAC teachers with double degrees feel the need for yet higher levels of oral and written proficiency in areas ranging from everyday language to subject-specific vocabulary and the language of classroom management. They also express the need to be able to produce and teach from advanced, general and specialised written and oral texts.

Any MLAC content teacher should, of course, also possess detailed knowledge of their subject, whether it is 'academic' like History or Physics, or vocational.

However, since MLAC depends on the use of a foreign language as a means of instruction, content teachers also need the ability to teach in the target language at a reasonable level of fluency. Clarity and accuracy in pronunciation and grammar are a must.

Subject-specific terminology

Subject-specific terminology is the special language used to describe the subject in question. As discussed in chapter 3, for MLAC purposes, it is also necessary to distinguish between the subject-specific terminology of the subject itself and that which is needed to teach the subject in the classroom. This language we will call 'subject-specific classroom discourse', an area of particular importance for MLAC instruction.

For example, in the Nordic countries, terminology in English is rarely a problem since most students at college or university will have read English textbooks in their academic studies. In larger language communities such as Germany, where more textbooks in German are used in the content courses, this is more of a problem. This situation may, at least in part, explain why the German MLAC teachers in the survey referred to above rank 'special terminology' as their most pressing need, unlike the Finnish teachers, for example. This need for subject-specific terminology is also felt in England and France and many other European countries.

Subject-specific classroom discourse is the language needed to run and organise a class in the subject in question, and comes in addition to what is needed to impart the subject. To use Chemistry as an example, teachers will most probably have learnt the terminology required to explain the effect of a catalyst on a chemical reaction from textbooks or articles. If not, they should be able to use their knowledge of the subject and the terminology in their mother tongue to pick it up fairly quickly. Nevertheless, the language needed to instruct pupils in setting up a laboratory exercise, including safety instructions, will not be so readily available. For more 'hands-on', vocational subjects such as car mechanics or building construction, in which teaching is more a question of guidance and organisation in work-related situations, the teacher's need to master the relevant classroom language will be even more pressing. In fact, classroom discourse might be a problem for foreign language instruction in general, not only for MLAC teachers. Even foreign language specialists often grope for words and expressions in classroom situations when they are outside the content proper of their subjects, or even revert to their mother tongue in these situations. In any case, the findings from the survey discussed above certainly indicate the need for increased focus on this in both foreign language and MLAC teacher education.

A final point concerning the language proficiency requirements of content teaching is connected to the production of subject-specific texts. For example, in a science course, it would be necessary to write laboratory reports in the target language. To what extent can content teachers be expected to teach this unless they have a language degree? Yet, a language specialist will often lack the necessary subject-specific terminology and knowledge to comment on more than language and structure. Either double degrees or team teaching have to be the solution.

What is required with regard to more 'traditional' foreign language skills in an MLAC environment? In part, this can perhaps be illustrated with an anecdote from a visit to a European school with an immersion programme. This school has an immersion programme starting at age 10 and continuing until graduation from upper secondary. One of the 'problems' that appeared there was that the senior students developed extremely advanced language skills. The school's teachers were hand picked, and had degrees in a language as well as in the non-language subject they taught. Nevertheless, many of their students who were receiving input in a number of subjects developed special language skills and proficiency beyond the level of many of their well-qualified teachers. We have included this example to make the point that teachers in *advanced* MLAC classes need to be able to speak and write the target language at very high levels indeed, whether they teach subject matter or formal FL classes, or both. Furthermore, this requirement goes beyond general fluency and vocabulary to include proficiency in and knowledge of LSP: special terminology, on the one hand, and the discourse features of special texts on the other. The need for teachers to have knowledge about the discourse features of both oral and written texts connects directly with the nature of the language proficiency developed by MLAC pupils (see Swain 1985, 2000).

Nevertheless, the situation is complex. Clearly, such advanced language and content skills are hardly needed for teachers at the elementary stage. Moreover, in contrast to the example cited above, research on French immersion programmes in Canada has revealed that while pupils developed near-native level receptive skills though exposure to the target language, this was not necessarily the case with the productive skills. In fact, the pupils' French was often so marred by grammatical and phonological errors that this caused serious criticism of the entire programme. Researcher Merril Swain claims that these deficiencies persist because learners need more than comprehensible output to improve:

> immersion students do not demonstrate native speaker competence, not because their comprehensible input is limited but because their comprehensible output is limited. It is limited in two ways. First, the students are simply not given – especially in later grades – adequate opportunities to use the target language in the classroom context. Second, they are not 'pushed' in their output. . . . There appears to be little social or cognitive pressure to produce language that reflects more appropriately or precisely their intended meaning. There is no push to be more comprehensible than they already are.

(Swain 1985: 259)

In other words, Swain claims that learners require opportunities to use the foreign language in extended discourse in a variety of genres and registers in order to develop advanced proficiency levels. When doing so, they notice the gaps in their linguistic and textual knowledge, and thereby become receptive to feedback on their errors and instruction on how to improve. In a more recent article about the field test of such a programme she reports:

> Verbalisation helped them to become aware of their problems, predict their linguistic needs, set goals for themselves, monitor their own language use, and evaluate their overall success. Their verbalisation of strategic behaviour served to guide them through communicative tasks allowing them to focus not only on 'saying', but on 'what' they said. In so doing, relevant content was provided that could be further explored and considered. Test results suggest that their collaborative efforts, mediated by dialogue, supported their internalisation of correct grammatical forms.
>
> (Swain 2000: 111)

Chapter 3 argued that a key challenge for MLAC teachers is how to create such an interactive language-learning environment. Ultimately, this will first and foremost require teachers with near-native proficiency in the foreign language both to keep up with the pupils and to be able to give them feedback on covert as well as overt errors. Overt errors are perhaps less problematical since they are generally easier to notice, such as the incorrect use of tense or prepositions. Finding covert errors, on the other hand, demands far more of the teacher since this can be a question of noticing instances of non-realisation. Examples would be non-use of the appropriate vocabulary or grammatical structures.

Giving feedback on errors, however, is only part of what is required. What will also be needed is teachers who are able to instruct pupils in how to produce these advanced oral and written texts as well as give feedback during the process and on the finished product. The skill and knowledge needed to teach MLAC pupils to produce advanced oral work and texts in both general and subject-specific genres must therefore be made an integral part of teacher education for MLAC. Fortunately, most foreign language departments at colleges and universities will have considerable expertise in these areas. There is also a need to plan and deliver lessons in line with what we know about cognitive process, thinking skills and learning strategies. Clearly, therefore, these topics must be given a prominent place in MLAC teacher education.

In sum, from the subject-matter perspective, the ideal MLAC teacher can perhaps best be described as two teachers in one: an expert on content matter (non-linguistic subject(s)) as well as on the relevant foreign language. From the pedagogical perspective, to which we will turn below, the ideal MLAC teacher can perhaps best be described as having a double grounding in pedagogical content knowledge in addition to appropriate teaching experience.

The pedagogical element

The pedagogical part is what an MLAC teacher needs to know in terms of theoretical understanding, as well as what they need to be able to *do* in the classroom. We can consider it in terms of *general educational theory* and *methodological knowledge*. These theoretical components complement the practical part of teacher education, which is provided by *student teaching practice* in pre-service training.

General educational theory deals with topics such as 'the aims of education in general', including 'aims orientated towards society' and 'individual-orientated aims', 'pupils' learning and general development', and 'planning, organising and evaluating teaching and learning'. With regard to an education for MLAC teaching, this component should be considered a basic requirement for all students in teacher education programmes, independent of the type and number of subjects studied academically.

Methodological knowledge deals with the teaching and learning of specific subjects in the educational system. 'Pedagogical content knowledge' is in fact a more comprehensive concept, and therefore more useful, than 'teaching methodology', which is essentially concerned simply with giving answers to the question of *how* in a school subject. The concept 'pedagogical content knowledge' includes answers to the questions of *what* and *why* in a school subject as well as the *how*. An interesting point in this connection is that the equivalent concept of 'subject didactics' is gradually becoming more common in a European context in spite of the somewhat negatively loaded English term 'didactics'. This word often indicates a moralistic approach to teaching. When used in connection with a person, it denotes someone who is too eager to teach people things or give instructions.[2] The equivalents to 'subject didactics' in some of the other European languages are not similarly loaded terms. This applies, for example, to the German term *Fachdidaktik* or the Norwegian term *fagdidaktikk*.[3] We may talk about the subject didactics of Mathematics, of History, of French as a foreign language, etc. Alternative terms used are 'subject-matter didactics' or 'subject-related didactics'.

Methodological knowledge varies to some extent depending on the type of academic subject involved. However, for all curriculum subjects, it does provide guidance to the what-, how-, and why- questions. It might be asked, for example, why a particular subject has a place in the school system in question. There are also all the more specific what- and how-questions – each of which must be justified in terms of answers to the why-questions. This methodological component includes, in other words, all matters relevant for a school subject and the teaching of it. This may be illustrated by the small selection of questions of relevance for most school subjects in table 11.1.

Our final component in the pedagogical part, student teaching practice, deals with the practical experiential aspects of teaching in the classroom. The trainee is usually supervised by an experienced mentor during their time spent in school-based teaching practice. As a rule, it implies observation of the mentor's own teaching in the relevant school subject(s), combined with the trainee's own teaching with feedback from the mentor and sometimes also from the class taught.

One of the main requirements of the MLAC teacher is the willingness to adjust the teaching of their subject to new circumstances, and the ability to find

Table 11.1 A selection of questions for the 'methodological knowledge' component of teacher education

---

What-questions
    What should the objectives of a
    course in the school subject be?
    What should the content be?

                Why-questions
                Why these objectives, this content, these
                measures, these types of teaching materials,
                learning activities, tests, evaluation criteria, etc.?

How-questions
    How should the content be dealt
    with (types of teaching materials,
    types of learning activities, etc.)?
    How should the progression of
    the students be evaluated (e.g. types
    of tests and evaluation criteria)?

---

solutions to problems that appear (see Hellekjaer 1996). Indeed, the teacher's confidence in their ability to cope with altered circumstances is perhaps the key factor determining whether they are willing to teach an MLAC course. Such confidence is supported by the knowledge needed to vary approaches to teaching as needs be. In a discussion of the qualifications of LSP teachers which is just as relevant for MLAC, Ian Tudor argues:

> The teacher . . . has to learn to 'listen' to learners and be willing to respond to their subjective learning needs – both as individuals and as members of a given socio-cultural community. This calls for considerable personal and cultural sensitivity from the teacher, flexibility in the terms of teaching style, and mastery of a wide range of methodological alternatives.

> (Tudor 1997: 99)

Teaching an MLAC class often makes teachers more critical of how they teach their subjects and thus increases their willingness to innovate. Furthermore, there is a general trend that teachers become more learner-centred in their teaching in MLAC contexts, and that they pay more attention to the development of study skills. Yet another effect is that they often develop a greater appreciation of how a school's ethos and organisation, also called a 'whole school policy' and, we may add, 'an across the curriculum policy', can help learning (see Baetens Beardsmore 1993). The question to ask here is whether all of the points mentioned above should not also be part of the repertoire of any subject-matter teacher.

    A willingness to innovate and adjust teaching according to circumstances is as relevant for teaching in general as it is for MLAC teaching. However, there is at least one crucial area of difference. MLAC subject-matter teachers will need to know how to help pupils sort out language problems, in particular, in elementary classes or when pupils are starting new subjects taught in a foreign language. It is a priority during the initial stages that pupils need help to bridge the gap between their actual language abilities and what is needed to function in the MLAC classroom (see Hellekjaer 1996; Johnson and Swain 1994). This aspect is situated squarely at the interface between pedagogical content knowledge and language proficiency. It applies to the willingness as well as the ability of the teachers to adjust their language and tempo, to speak clearly and distinctly, avoid idioms and colloquialisms, and to make extensive use of visual aids to support comprehension. Furthermore, it applies to a knowledge of how to enhance students' listening or reading comprehension skills, for instance, through pre-reading or listening exercises. These approaches are important if MLAC is to engage with the cognitive approach to language teaching outlined in chapter 3. In addition, it means knowing enough about language acquisition to imbue students with confidence that their language skills will improve and knowing how to enhance this process. This, of course, relates to the motivational aspects of language learning also referred to in chapter 3.

How can a 'pure' foreign language teacher on the one hand and a 'pure' subject-matter teacher on the other support each other for mutual gain in the language learning process? To give examples, there are numerous opportunities to use the target language actively in the subject matter class, for instance, in group work, oral presentations, or panel discussions, or in the writing of everything from laboratory reports to essays on topical subjects. An experienced subject-matter specialist using a learner-centred approach will make the most of these opportunities. But how well a teacher with a single subject-matter degree functions will depend on what degree of interest and knowledge they bring to the classroom.

One solution is, of course, that a parallel foreign language class can function as a support for the subject-matter teacher. So, the subject content is approached from two directions: one in the subject specialist class; the other involving coverage of a similar subject and issues in the foreign language classroom. The Longleat example in the last chapter adopts this approach. We may call this a kind of 'team teaching'. In another example, a panel discussion might draw upon an ethical problem from Biology, such as biotechnology, which could take place in a Biology lesson or in a foreign language lesson. The history materials in the last chapter involve similar parallel coverage. The foreign language teacher in the team will usually be better qualified to give feedback on mistakes, help with language problems, and teach pupils how to produce the required texts at the appropriate discourse level (see Hellekjaer 1998a). This type of team teaching will, of course, depend on a willingness on the part of the foreign language teacher to learn enough about the subject-matter topics in question, and a willingness from both parties to co-operate when required.

An agenda for educating MLAC teachers

The subject-matter element

In many European countries, it is unlikely that existing teacher education pro-grammes will be able to meet the immediate need for qualified MLAC teachers. The number of people who take double degrees is small, although increasing. However, many graduates do not choose careers in teaching. In the mean time, a short-term solution would be encouraging students within current systems to qualify themselves for MLAC by choosing appropriate combinations of subjects.

Students starting their academic studies can be made aware of the possibil-ities of an MLAC teaching career if they choose an appropriate combination of academic disciplines (in their degree). We may call this 'a guided choice of academic disciplines' versus the traditional 'free choice of academic disciplines' in the subject-matter part of teacher education. On the basis of what is said above, an appropriate combination for MLAC purposes is a foreign language combined with a non-language subject. To some extent, the appropriate combi-nation will vary from country to country, depending on the language situation in the country as a whole and the foreign language(s) offered in the school system. The choice of the non-language part of the combination depends on the non-language subjects offered in the school system involved. In the Nordic countries, for example, the combination may consist of English and Physics or Mathematics, German and History, or French and Geography, etc. An alternative solution for subjects that are rarely combined with a foreign language would be studying the subject, wholly or in part, in the target language country. In any case, with or without an MLAC teacher education programme, student counselling to ensure 'a guided choice of academic discipline' will be important while MLAC teacher education programmes are being developed and set up.

In what follows, we will look at the subject-matter part, starting with content and continuing with foreign language education. Perhaps the best way to start is by asking what the MLAC content teacher needs to know that is not also required for teaching in the mother tongue. Being a specialist in the subject or trade in question is of course indispensable. Chemistry is Chemistry whatever the language, and the same goes for car mechanics or welding.

Furthermore, with regard to teaching, teachers in all walks of life and languages need 'sensitivity to learner needs' and 'mastery of a wide range of methodological alternatives' (Tudor 1997: 99). The same goes for the ability to innovate, the ability to solve problems, and awareness of the importance of a school environment for any programme (see Hellekjaer 1996; Baetens Beardsmore 1993). The main difference is that the MLAC subject-matter teacher must be able to teach their subject in the target language. This is a question of general proficiency in the target language, involving fluency, pronunciation, and accuracy on the one hand and subject-specific terminology, classroom discourse, and the discourse features of relevant, subject-specific, oral and written texts on the other. Consequently, a precondition for a course for subject-matter teachers is a given level of general proficiency in the target language, documented either through a language certification programme (see below) or, preferably, through a double degree including the target language. Nevertheless, this will remain a utopian goal with many subjects such as the natural sciences. Thus, we require a programme capable of accommodating trainees with language degree backgrounds acquired by different routes.

It has been suggested in this book that a good way to learn languages is by learning the subject and language simultaneously through an MLAC module (cf. Hellekjaer 1998b). Frøydis Hertzberg (1999) uses what she calls *exemplary practice* for teacher education in classroom methods in order to bring this about. This approach entails using the same teaching techniques students are supposed to use as future teachers, which would here be a module of the subject-matter degree taught in the target language and an MLAC content module comprising teaching and textbooks in the target language. The optimal solution would be that this module is made part of an exchange scheme, where institutions in different countries offer specialised modules. Such modules should have three main elements:

1   The subject taught in the target language and with textbooks in the target language;
2   A language component comprising language development with particular emphasis on producing subject-relevant texts;
3   A practice component allowing the learning of the relevant classroom, or work-related, language/discourse.

To use the example of a vocational subject for an advanced learning context, a teacher of car mechanics would do part of their content study in the second language – for example, Spanish, in or outside Spain. Parallel to this course would be a collaborative language course in which the teacher would compile a portfolio of subject-specific texts; anything from an instruction manual to a damage report or automobile brochures. Finally, there would be a practice period in relevant situations, either in a garage in Spain or at a school providing courses in car mechanics. Here, they might be requested to produce their own dictionary of key classroom- or work-related terms and expressions. If longer stays are not possible, an alternative approach to the learning of classroom or work-related language might be shorter visits to schools or places of work to target language communities, or, for instance, transcribing a selection of videos of authentic, subject-relevant classroom situations.

The foreign language component

As with the content component, it is relevant to ask how such a module would differ from traditional foreign-language teacher education courses. There is a clear need for additional components and changes in focus to prepare second language specialists for teaching in an MLAC programme.

To start with, as suggested above, where there is the need for near native-speaker levels of language proficiency, one solution would be to encourage students to study for all or part of the course in the target language country. This arrangement would certainly be indispensable for the less common languages. Nevertheless, such stays would be hardly possible for all MLAC students, and not even necessary where MLAC teaching is targeting beginner learners.

Where advanced teaching is to take place, there is a need for a much stronger emphasis to be placed on developing the student's oral and written language proficiency in undergraduate programmes. As part of this effort in foreign language learning, as with the content part, the use of specific examples of good practice is important; students are encouraged to use the same teaching techniques of modelling as are future foreign language teachers. For MLAC teacher education, this could mean combining instruction in key aspects of linguistics – genre, text and register, for example – with the actual production of advanced oral and written texts in an interactive learning environment (see Kowal and Swain 1994; Swain 2000). If this language production could be integrated with examination requirements, so much the better; for instance, MLAC teachers might compile a portfolio of advanced oral and written texts for examination purposes which would involve mastering discourse and narrative techniques they could then teach to their future pupils and students. Thus, future teacher trainees would not only be required to undergo the demanding process of developing their language proficiency, but would also be getting practical, hands-on experience with precisely the methods they would be using in their MLAC classes. This work could be based in part upon traditional literary, social, and linguistic topics, which would enhance the content element as well. It is not necessary to demolish the traditional components in second language teacher education. However, for MLAC purposes these need to be supplemented by a grounding in language for special purposes, both as spoken language and as written texts. Part of this work could consist of producing subject-specific texts for inclusion in the MLAC student portfolio. A similar principle could be applied to classroom language in order to be able to teach a foreign language class.

The pedagogical part

Of the normal elements in the pedagogical part of *initial* teacher education, the component 'general educational theory' will apply to both groups of students described above: students with 'a guided choice of academic disciplines' as well as students with 'a free choice of academic disciplines'. However, it is when it comes to the components 'pedagogical content knowledge' and 'teaching practice' that a differentiation must take place.

With regard to the 'pedagogical content knowledge', or methodology, component, ideally there would be two distinct courses for students whom we have described as having double degrees: in a curricular subject and in language. Here, we will only go into detail in relation to a 'pedagogical content knowledge' course in a foreign language. However, it must be kept in mind that a methodology course in a non-language subject will have to be constructed in more or less the same way. For MLAC purposes, there will be some areas of knowledge in common to both the subject matter teacher and the foreign language teacher. One such area is the need to be able to help students sort out language problems, for instance, with listening to teaching or with the reading of difficult textbook passages. A language teacher does need a variety of strategies, such as the pre-listening or reading activities discussed in chapter 3, to activate mother–tongue knowledge that will ease the learning process or work with unfamiliar language items.

It is possible to design a series of modules to deal with the methodology course of one specific foreign language, and require that all the students with that particular foreign language follow them. Some of these modules will have to be made compulsory, and others optional. Among the compulsory modules we would expect such 'traditional' themes as: the history and the characteristics of the foreign language in the school system of the country; theories of language acquisition/learning and language teaching; planning and organising teaching; the teaching of culture; evaluating student language; constructing tests, etc. (see Simensen 1998). Among the optional modules, there would be units specifically constructed for students with 'a guided choice of academic disciplines' and thus to be considered a prerequisite for future MLAC teaching. Such modules would concentrate on topics such as bilingualism, syllabus design and teaching materials for MLAC teaching, and various other questions in relation to the foreign language as the medium of instruction. To be able to give all students in the pedagogical part of teacher education the same opportunity for 'specialisation', there should also ideally be modular options for students with a 'free choice of academic disciplines'. These options could include, for example, some sort of advanced course in teaching, supported by information and communication technology, project work, internationalisation, etc.

When it comes to the component 'student teaching practice', we will deal with it here solely from the perspective of prospective MLAC teachers. Two options are outlined here. We label these a 'half-and-half-option with extra cost compensation' and a 'double practice option with extra cost compensation'.

In the 'half-and-half option', half of the time is spent on teaching practice within the national school system, if possible also with some practice in MLAC classes. This arrangement would ensure a familiarity with and an understanding of a local school as well as the national school system. The other half of teaching practice would be taken in the target language country, with the trainee teaching in their non-language school subject(s). Such an arrangement could, for example, involve a trainee teaching physics in English in Britain, Geography in German in Germany, or History in French in France, etc. Extra costs in connection with the stay abroad might be covered though European Union support; for example, either the EU/EEA programme Comenius 2, 'Language assistants in schools', or a similar programme (see European Commission 2001a).

The 'double practice option' implies that first the trainee undertakes the same period of teaching practice as any other student along more or less traditional lines within the national school system. Then, as the name indicates, the MLAC trainee undertakes an extra period of teaching practice in the target language country in the non-language school subject(s) of the trainee. The extra costs are covered along the lines described above.

In-service training, continuing education, and additional certification

Experienced teachers will be an important resource for MLAC teaching. Therefore, it is necessary to provide opportunities for qualified teachers to add to their existing qualifications for MLAC purposes. For qualified teachers with two or more academic subjects appropriate for MLAC teaching, some sort of in-service or continuing second language education arrangement would be the best option. In addition, teachers should be able to add relevant MLAC modules on methodology to their subject qualifications. They must also be given the opportunity to undertake a period of teaching practice abroad along the lines outlined above in the section on trainee teaching practice.

Similarly, it is necessary to provide for the possibility of qualified second language teachers adding one or more academic subjects to their existing subject qualifications. For the purpose of future MLAC teaching, both a foreign language subject and a non-language subject are appropriate, depending on the teachers' existing qualifications. Therefore, a subject specialism would enhance their portfolio of expertise to teach in a language-subject integrated way. Like trainee teachers, they could be offered the same opportunities to study selected components abroad and to get financial support on a par with trainees in their initial teacher education programme, as discussed above.

There are probably a number of qualified teachers with only non-language academic subjects as formal qualifications, but with foreign language skills. Their linguistic competence may be the result of work experience abroad, for example, as a teacher in a developing country where French, German, Spanish, or English is used as the language of instruction. Or, their abilities in a second language might have been gained in social and/or family contexts. Clearly, appropriate certification programmes in foreign languages are needed in order to recognise their competence. Such certification needs to be made easily available for this group of teachers for the purpose giving formal recognition to their ability to use the relevant second language *as a medium of instruction* in their teaching. A series of tests for certification already exists. However, it is important to choose the right kind and level of test. In future, this may be done through a system that will direct users to tests that are appropriate and will certify their levels of proficiency, for example, Dialang. Dialang is a project for the development of diagnostic tests in a number of European languages (see http://www.dialang.org/). It is supported by the European Commission under the Socrates programme, Lingua Action D (see European Commission 2001b), and offers certification which can be recognised across European member states.

International co-operation, the use of information and communication technology (ICT), and distance learning

An MLAC teacher education programme will profit from extensive co-operation between institutions, particularly at an international level. A few areas only for such co-operation will be outlined in the following.

First, there is the need for co-operation between institutions in different countries in relation to establishing subject-related modules. For example, these modules might be a course in History or Science (or any other curriculum subject) taught in the relevant target language. Such a module might receive the same credit-value as a module in a home institution. It would probably be most practical to encourage a number of institutions to form a network, each specialising in one or more subjects for students from several countries. These same institutions could also be responsible for compiling electronic data bases of subject-specific termi-nology and subject-specific classroom language in the area in question. On the basis of this, it would be expected and appropriate for these institutions to produce teaching materials, ranging from books to audio-tapes and videos, in particular for use in distance learning.

For initial teacher training schemes in the pedagogical part of teacher educa-tion, international networks should be responsible for organising teaching practice in schools of the relevant target language communities, for example, as part of a 'half-and-half' or a 'double practice' model, as discussed above. For in-service programmes, there will be a similar need for co-operation in organising 'shadow schemes', in which teachers visit schools or places of work to be exposed to classroom or work-related language.

Finally, international co-operation is clearly a desirable element in running distance learning schemes with an ICT element, either as part of an initial training programme or for in-service or continuing educational purposes. Distance learn-ing schemes could, for instance, focus on the subject and/or classroom language and/or teaching methodology. Teaching could take place either on satellite television, through standard video-conferencing, or through the use of inexpen-sive, Internet-based solutions such as CUSeeMe or Microsoft NetMeeting (see Hellekjaer and Paulsen 1999). If the types of relevant electronic data bases mentioned above were available, they would become an important part of target-language education.

Summary: key requirements for MLAC teacher education

When outlining a programme of MLAC teacher education, deciding which skills and what areas of knowledge are essential is both very important and highly problematical. One difficulty is deciding which aspects belong to traditional teacher education and which are particular to MLAC. Another is sorting out what is typical of the non-language subject content as compared with the foreign language, and the degree to which they overlap. Table 11.2 lists the skills and knowledge which must be included in an MLAC teacher education programme.

Conclusions

This chapter has dealt with the education of teachers for MLAC teaching in schools. The discussion of diversity in existing teacher education has been limited to the situation in Europe. We have looked at teacher education for MLAC from a subject-matter as well as a pedagogical perspective. On the basis of teacher experience with this type of teaching, we discussed the requirements for various types of MLAC teaching, seen in relation to subject-matter content knowledge, foreign language skills, pedagogical knowledge and practical classroom skills. Finally, elements of an agenda for educating MLAC teachers have been suggested. The focus here has been on initial education, although the possibilities for in-service, continuing education and additional certification have also been mentioned. Of course, an important aspect of this agenda is international co-operation for the establishment of networks of educational institutions. It is

Table 11.2 Key requirements for MLAC teacher education. (Components roughly ranked by area and in order of importance)

Subject-knowledge requirements		Pedagogical requirements	
Foreign language	*Content*	*Pedagogical content knowledge*	*Student teaching*
Advanced oral and written proficiency, comprising language for classroom management and for social interaction	Adequate target-language proficiency comprising subject-specific terminology and classroom/work-related discourse	MLAC theory, comprising: • language acquisition and development • bilingualism • school policy • materials development • assessment	National teaching practice, including MLAC classes Teaching practice in target-language communities
General textual competence, knowledge of the discourse features of spoken and written texts	Knowledge of the discourse features of relevant subject-specific texts	Subject-specific pedagogical content knowledge, in particular methodological flexibility in relation to MLAC teaching	
Language for Special Purposes knowledge, terminology, and discourse features			

Linguistic problem solving, i.e. reading and listening strategies; study skills

Studies in target-language community, theoretical as well as practical, made possible through international co-operation probably at this level that we feel MLAC has most to offer: as a means of bringing national and institutional policy and practice together and focusing on common pedagogical and linguistic goals.

Notes

1   See, for example, Martin 1976, one of the first books in the 'movement'.
2   *Longman Dictionary of Contemporary English*, Harlow: Longman, 1995.
3   The newly completed subnetwork E 'Searching for a missing link – subject didactics as the science of a teaching profession?' may be mentioned in this connection. This was part of one the Socrates-supported thematic networks, the Thematic Network on Teacher Education in Europe (TNTEE), and published in the report *'Didaktik/ Fachdidaktik as the Science(-s) of the Teaching Profession (*Hudson et al.1999; see http:// tntee.umu.se/subnetworks/subnetwork_e/).

References

Baetens Beardsmore, H. (1993) 'Bilingual learning: institutional frameworks – whole school policies', *Council of Europe, CC – Lang (93) Workshop 12A*.

Dialang, Dialang-Project and System, Internet, 5 March 2001. Available at: http:// www.dialang.org/.

European Commission (2001a) 'Comenius: European co-operation on school education', Internet, 5 March 2001. Available at: http://europa.eu.int/comm/ education/socrates/comenius/activities/comenius1.htm#Assistant.

—— (2001b) 'Socrates, the European Community action programme for co-operation in the field of education', Internet, 5 March 2001. Available at: http://europa.eu. int/comm/education/socrates/lingua/comp/list-96.html#list.

Hellekjaer, G. O. (1996) 'Easy does it: introducing pupils to bilingual instruction', *Språk og Språkundervisning* [Oslo] 3: 9–14.

—— (1998a) 'Teaching LSP: methods and misconceptions', *Fachsprache*, Heft 3–4/98: 149–55.

—— (ed.) (1998b) *Report from Workshop No. 18/97, Redefining Formal Foreign Language Instruction for a Bilingual Environment*, Graz: The European Centre of Modern Languages.

Hellekjaer, G. O. and Paulsen, T. R. (1999) 'Seeing is believing: CUSeeMeInexpensive video-conferencing', *Språk og Språkundervisning* [Oslo] 4: 28–32.

Hertzberg, F. (1999) 'Å didaktisere et fag – hva er det?', in C. Nyström and M. Ohlsson (eds) *Svenska i utveckling: en vänskrift til Birgitta Garme på 60-årsdagen den 24 november 1999'*, Uppsala, Uppsala Universität.

Hudson, B., Buchberger, F., Kansanen, P., and Seel, H. (eds) (1999) *Didaktik/ Fachdidaktik as the Science(-s) of the Teaching Profession? TNTEE Publications 2.1*, Umeå: Thematic Network on Teacher Education in Europe.

Johnson, R. K. and Swain, M. (1994) 'From core to content: bridging the L2 proficiency gap in late immersion', *Language and Education* 8 (4): 211–29.

Kowal, M. and Swain, M. (1994) 'Using collaborative language production tasks to promote students' language awareness', *Canadian Review of Studies in Nationalism* 3 (2): 73–93.

Martin, N. (1976) *Writing and Learning across the Curriculum*, Schools Council Writing Across the Curriculum Project, London: University of London, Institute of Education.

Räsänen, A., Kaasik, T., Mathews, H. D., Oresik, H., and Sentocnik, S. (1996) 'Profile of teacher qualifications required for bilingual education programmes', *Report on Workshop 12B, Bilingual Education in Secondary Schools: Learning and Teaching Non-Language Subjects through a Foreign Language*, Echternach, Luxembourg: Council of Europe, 277–92.

Sander, T. (ed.) (1999) 'Teacher education in Europe in the late 1990s: evaluation and quality', TNTEE Publications 2.2, Thematic Network on Teacher Education in Europe, Internet, 5 March 2001. Available at: http://tntee.umu.se/publications/publication2_2.html.

Simensen, A. M. (1998) *Teaching a Foreign Language: Principles and Procedures*, Bergen: Fagbokforlaget.

Swain, M. (1985) 'Communicative competence: some roles of comprehensible input and output in its development', in S. Gass and C. Madden (eds) *Input in Second Language Acquisition*. Boston: Heinle & Heinle.

—— (2000) 'The output hypothesis and beyond', in J. P. Lantolf (ed.) *Sociocultural Theory and Second Language Learning*, Oxford: Oxford University Press.

Tudor, I. (1997) 'LSP or language education?', in R. Howard and G. Brown (eds) *Teacher Education for Languages for Specific Purposes*, Clevedon: Multilingual Matters, 90–102.

Wolff, D. (1999) 'Content-based language learning: some critical issues', in D. Marsh and B. Marsland (eds) *CLIL Initiatives for the Millennium: Report on the CEILINK Think-Tank*, Jyväskylä: University of Jyväskylä, 122–4.

12 Teacher education: practical materials

Cheryl Hardy and Michael Grenfell with
Kim Brown, Rosanna Raimato and Melanie Valet

This chapter continues the exploration of teacher education in Modern Languages Across the Curriculum. It is concerned with strategies and practical activities that could create immediate opportunities for a teacher, a school or a training institution to begin to teach in this way. Several activities are included here as models for in-service or initial teaching training workshops. They are organised around three distinct aspects: 'teachers' knowledge bases', 'progression and planning' and 'learner strategies in MLAC'. The teacher education activities are illustrated by three practitioner examples: Kim Brown working with post-graduate trainees; Rosanna Raimato working within a whole school approach to language; and ideas from Melanie Valet in the context of cross-curricular work with other departments in her school. Each of these examples is accompanied by activities which might be used within pre-service and in-service teacher education. We conclude the chapter with some methodological principles underpinning MLAC teacher education.

In the previous chapter, the long-term demands for teacher education of Modern Languages Across the Curriculum were explored from the point of view of developing accredited training programmes which would produce well-qualified, expert teachers. Unfortunately, long-term programmes for teachers with dual expertise are expensive and demanding and will probably appeal to only a few individuals. None the less, the remarks made in chapter 11 about the nature of the knowledge needed to teach Modern Languages Across the Curriculum successfully apply equally to a more diverse view of training MLAC teachers. This chapter considers principles and practice which underpin the provision for expert courses, and support smaller-scale training enterprises such as short courses for experienced teachers, inputs into existing initial teacher training courses for Modern Foreign Languages (MFLs) trainees, or simply practical guidelines for the teacher who 'wants to have a go'.

Teachers' knowledge bases

The types of knowledge needed to teach MLAC effectively are identified in chapter 11 as stemming from foreign-language competence, expert subject knowledge and knowledge about how to teach – pedagogical knowledge. In the context of MLAC, these categories can be subdivided further to include issues of subject specific vocabulary and language forms, and the language needed for classroom organisation and control. Figure 12.1 offers an analysis of the range of pedagogical and language knowledge bases which are implicated in planning and teaching MLAC.

The model in figure 12.1 gives a basis for establishing which knowledge domains are already available to a particular teacher and could be used for a range of targeted courses which address specific shortfalls. Points to bear in mind for MLAC teachers cover a range of issues. For example, a native speaker who has a subject-specific degree or a subject specialist who has language competence would need no additional content or language knowledge, but would benefit from the opportunity to consider specific pedagogical knowledge either by study or through supported practical experiences. Furthermore, a trained MFL teacher might only require some additional content knowledge to be able to plan and teach MLAC independently. Where two or more teachers co-operate to present MLAC activities, it is likely that, although no one teacher has all of the competencies required, within the group of teachers involved the necessary

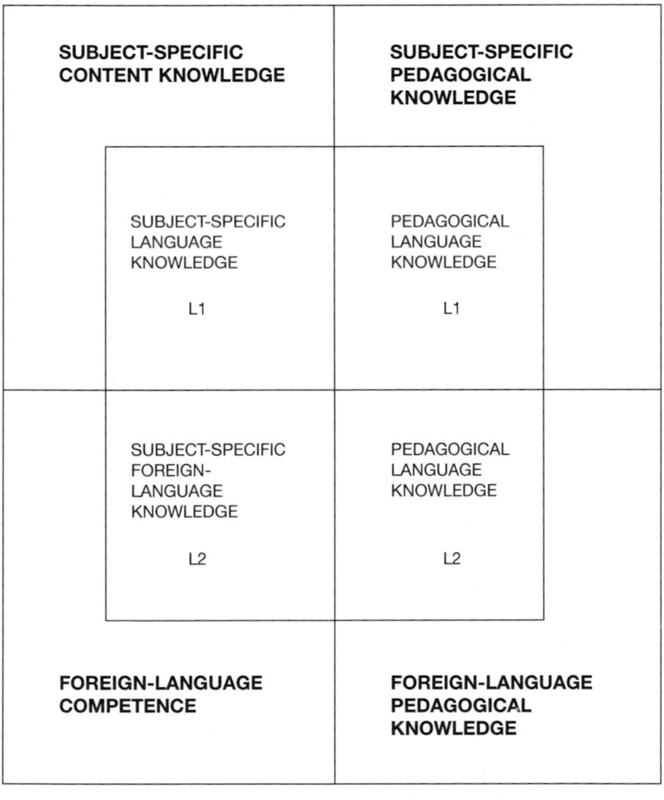

SUBJECT-SPECIFIC CONTENT KNOWLEDGE		SUBJECT-SPECIFIC PEDAGOGICAL KNOWLEDGE	
	SUBJECT-SPECIFIC LANGUAGE KNOWLEDGE L1	PEDAGOGICAL LANGUAGE KNOWLEDGE L1	
	SUBJECT-SPECIFIC FOREIGN- LANGUAGE KNOWLEDGE L2	PEDAGOGICAL LANGUAGE KNOWLEDGE L2	
FOREIGN-LANGUAGE COMPETENCE		FOREIGN-LANGUAGE PEDAGOGICAL KNOWLEDGE	

Figure 12.1 Language knowledge bases applicable to MLAC teachers

knowledge bases are available. If several teachers are motivated to plan and teach in partnership with one another, the training needs of each individual are greatly reduced since a broader range of knowledge bases are available, at least for planning purposes. For a teacher educator, intent upon developing courses which address MLAC needs, this all suggests that establishing co-operative working between teachers from language and non-language backgrounds minimises the need to make subject-knowledge inputs.

For example, if a small-scale project is envisaged, centred around a particular topic area – for example, the French climate – then the additional language-specific, content-specific or pedagogical knowledge which each teacher needs is reduced still further. Experienced teachers might well teach each other any necessary knowledge in the course of their joint topic planning. A teacher education institution could plan a short training course to equip teachers for teaching one particular MLAC topic and a complementary course on the same topic with its trainee teachers, and then arrange for students and their training mentors to work together in school.

For language teachers, one positive outcome of planning and teaching cross-curricular language lessons is an increased awareness of the context of their language teaching. In chapter 10, Kim Brown writes about her experiences of teaching language across the curriculum. Here she offers her experience of working with trainee teachers on fables and stories from other cultures.

Trainee teachers were asked to complete an evaluation of a term of project work that we had done on cross-curricular teaching in modern languages. They had been introduced to fables, stories and poems from around the world, to issues of national, international and global concern and to resources and strategies to support cross-curricular teaching in language lessons. In their evaluations, trainees talked about the ways in which their own knowledge and perceptions about the world had been challenged and extended by these approaches:

'it has made me realise how "limited" my experience was in this particular aspect';

'it reminded me that at times I suffer from *little England syndrome*';

'all the activities we did made me think about language teaching in a different way, especially activities aimed at developing pupils' understanding of other cultures and their own culture'.

Cross-curricular teaching makes demands on teachers in terms of their own professional development. It brings them up against the limits of their knowledge and understanding of the world and challenges them to move forward in ways that will support their effective teaching of languages through other topics and subject areas. One trainee saw this clearly after the work we had done:

'I did not know that so many countries in the world are francophonic [*sic*]. It is shocking that having just completed a French Studies degree, I was unaware that the number was so great. It reveals a large gap in my and, obviously, others' education and teaching.'

We cannot assume that undergraduates leave university fully prepared to teach languages effectively to pupils. In many cases in the UK, trainees on modular courses or those combined with subjects such as Business Studies or Economics might not have studied any literature at all in their degree course. Often, this is a matter of choice. In the same way, students might not have considered the francophone world in their French degree or world issues relating to German or Spanish speakers beyond those on the European mainland. If cross-curricular teaching is to be effective, individual teachers, as well as those responsible for initial and continuing teacher education, need to take responsibility for professional development in these areas. Without a full understanding of issues relating to communities in the Southern Hemisphere, for example, or of different interpretations of democracy and citizenship or cultural awareness, teachers run the risk of reinforcing stereotypes and of tokenism in their teaching. Cross-curricular teaching demands a clear rationale and a sustained approach from teachers who might not have thought about their teaching in this way before.

In chapter 10, Kim Brown offered some examples of the specific MLAC activities which her trainees had undertaken and which led to this wider view of teaching languages in context. This aspect of increasing teachers' awareness of their own knowledge bases and of the gaps in them is one that can be addressed directly through specific teacher education activities. For example, one possibility is offered here as a sequence of resource sheets. Activities with trainee teachers or with more experienced teachers might be organised as shown in the 'Activity 1' box.

Activity 1: Teachers' knowledge base
In this activity, the tutor explains the connections between language and content appropriate for MLAC, using figures 12.2–12.4. With figure 12.2 the tutor would offer specific examples from their own classroom experience and would ask teachers to suggest examples from their teaching experiences. Teachers then briefly discuss the diagram in pairs, identifying

further examples from their own everyday and/or teaching experiences of the sorts of things which could be placed under each heading, for example, knowledge of subject content or language needs.

The second sheet – figure 12.3 – suggests a specific MLAC topic – in this case, the French Revolution and the past tense in French. Tutor and teachers together identify what the learning needs for each topic would be, paying particular attention to common features.

A specific MLAC topic is now chosen by the group. Teachers work in pairs to complete a blank grid – figure 12.4 – for their chosen topic. Teachers then share their ideas across the whole group and construct a single grid between them. Finally, each teacher is asked to focus on their own subject, language and pedagogical knowledge when they are asked:

- what have you learnt through this activity?
- would you be confident to teach the topic in question?
- what else might you need to know?

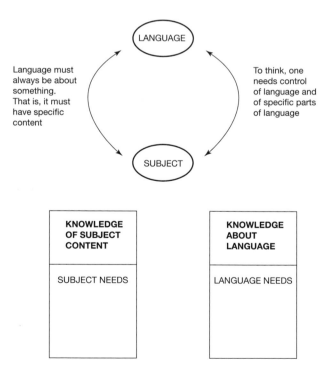

Figure 12.2 Language/subject knowledge links

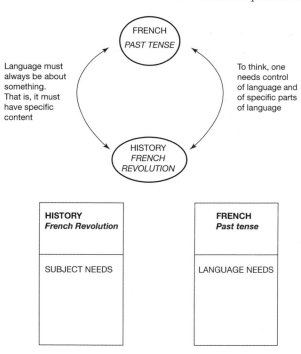

Figure 12.3 Language/subject knowledge links – a History example

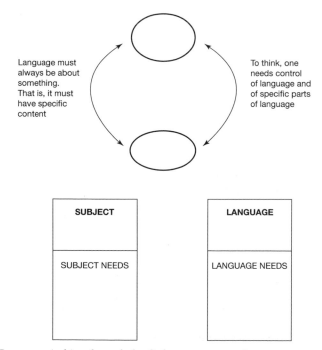

Figure 12.4 Language/subject knowledge links – own example

This activity could serve as a preliminary activity to planning and teaching any MLAC topic, since it raises teachers' awareness of the diversity of subject and language needs for any particular subject whilst providing an opportunity to identify any shortfalls in their own knowledge bases. MLAC teacher education activities of this sort could become an integral part of every language teacher's initial training. They can also play a useful part in the professional development programme of a school and contribute positively to the continuing education of experienced teachers through short professionally based or accredited courses.

Progression and planning

In this section, we look at the ways in which teachers may plan MLAC activities in order to ensure progression in pupils' learning. Here, we complement the discussion by offering a practitioner example of how planning can address the language learning needs of pupils at the same time as meeting the demands of another curriculum subject area. Ideas for teacher education activities are based around this example.

Central to any discussion of accountability is the basic need to ensure that pupils' learning follows an appropriate progression. In foreign language teaching, progression most often refers to the systematic development of each of the four skills: listening, speaking, reading, writing. In MLAC teaching, the skills progression from another subject context must also be incorporated into second language lessons. Teachers need to understand the complexity of this task, which demands detailed planning against appropriate subject and language frameworks to ensure that MLAC contributes positively to skills development and understanding in both subject domains. Figure 12.5 might be used with teachers in order to relate subject progression with language progression and explore these

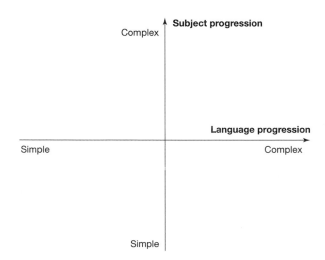

Figure 12.5 Progression in MLAC

as continua. We offer a practical activity linked to this relationship later in the chapter where separate activities are located at different points in the diagram.

Central to ensuring progression in the two distinct domains of language and subject knowledge must be *planning*. Planning is the focus of the next series of teacher education materials. 'Linking across the curriculum' – Activity 2 – is set out in three parts. Firstly, a case exemplar with related activities. These are presented as an introductory worksheet and a description of the case, including three tables of the school's own overview materials. Secondly, we offer a practical planning activity, which might be used either by teachers on their own or as part of a professional teacher education training course. This activity includes a worksheet and two planning sheets. Thirdly, we return to the idea of mapping language complexity against subject demand first referred to in chapter 3 and taken up again in figure 12.5. Here, we give an example of how one topic can be mapped against the two continua and encourage would-be MLAC teachers to try for their own programme of work.

The exemplar illustrates how a whole-school approach to cross-curricular planning for language was undertaken. It is based on materials provided by Rosanna Raimato. A more detailed account of MLAC pupil activities mentioned here for Art and MFLs and for German and Business Studies can be found in chapter 10.

Activity 2: part 1

Linking across the curriculum
Worksheet 1
Read the exemplar – A whole-school approach to MLAC.

Think about your own school or college setting and answer the following questions:

- Do you think that the key features of the MLAC course described in the case example would apply in your school or college (table 12.1)?
- How might you modify them?
- Would the same key objectives for the topic of Festivities and Celebrations (table 12.2) be appropriate for the curriculum requirements in your region?
- Would you prefer different learning objectives for this topic?
- In the MLAC Topic Overview (table 12.3), would you choose the same language objectives, grammar or linguistic activities for your students? Would you modify this overview so that it is appropriate for your own students and educational setting?

When you have tried to answer these questions on your own, discuss your ideas as a group. Are there any common features? Any major differences? Talk about a range of ways of teaching this MLAC topic.

Case example 1: Linking across the curriculum

This account offers an example of MLAC innovations, which are part of a nation-wide UK initiative to develop language learning through designated specialist language colleges. Within a given framework, each school chooses for itself how to approach language, what to prioritise and whom to involve, but language teaching and learning must be a central focus in the whole school's development. In many of these schools, cross-curricular co-operation by teachers is actively supported, provided one of the subjects to be taught is a language-based one, that is, Modern Languages Across the Curriculum. It is relatively easy for teachers to exploit opportunities to work together on joint projects. In this school, three objectives are identified and shared with all staff:

- Providing a distinctive curriculum in a language college;
- Establishing a new perception of teaching and learning using more than one language;
- Developing language competence as a transferable skill.

Since January 2000, language teaching at the school has emphasised communication with students and schools abroad, including e-mail links, and has encouraged the active use of information technology in learning through language software, the making of videos or desk-top publishing of newspapers or magazines. Cross-curricular links have been introduced as a part of the school's formal curriculum; for example, there are MLAC activities to teach MFLs and Art together which were planned from the national programmes of study for each subject. Two or more teachers plan together, but then teach in individual classrooms.

Longer-term projects like German and Business Studies lead to nationally accredited vocational qualifications. Staff development for these MLAC integrated courses occurs within the school through staff meetings, faculty meetings and joint planning. Languages staff have identified the key features in table 12.1 as essential elements of what they do.

Table 12.1 Key features of MLAC courses

Integrated courses – how have they worked?

Features of the courses:

- One hour per week is taught by a linguist.
- The lessons are time-tabled as 'Art', 'Humanities', 'Religious Studies' so that the remaining lessons are delivered by the specialist subject teacher.
- Initial conferences take place between the teachers. Subsequent meetings are used to decide on subject content and MFL links.
- Regular planning meetings are held to assess progress and clarify future units of work.
- Subject-specific teaching styles, key words and concepts are adopted for linked MFL lessons.

Mixed-ability groups range in size from 12 to 25 students.

These key features are exemplified in the example of an integrated course for French and Religious Education shown in table 12.2. The topic was taught to 11–12-year-old students in Year 7. For most pupils in Britain, this would be the first year of learning a foreign language.

Table 12.3 gives an overview of the topic to be covered. It is not a lesson-by-lesson guide. Suggestions for appropriate grammar and useful resources are given here. Shared resources are used, and your own ideas can be contributed.

Table 12.2 MLAC topic objective

Year 7 Second Language Course

Unit title: Festivals and Celebrations

Unit length: 6 (+) lessons – approximately 6 hours

Aim of unit: To exploit opportunities within the Year 7 Religious Education unit on festivals and celebrations as a context for using and extending FL skills and knowledge. Reference should be made to the work pupils are doing in the RE lessons and contributions drawn from students in order to link the two subjects.

Students should be able to:

*   Consolidate FL language covered in earlier units of work.

*   Develop cultural awareness of the country of the language studied through learning about special dates and occasions and how they are celebrated.

*   Describe their own daily routines on special days and compare them to those of students of their own age in other countries.

*   Communicate this information verbally and in written form.

Table 12.3 MLAC topic overview

Topic	*Grammar + structures*	*Resources*
• Revision of dates and months of the year, e.g. ask for and give the date. • Understanding important dates in the year for the target language country and their equivalents in UK, e.g. Christmas, New Year, Easter, public holidays, etc. • Learn greetings for specific events, e.g. birthdays, Christmas etc.	• **Present tense** of verbs relevant to this context: • **First person singular** for all pupils • **Third person singular** can be used as an extension activity for high achievers. • Verbs and phrases for **expressing opinions**.	For French • See *Encore Tricolore* 1, Unit 6. • The MGP magazines also have some useful materials. • ICT. Essential for dates etc. Internet and Encarta for more general cultural research

continued

Table 12.3 (continued)

• Practice times and
  parts of the day, e.g.
  morning, evening etc.

• Speaking about
  what you do on
  special dates including
  daily routines.
  Compare these
  with TL country.

• Identify foods,
  gifts related to the
  special events and
  relevant vocabulary.

Possible linguistic activities:	National Curriculum references:
• Pair work	
• Role plays	1 Acquiring Knowledge – a, b, c,
• Class repetition	2 Developing language skills – a, c, d, f, g, h, j
• Creative writing	3 Developing language-learning skills
• Oral work	– a, b, c, d, e
• Taped or video activities	4 Developing cultural awareness – a, b, c, d
• Poster presentations	
• Songs and poems	

Activity 2: part 2

The next activity is best tackled in groups, preferably with teachers from different subject backgrounds so that objectives and activities can be planned from the point of view of the curriculum subject area and from FL viewpoint.

Activity 2: Worksheet 2

Working with at least one other teacher,

• Choose a cross-curricular topic, which you might plan together.
• Identify key pupil learning objectives for your MLAC topic.
• Agree a topic plan.

Either use the exemplar you have just read as a model

or

Record your decisions using planning sheets 1 and 2 for Activity 2.

Activity 2   Linking across the curriculum   Planning sheet 1

LANGUAGE / SUBJECTS	MLAC TOPIC 1 When? How long? Which pupils?	MLAC TOPIC 2 When? How long? Which pupils?	MLAC TOPIC 3 When? How long? Which pupils?
English			
Mathematics			
Science			
Design and Technology			
Information Technology			
History			
Geography			
Art			
Music			
Physical Education			
Religious Education including Citizenship			

Figure 12.6 Planning an MLAC topic (1)

Activity 2   Linking across the curriculum   Planning sheet 2

Modern foreign language learning objectives can be linked to another subject. Teaching is in L2. Lessons provide a context and an opportunity to apply, practise and consolidate knowledge, skills and understanding in the additional subject.

LANGUAGE   ———————————————————————————————————

LEARNING OBJECTIVE   ———————————————————————————

SECOND SUBJECT   ————————————————————————————————

LEARNING OBJECTIVE   ———————————————————————————

DESCRIPTION OF UNIT OF WORK (lesson or series of lessons)

Figure 12.7 Planning an MLAC topic (2)

Activity 2: part 3

In chapter 3, the relationship between the language-learning context of an activity and its cognitive demands was discussed. Here, we have adapted the same idea and present the grid, firstly, using the contextual example of 'Festivals and Celebrations' from the exemplar above, and secondly, using a blank grid for any MLAC topic. These grids are a useful check to ensure that there is a balance in the types of challenges presented to pupils. Worksheet 3 indicates how teachers would work with the grids.

The learning objectives and activities from 'Festivals and Celebrations' are mapped onto the first grid in order to show how particular language- and subject-based activities interrelate and have consequences in terms of the 'embedded-ness' of the subject context and the cognitive demands of tasks. In teacher education situations, the activity would then be to fill in the second grid for a new and different topic or subject area.

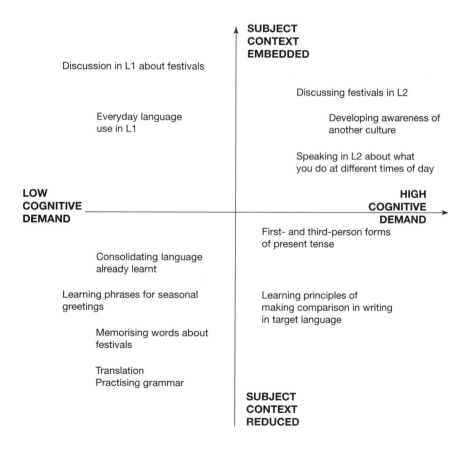

Figure 12.8 Cognitive demand and context: 'Festivals and Celebrations'

Activity 2: Worksheet 3

Review the cognitive demand of the topics you have planned by plotting your objectives and/or pupil activities on a copy of sheet 3.

You may wish to modify your plan to ensure that pupil activities are challenging, but not impossible.

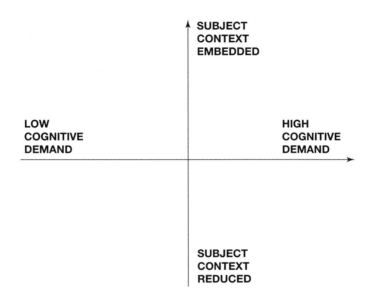

Figure 12.9 Cognitive demand and context for an MLAC topic

Learner Strategies in MLAC

It is clear from the discussions in this book that Modern Languages Across the Curriculum must involve developing common learning strategies between the subject and language content of lessons. This section offers a further practical illustration of MLAC planning followed by an activity, which could be used with would-be MLAC teachers.

Our example is of a school where inclusion of learning strategies is an integral aspect of planning. Here, the modern languages department has worked with several different subject teams to produce a series of MLAC topic plans. Although the lessons are taught within the languages department, the content and pupil activities are jointly planned with other subject teachers to ensure that the learning outcomes fit within the individual subject curriculum – several teachers plan, but only one teaches. Three different aspects of learning are integrated into these MLAC topic plans: content objectives, language objectives and learner strategies.

In Britain, National Curriculum Key Skills would offer a possible framework for choosing learner strategies. The topic plans show lessons where new vocabulary is introduced to meet practical needs. Ideas from Science, Geography, etc. are consolidated and learner strategies are also identified as learning outcomes of these topics; for example, developing research skills. The positive outcomes of MLAC work like this are not only language lessons which actively involve pupils but, for the teachers, a greatly increased understanding of other subject knowledge bases and of the generic skills or learner strategies which are common to the subjects. In this case, the content of lessons is planned against three distinct progressions: strategic progression; language progression; subject progression. In tables 12.4 and 12.5, plans are given for two MLAC topics: the Solar System (Science) and multicultural houses (Geography). Suggestions for how these topic plans can be used in a teacher education context are given in Activity 3.

Activity 3: Planning learner strategies into MLAC
Worksheet 1: Learning strategies and MLAC

Read the two MLAC topic plans for Science and Geography.

Could you use these plans in your own educational setting?

* What features would you keep?
* What would you modify?
* What would you leave out?

In both of these MLAC examples, the learner strategies planned are complex ones so that the topics could be seen to give priority to pupils developing the learner strategies in question rather than learning new language structures.

> Try to replan one of these topics with less demanding learner strategies and more demanding language content objectives.
> Discuss this within your group.

Working in pairs,

> *Choose* your own MLAC topic.
>
> *Identify* learning objectives:
> – from subject-specific progression
> – from the language progression you use
> – from a learner strategies progression.
>
> *Plan* a series of lessons which match your chosen objectives.
> Use the examples here as a model, or use planning sheets 1 and 2 to record your answers.

Table 12.4 Planning learner strategies into an MLAC/Science topic

Cross-curricular science	Solar system

Objectives
- Students will know the order of the planets in the solar system.
- Students will extend their knowledge of the solar system and the individual planets.
- Students will extend their grammatical and lexical knowledge of the solar system in the target language.

Learner strategies
- Developing students' research skills
- Developing group/project work
- Developing autonomous learning

Resources
ICT, library, polystyrene balls, wire, paints, paper

There are many children's books which are now available in French, Spanish, German and Italian, that come with stickers, grids, etc. which can be adapted to transparencies and worksheets.

Useful websites:
- yahoo!France (or other target language versions) – astronomy
  These sites have clips, show reels and other wonderful images that really make the solar system alive!
- www.bath-preservation-trust.org.uk/museums/herschel/index.html – (version in French)
  This site gives the history of astronomy and the discovery of Uranus.
- www.exmachina.be/galaxiens/
  This one is a French cartoon with games and opportunities for using CD-ROMs.
- www.alphagalileo.org/
  This is the latest Science source (French, German, Spanish, Italian).

There are also CD-ROMs that can be bought from the target-language country.

Class dynamics	Time
Group work, pair work and independent learning	4–6 lessons

Lesson content

1 Basic fact finding about the solar system which students can convert into the target language.

2 Students already know systems for remembering the order of the planets (My Very Easy Method Just Speeds Up Naming Planets – Mercury, Venus, Earth, Mars, Jupiter, Saturn, Uranus, Neptune, Pluto). Ask students to make systems for remembering in the target language.

3 Devise gap-filling grids that students can complete (period of rotation, length of day, distance from the sun, etc).

4 Allow the students to work in groups to research one planet. They will then use the research of the planet to write a piece for display. Then students feedback to each other.

5 Students then use their information to build a model of their planet (correct colour, size, etc.). These models will be used to become a mobile of the solar system for the classroom.

Table 12.5 Planning learner strategies into an MLAC/Geography topic

---

Cross-curricular geography
house and home/where I live
Year 7

Cultural abodes

Objectives
* Students will be able to use habitual phrases (pronouns + live, in, at, it is + adjectives).
* Students will use these L2 phrases to learn about different cultures and habitats/ abodes around the world.
* Students will develop empathy for different cultures around the world.
* Students will increase their geographical awareness.

Learner strategies
* Developing ICT skills (Internet, word-processing)
* Developing students' research skills
* Developing group/project work
* Developing autonomous learning

Resources
Coloured A4 pictures/transparencies of different cultures and their abodes. Smaller copies of the same pictures. Enlarged maps of the world. Atlases. Access to the library and to the Internet. Sugar paper.

Class Dynamics	Time
Group work for projects	3–5 lessons

Lesson content

1 Students will transfer their language knowledge to group work which consists of researching a particular culture, for example:
* Inuit
* Masai Mara
* Native American
* Jewish
* Japanese

2 Students will design a display that could be:
* visual
* audio-visual
* in book format
* in display format
* in a mixture of the styles of their chosen culture.

   The display should depict where people live and how they live.

3 Students will carry out a short oral presentation in the target language to the rest of the class.

	MLAC Topic 1		MLAC Topic 2	
LEARNER STRATEGY	Subject	Language	Subject	Language
Ordering information				
Sequencing				
Classifying				
Brain-storming				
Decision making				
Planning				
Generating options				
Making predictions				
Testing				
Drawing conclusions				
Generating ideas				
Formulating views				
Problem solving				

Figure 12.10 Planning learner strategies into an MLAC topic (1)

Activity 3 Planning sheet 2

Planning language-aware learning

A curriculum subject is taught in L2 rather than L1 in order to provide a context for learning the target language. Opportunities to use Key Skills, such as finding information, problem solving or thinking skills, are also planned into the lesson.

SUBJECT LEARNING OBJECTIVE	
LANGUAGE LEARNING OBJECTIVE	
LEARNER STRATEGY (or Key Skills objective)	

DESCRIPTION OF WORK (lesson or series of lessons)

Figure 12.11 Planning learner strategies into an MLAC topic (2)

This activity consists of a worksheet, the two topic examples, and two planning sheets. The idea would be for a group of teachers or trainees to do worksheet 1 and then plan their own series of MLAC lessons using the two planning sheets (figures 12.10 and 12.11).

The strategies listed in figure 12.10 are based on the thinking skills and strategies listed in chapter 3. Figure 12.11 provides a recording sheet for identifying learning objectives from the three skill progressions: subject learning; language learning; learner strategy.

In this third activity, topic or lesson planning is at its most complex, since language and subject outcomes are considered in relation to activities designed explicitly to develop learner strategies. The range of pedagogical and subject knowledge which is needed to plan for learning of this type is broad and is most easily met through co-operative working by teachers with distinct subject expertise. Teacher education must take these needs into account. Whilst an expert MLAC teacher with dual subject interests and pedagogical training in both language and subject content would be able to plan and teach lessons independently, teachers with this very specialist training are not abundant. In Britain, at least, the most practical route to the continuing development of Modern Languages Across the Curriculum is as suggested by the examples above: for teachers to plan topics together but then to teach lessons in parallel, not necessarily at the same time or in the same place.

Conclusion

In this chapter, we have set out some ideas for activities which teachers and teacher educators might use to 'get started' in MLAC – in whichever country or language they teach. The activities would form the basis of a series of introductory sessions as part of an initial teacher training course, but could equally well be adapted for experienced teachers to use as part of informal school-based training or when undertaking further formal study.

The presentation of these ideas has been underpinned by four key methodological principles:

- MLAC teacher education is best tackled by working co-operatively with other teachers, possibly on a short course;
- Since planning is central to the success of MLAC, sufficient time must be available to develop specific activities for different settings;
- Practical classroom application is essential;
- The evaluation of both planning and classroom work is an essential element for every teacher wishing to develop MLAC skills and to undertake further exploration.

There are two key elements which must be addressed in any teacher education for MLAC – at whatever level this is offered. Firstly, increasing teachers' awareness of their own *Knowledge bases* and of how these might be supplemented to provide the necessary range of expertise for MLAC. Secondly, *Planning* as a means of focusing teachers' intentions on what is to be learnt and how. Teachers need to review the balance of learning demands between different learning outcomes so that activities are challenging, but accessible. The additional time needed to plan effective MLAC activities does, however, offer significant payback. For example, planned and accountable consolidation of ideas from one subject domain can occur symbiotically with the acquisition or application of ideas from different subject domains. MLAC therefore becomes an exciting part of every pupil's education by providing curriculum enrichment, together with curriculum accountability through clearly defined learning objectives and language, subject and learner strategies.

Conclusion

Michael Grenfell

The introduction to this book promised that it was about 'broadening horizons' and in the course of its four parts and twelve chapters we have seen the multifaceted nature of our topic. The year 2001 was the European Year for Languages. As a result, we began the new millennium with renewing our commitment to language as a central vehicle for achieving our social, economic and cultural goals. I wrote also in the introduction that, in the twentieth century, the philosophy of language was the philosophy of man (*sic.*). We define ourselves in linguistic terms, and communication is an essential component in our high-tech, global 'village'. We can therefore assume with some confidence that language matters and systems of communication will continue to define the way we think and act, and to increase at an exponential rate. But these ideas are not simply a pragmatic response to external demands. Besides meeting the communication needs of the modern economy, language is also probably the most embedded aspect of an individual's personality. What language? Where? When? Why? These are questions laden with personal repercussions for the individual as much as for international ambitions. So, as soon as we involve ourselves in language, we evoke a whole set of actions and reactions as a consequence. It could be argued that questions of language teaching and learning are a rather small part of the vast field of intercultural preoccupations. However, we have seen here how many facets of theory and practice of just one area of it – Modern Languages Across the Curriculum – link with a range of social and individual processes. Starting with methodological and pedagogic concerns, it has been necessary to raise a whole set of questions about values and actions in order to understand present practice and future possibilities in connecting life and language. In this conclusion, I want to sum up the range of concerns and issues raised in the course of the book, taking Modern Languages Across the Curriculum as our point of reference.

There is the issue of the rubric itself. Modern Languages Across the Curriculum, Content and Language Integrated Learning, Immersion Programmes, Sections bilingues, Bilingualism: all of these have been used at some time to describe the approach to language learning and teaching explored in this book. But they have often been employed with different, if complementary, objectives in mind, with different emphases of language and content, and in very different cultural contexts set in particular time periods. The adoption of an MLAC approach is significant in marking a fresh international perspective on language matters; what might be done and why. At its simplest level, we have seen how MLAC might simply be regarded as a methodological trend or development – a latest version of Communicative Language Teaching. There are real pedagogic implications based on practical experience with CLT, research and theoretical developments. MLAC is rooted in what we now know about teaching and learning in second languages. However, in our historical overview, the case examples, our contributors' comments, practical materials, and discussion of teacher education, we have seen the political, social, economic and cultural issues also apparent in this approach to language learning. Modern Languages Across the Curriculum in its narrowest and simplest sense is about teaching a second language and a curriculum subject together for pedagogic reasons. However, we have seen this approach from the viewpoint of different linguistic contexts: minority languages (for example, Turkish), or regional languages (for example, Catalan, Basque), or national bilingual contexts (for example, Flemish, French, German). These scenarios for MLAC necessarily imply distinct *raisons d'être*. The nation's requirement that its citizens should learn second languages contrasts with the personal ambitions of its people in response to tensions between instrumental and integrative motivations at both these levels. There is a distinction between *need* and *desire* – one is a necessity; the other is an option. In either case, there may be tensions between national and personal perspectives. Choice is involved here, and choice made as a calculation of time, expenditure and effort compared with likely returns. Again, these choices imply decisions made by the European Union on behalf of its member states, or by particular countries for their citizens, or by individuals in terms of their own perceived strengths, weaknesses, opportunities and threats.

Language policy and content

There is no shortage of language policy, distinct as it is from practice. As mentioned above, the driving force for *communicative* language teaching was never simply utilitarian. The notion of *communicative competence* had at its core a psycholinguistic definition, but it also related to the ability to *be* social. The German philosopher Habermas (1984, 1987) saw such competence as the basis for communicative *action*: new ways to form relationships and interact free from constraints. Our aim, then, is to create these conditions, liberated from past forms that have already proved inadequate in providing what was needed for a modern world. In a continent which has suffered war and revolution to the extent that Europe has in the past two centuries, communicative action and competence are important principles of practice. In effect, developing an effective language policy delivers on the levels of interpersonal *and* of international communication. But what might such a policy look like in practice?

The *Common European Framework of Reference* (1996) offers us a state of the art description of key issues connected with the teaching and learning of second languages. Essentially it is an assessment framework with which EU member states can review and revise the content and levels of linguistic competence against which their learners are judged. The European White Paper of 1995 takes a broader view. It sets out the goal that every citizen should be proficient in three European languages. But this ambition immediately raises differentials between countries. In non-English-speaking bilingual countries (for example, Belgium) this can be achieved when people are learning English as one of the three. Whether we like it or not, English has become a *lingua franca* and seems unlikely to lose that status. Indeed, in some of our case examples, bilingualism simply means teaching in English. However, in a region with a local language, Catalonia, for example, people may need to retain their own language whilst learning that of the nation state, then English *and* then another major European language in order to meet all of their linguistic needs. Indeed, French, German and Spanish take on the status of 'major' European languages and join English as the principal linguistic acquisitions. Modern Languages Across the Curriculum therefore raises the question of linguistic choice and status – which languages and where? It also highlights the way policy runs ahead of practice, or ideals grate with reality. Any pragmatic approach here is likely to be bought at the cost of promoting some languages and, consequently, demoting certain other languages in relation to each other.

European citizens do have a right to develop their mother tongue for use in a range of personal and professional contexts. They also have a right to know about language as it operates as a medium of communication across the European Union and the world. However, such knowledge only really shapes individual action and identity when second languages are also learnt to a level of reasonable competence. We can see here language learning as a 'right', and language learning with a particular style and content. One that sees an intimate relationship between mother tongue and second languages. Such a perspective needs a language policy which advocates links with 'knowledge about language' *across the curriculum*.

Language policies raise issues of organisation, individual autonomy and macro-management. Clearly, the links between regional authorities, national governments and Europe-wide administration have to provide systems of communication which put policy into practice towards common goals whilst protecting independent choice. There is no overestimating the tensions in achieving such agreements. For some, Europe consumes individual autonomy and character; for others it offers protection.

These issues of size and scale raise questions about what is transmitted in language learning and teaching. We have seen that virtually any subject can be used as a basis for learning a language. In discussing language skills, it is clear that competence cannot be defined purely in terms of linguistic effectiveness. Rather, we draw attention to the values transmitted through language. In the English National Curriculum such values are defined in terms of the moral, spiritual, cultural and social. No language learning is value-free. There is an incipient consumerism in the 'pupil as tourist' content which grips a good deal of Communicative Language Teaching. The topics we have seen in our practical examples certainly use language content to broaden and enhance appreciation in an aesthetic sense as well as increasing understanding of socio-cultural processes. What is perhaps emerging is a view of the twenty-first century European citizen. They are likely to be multicultural in their patterns of travel and consumption and hold international perspectives through systems of communication. They will be flexible and be able to 'switch' identities according to context. They will experience life on an increasing range of levels: personal, social and virtual. Such adaptability will require affective control as well as social and linguistic content know-how/ know-what skills to manage the scope of this discourse. The *Common European Framework* sums up this range as *savoir-faire* and *savoir-être*; in other words, not only how to get things done but also how to develop personalities that hold together in the face of cultural diversity. Such knowledge is ultimately empowering on a personal as well as a professional level and leads to an appreciation of European values, of national and regional heritage, and of personal positioning and trajectories.

Language learning

If Modern Languages Across the Curriculum can be understood as the youngest offspring of Communicative Language Teaching, it is because it raises new perspectives on the processes of language *learning* which can be reflected in our twenty-first-century approach to language *teaching*. Most salient of recent developments in linguistic research is the so-called *cognitive* approach to learning processes. In chapter 3, we saw that these trends were not 'new' at all, but formed a part of a research tradition that goes back many decades. What is perhaps most appealing about the approach is the way it has clear and direct pedagogic implications and applications. So, to regard a language classroom as a social context is immediately to include the spectrum of cultural content and values alluded to in various parts of this book. It puts the accent on the group and the individual within the group. It sees language as a social construct with direct consequences for individual psychologies. It sets competence as an *individual* condition but formed within a *group* condition. Modern Languages Across the Curriculum involves a content-rich environment as an enhancement of cognitive processes; in other words, the medium of ideas carried through language in the development of thinking and language. Of course, we have seen how this content focus matches the ideas of 'comprehensible input' coming from the tradition of 'deep structure', Universal Grammar and the Language Acquisition Device. It also connects with the idea of 'negotiated meaning'; of developing competence through direct interpersonal linguistic interactions. However, the cognitive approach does not remain at the level of individual/group linguistic penetration. There is a 'meta' level involved in cognition: to think in language and use language processes, but also to think *about* and reflect *on* this thinking and about these processes. Central to Modern Languages Across the Curriculum is, therefore, the notion of learning strategies: techniques, skills and tactics for dealing with second language, and for planning for monitoring and evaluating this process. The distinction between first and second languages makes this cognitive dimension not only available but necessary to developing linguistic systems in more than one language. In this respect, traditional approaches to Communicative Language Teaching are found to be no less wanting than traditional approaches to grammar, since neither approach provides this socio-cognitive element as central or offers opportunities to reflect on its features in terms of a personal level of competence. Mimicking communication in the belief that direct acquisition follows is no less narrow in its approach than learning an abstract grammar rule.

A cognitive dimension to language learning is not conditional on developing a programme of Modern Languages Across the Curriculum. However, we have seen that MLAC does offer enhanced opportunities to marry language with thinking skills, to plan lessons in terms of content embeddedness and the level of cognitive demand, and to develop learning skills in line with potential learning strategies. In this way, thought and language form parts of an approach that is congruent with pedagogic principles and practice. We have also seen the implications of this cognitive approach for the particularity of task design and application: in the planning that occurs, as in the task response and follow-up. All stages of learning and teaching should be seen as serving a cognitive purpose. Such an approach raises the possibility of the enhanced autonomy of the learner; something which is synonymous with successful language learning. This autonomy and this content-rich teaching have been linked with motivation and the way positive affective responses and attitudes impact on the successful outcomes of language learning.

Language skills can have a broad or a narrow definition. In the most restricted sense, they are often referred to as listening, speaking, reading and writing. Traditionally, Communicative Language Teaching has been preoccupied with oral/aural skills. One thing which is clear about Modern Languages Across the Curriculum is that this situation can be supported no longer. MLAC involves all four skills in cross-curricular language policy and practice, and subject-content integration. It is possible to see the curriculum redefining itself; no longer as language lessons *and* subject lessons but subject lessons *as* language lessons. In other words, MLAC is not simply about enhancing linguistic competence but also about enhancing subject competence by the emphasis that is now put on language as the vehicle for developing thinking *about* content. The curriculum itself may develop away from the narrow confines of single subject disciplines – History, Geography, Mathematics, etc. – to broader areas of accessing information and using it for particular personal, group and professional purposes. To this extent, questions of which languages in which subjects are just the starting point for a renewed investigation of where we start in curriculum design, and for what purposes.

A wider definition of language skills therefore includes information-accessing skills – from the Internet or via other ICT systems. *Using* language becomes a means to an end. In this case, we can imagine a scenario where the accent shifts away from oral/aural skills, with its view of language as an interpersonal interaction, to reading and writing skills in note-taking, text comprehension and knowledge gathering for a subject-specific purpose. MLAC often starts with a printed text rather than a dialogue. Many of these information-processing skills are transferable across languages. It may well be out-of-date to think in terms of a single language-specific competence as if it were a linguistic monolith. Rather, we can foresee competence as an overarching condition, which spans a range of languages. There is the case of the advanced bilingual learner, but there is also the case of those who use 'micro' languages within narrowly defined fields of applications; in other words, those who use many languages but only within a very specific limited scope. All this becomes possible with just a little imagination, vision and pragmatism. Modern Languages Across the Curriculum is rooted in language learning and teaching but implicates our understanding of what we mean by these terms and what they could imply. In this sense, the 'theoretical' impacts on practical possibilities.

Support and training

These ideas are heady and, in the conclusion of a book which has spanned such a wide range of theory and practice, contexts and values, we can perhaps be excused for giving in to the temptation of foreseeing the future. However, all these potential scenarios and possible developments always have to be translated through organisational structures, resource provision and practical support and training.

It is clear that Modern Languages Across the Curriculum may mean different things in different times and places – working within a consensus of principle. But there are also very specific decisions to be made about the organisation of the curriculum across age phases and according to the type of institutions where learning takes place, and about the training and support for teachers. What will MLAC look like across different phases of primary, secondary and higher education? It is perhaps easy to imagine a group of adult students studying Chemistry through German, but what about primary pupils? Will such specialisation run counter to the holistic curriculum? Should second language teaching target the development of 'hard' linguistic competence, or should it go for a 'sensibilisation' model (where there is a raising of second language awareness rather than expertise)? Is there a *minimum savoir* which can be defined for each phase, and how do they dovetail with the one that proceeds or succeeds it? Indeed, are these age phases necessarily the best way to think about organising learning?

Our case examples named a range of scholastic institutions in various countries, such as European schools, language-medium Schools and bilingual schools. The age of institutional diversity is clearly upon us. In England, we have embarked on a programme of 'specialist colleges', one type of which is the 'language college'. The brief for these colleges is to increase language provision and linguistic performance for their pupils and students. Such institutions necessarily have to develop their own independence in how to organise learning. Links with other countries will be essential in providing the structures of communication and international contact in order to open fully the doors of Europe and the world beyond and to broaden personal and professional horizons. For such contacts and relations to be sustainable, flexibility will need to be a defining principle: flexibility in language taught, but also flexibility in approach, availability and recognition. Both the school week and the school year will have to become more adaptable to varying patterns of institutional activity. Increased autonomy will be a necessary condition of this flexibility. Learners learn and teachers teach. However, increasingly these processes will not necessarily take place at the same time. Rather, teaching and learning will occur when both the individuals involved and the systems they utilise are available, which may be different for the learner and the teacher. This range of operations needs to be recognised as legitimate. As do their outcomes. There is a pressing need for EU wide recognition of common linguistic criteria in both the narrow and the broad definition of language skills. This possibility has only just begun with the *Common European Framework*. National curricula need defining in terms of the framework and also of a common language policy developed for integrating mother tongue and second language studies across the curriculum. But change entails risks, which can be interpreted as threats and are often fought against as undesirable. A major concern in trans-national recognition of teaching and learning outcomes is the comparability of levels and associated standards. It is all the more important therefore to stipulate what are the aims and objectives of Modern Languages Across the Curriculum, how they are assessed and against what criteria, and how outcomes should be accredited. We need a system that is integrated and recognised across Europe.

The final theme of this conclusion is perhaps the most crucial: teacher education. The recognition of standards, criteria, aims and objectives alluded to in the last section needs to extend to a common recognition of teacher qualifications. Modern Languages Across the Curriculum is synonymous with teacher mobility, as well as recruitment and retention issues. Content and Language Integrated Learning only makes sense if subject teachers can see their subjects taught in different cultural environments. Similarly, teachers, whether of the mother tongue or a second language, need also to experience language as a first *and* a second language. Otherwise, there is no inter-penetration of knowledge about language in first, second and bilingual contexts. What it is like to be a native speaker in a subject-specific context is distinct from approaching the same subject as a second language speaker. And here we have to recognise that, pragmatically speaking, it is never going to be the case that all language teachers will have, or want to have, bilingual competence in their second language, let alone their third and fourth. Learning strategies, learning skills, thinking skills can be overly embedded in either language *or* the subject base; whilst what is wanted is their integration. This integration needs to be experienced first hand in various European countries, not simply justified in theoretical terms. In order to enhance teacher mobility, common certification to gain 'Qualified Teacher Status' is therefore a must. Such recognised qualifications might be at a supplementary level, of course, and do not preclude maintaining particular teacher-education traditions and systems in individual European states.

The book has tried to strike a balance between the personal and the public aspects of language learning and teaching. There are tensions in the quest for a united Europe whilst cultural, economic and political diversity are defended.

Individual teachers and learners have personal needs, wants and responsibilities to be met through MLAC. There are also national and international pressures to conform to one form of teaching and learning or another. It takes a *broad* mind to appreciate these *broad* horizons, which hardly imply absence of conflict. This book has focused on a new direction in language teaching; one which offers a response to the perceived limitations of past methodologies. There is consensus over where we have been and what we have experienced, albeit filtered through our personal and cultural-specific lens. What is exciting about Modern Languages Across the Curriculum is that it not only offers a methodological response, but also raises questions which involve identity, behaviour and organisation. Within the issues of theory and practice, policy, materials and curricula design, it therefore also includes institutional organisation and professional support and training. As we write, we are only just at the beginning of the new millennium. What is emerging is the outline of a new language learning and teaching agenda to shape the immediate coming years. In one form or another, this agenda will be constructed around the themes of Modern Languages Across the Curriculum.

References

Commission of the European Communities (1995) *Teaching and Learning: Towards the Learning Society*, Brussels: DGV.

Council for Cultural Co-operation Education Committee (1996) *Modern Languages: Learning, Teaching and Assessment: A Common European Framework of Reference*, Strasbourg: Council of Europe.

Habermas, J. (1984) *Theory of Communicative Action*, 2 vols, Oxford: Oxford University Press.

—— (1987) *Knowledge and Human Interests*, Cambridge: CUP.

Index